Love, Sex,
and Marriage

To Donna and David
Judith and Ray
*May their love be
consecrated anew each day*

Publication of this volume
was made possible by a grant from the
MEMPHIS-PLOUGH CHARITABLE TRUST
in Memory of
MOSES and JULIA PLOUGH

New Edition

Love, Sex, and Marriage

A JEWISH VIEW

RABBI ROLAND B. GITTELSOHN

*By this ring you are consecrated unto
me as my wife, in accordance with
the faith of Moses and of Israel.*
FROM THE TRADITIONAL JEWISH
MARRIAGE CEREMONY

UNION OF AMERICAN HEBREW
CONGREGATIONS, New York

Library of Congress Cataloging in Publication Data

Gittelsohn, Roland B.
Love, sex, and marriage.

A combined revision of the author's works: Consecrated unto me
(1965) and its supplement, Love, sex, and marriage (1976)
Includes bibliographical references.
SUMMARY: A textbook, with a Jewish viewpoint, on all aspects
of male-female relationships from dating to love, sex, marriage, and
divorce.
1. Marriage—Jews. 2. Sex instruction for youth. 3. Sex and Judaism. [1. Marriage—Jews. 2. Sex instruction for youth] I. Gittelsohn,
Roland B. Consecrated unto me. II. Title.
HQ525.J4G542 306.7'089924 80-17632
ISBN 0-8074-0046-7

MANUFACTURED IN THE UNITED STATES OF AMERICA
10 9 8 7 6 5 4 3 2 1

Contents

EDITOR'S INTRODUCTION   vii
PREFACE   viii
ACKNOWLEDGMENTS   x

1   Marriage: heaven or hell?   *1*
2   What is love?   *9*
3   Love and the family   *26*
4   A family is more than two   *48*
5   Old enough to love?   *64*
6   How to make the right choice   *81*
7   Recipe for success   *102*
8   Sex is here to stay   *122*
9   The same, yet different   *154*
10   Do all religions agree on sex?   *176*
11   To wait . . . or not to wait   *190*
12   Not to wait   *204*
13   To wait   *213*
14   New trends . . . and newer   *242*
15   The stakes are high   *270*
16   How important is religion?   *289*

Notes   *303*

UNION EDUCATION SERIES
Edited by
DANIEL B. SYME, *National Director of Education*

Editor's
Introduction

MANY PEOPLE HAVE come to refer to the 1970s as the "me decade." During that ten-year period, we witnessed profound changes in the nature of man/woman relationships, marriage and family life. Formerly inviolable, societal mores crumbled along the way in the individual's search for self and self-fulfillment.

Yet, as so often happens in the wake of revolutions, what became known as the "sexual revolution" ultimately led to a desire for a return, at least in part, to more traditional values. Thus, as we enter the 1980s, we find a new generation of youths and adults engaged in careful examination of the effects of total self-orientation, still committed to self-realization, but also desiring meaningful relationships based on trust, affection and a *sharing* of self.

As is the case with all human situations, Judaism has something important to say about love, sex and marriage. In this major new volume, Rabbi Roland B. Gittelsohn builds on his previous two works on the same subject, *Consecrated Unto Me: A Jewish View of Love and Marriage,* and *Love, Sex and Marriage: A Jewish View.*

Rabbi Gittelsohn's absolute candor in acknowledging societal realities blends with sound psychiatric insights, Jewish content and, most importantly, Jewish values that can inform and guide our daily lives and critical life choices.

We hope that you will find this book an important addition to your home and classroom study of Judaism. As always, we welcome your comments and suggestions.

Rabbi Daniel B. Syme, NATIONAL DIRECTOR
UAHC DEPARTMENT OF EDUCATION

Preface

I AM INDEBTED far beyond my utmost capacity of expression to loving friends, without whose generous assistance this volume would have remained an idle dream.

Foremost among these are the several hundred high school students whose response to my course on marriage at Temple Israel of Boston encouraged me to publish the original edition of this book in 1965. Others who helped immeasurably at that time were Rabbi Alexander M. Schindler, president of the Union of American Hebrew Congregations, Mrs. M. Myer Singer, Rayanna Simons and Rabbis David S. Hachen, Henry F. Skirball, Leon Fram, Samuel Glasner and Jack Stern, Jr.

Neither time nor fatigue was ever an obstacle to my devoted secretary, Bessie R. Berman, in her several typings of this work. Additional typing for this revision was done by Barbara Gantshar, Dorothy Grishaver Levinson and Vivian Mendeles.

The world in which we live now is vastly different from that of a decade and a half ago. Especially regarding the mores of marriage and sex, the changes have been kaleidoscopic.

I do not believe that the sexual ethics of Judaism have changed or have become outmoded. But our presentation of them to young people can no longer be as dogmatic as mine was in 1965; perhaps it should have been less monolithic even then. Today we must offer young people more alternatives; we must give them both sides of such controversial questions as the advisability of premarital intercourse, then trust them to arrive at their own decisions.

In addition to the difference in approach, such subjects as the women's liberation movement, deviant or variant sexual behavior and alternatives to marriage—scarcely topics of major interest in the mid-1960s—are here treated with open honesty. My previous very brief references to masturbation and petting are also treated more fully and, I hope, more adequately.

The changes, deletions and additions in this new edition add up to considerably more than a brief *précis* would suggest; in many respects, this is a different book.

Limitless encouragement and help in the preparation of new material have been given me by the late Abraham Segal and by Rabbis Daniel B. Syme (director of the Commission on Jewish Education), Leonard A. Schoolman and Bernard Kligfeld. Dr. Abraham Franzblau added a psychoanalytic perspective. One of my former students, Claudette Kisliuk Beit Aharon, and a teacher in our religious school, Alice Lanckton, offered numerous suggestions and insights. Dr. and Mrs. James Wiener contributed doubly: as parents of two intelligent, perceptive teenagers and from a professional psychiatric point of view.

I invited Judith Fales, a capable and sensitive sociologist, to write Chapter 12 because I wanted the case for a permissive attitude toward premarital intercourse to be presented more fairly than I, as an opponent, could manage. I am confident that our readers will be grateful to her, as I am.

To all those mentioned above and to many others who helped in smaller ways—*Todah Rabah!*

As *Love, Sex, and Marriage: A Jewish View* is offered to the public, my hope is a simple one. May an insight here, a suggestion or comment there touch the hearts and minds of many among my readers—helping them to a higher evaluation of themselves and a more wonderfully happy marriage!

Roland B. Gittelsohn

Acknowledgments

THE AUTHOR WISHES to acknowledge his gratitude to the following authors, cartoonists and publishers for permission to reprint material from their works:

THE AUTHORS AND PUBLISHERS

Association Press for *Love and the Facts of Life,* by E.M. Duvall (© 1963), *Sex Ways in Fact and Faith,* by E.M. and S.M. Duvall, editors (© 1961), *Before You Marry,* by S.M. Duvall (© 1949), *Ethics in Sex Conduct,* by C. Leuba (© 1948).

Behrman House, Inc., for *Talmudic Anthology,* by Louis I. Newman (© 1945).

Eugene B. Borowitz and Schocken Books for *Choosing a Sex Ethic,* by Eugene B. Borowitz (© 1969).

Malcolm Boyd and Doubleday & Company, Inc., for *Take Off the Masks,* by Malcolm Boyd (© 1978).

Boyd Cooper and Charles Publishing for *Sex Without Tears,* by Boyd Cooper (© 1972). *Current Medical Digest* for January 1956.

The Dial Press, Inc., for *Sex and the Adolescent,* by Maxine Davis (© 1958).

E.P. Dutton & Company, Inc., for *Everyman's Talmud,* by A. Cohen (© 1949).

Fortress Press (Muhlenberg Press) for *Better Ways of Growing Up,* by John Crawford and Dorathea Woodward (© 1964).

Harcourt, Brace & World, Inc., for *A Sane and Happy Life,* by Abraham and Rose Franzblau (© 1963).

Harper & Row for *Love and Marriage,* by F.A. Magoun (© 1956), *Sexual Revolution in Christian Thought,* by D.S. Bailey (© 1959).

Rafael Loewe and Macmillan & Company, Ltd., for *A Rabbinic Anthology,* by H. Loewe and C.G. Montefiore (© 1938).

The Nation for February 8, 1958.

The New York Times for May 6, 1962, January 31, 1965, September 21, 1977, by The New York Times Company (© 1962, 1965, 1977).

Redbook for April 1962.

The Ronald Press Company for *Why Marriages Go Wrong,* by James H.S. Bossard and Eleanor Stoker Boll (© 1958).

Saturday Review for "What the Girls Told," by Dr. Karl Menninger (September 26, 1953), "Letter to the Editor" (August 15, 1964).

Charles Scribner's Sons for *Hasidic Anthology,* by Louis I. Newman (© 1935), *Toward a Successful Marriage,* by J.A. Peterson (© 1960).

Judith Viorst and The New American Library for "True Love" from *It's Hard to Be Hip Over Thirty and Other Tragedies of Married Life,* by Judith Viorst (© 1968).

Judith Viorst for "Growing Up and Other Small Tragedies" by Judith Viorst (© 1973).

THE CARTOONISTS

Chapters 1, 2, 7: Mell Lazarus and Field Newspaper Syndicate for "Miss Peach," by Mell Lazarus.

Chapter 3: Don Orehek and *Cosmopolitan* (© 1978).

Chapter 4: Johnny Hart and Field Newspaper Syndicate for "B.C.," by Johnny Hart.

Chapter 5: Mell Lazarus and Field Newspaper Syndicate for "Momma," by Mell Lazarus.

Chapter 6: V. Gene Myers and *Cosmopolitan* (© 1979).

Chapters 8, 13, 14: Bill Hoest and *Saturday Review* (© 1969).

Chapter 9: Randy Hall and *Cosmopolitan* (© 1979).

Chapter 10: Cathy Guisewite and Universal Press Syndicate for "Cathy," by Cathy Guisewite.

Chapter 11: Ed Arno and *Cosmopolitan* (© 1978).

Chapter 12: John Milligan and *Saturday Review* (© 1971).

Chapter 15: Robert Censoni and *Saturday Review* (© 1970).

Chapter 16: Mort Gerberg and *World Magazine* (© 1972).

Marriage: heaven or hell?

The most important decisions you will ever make are your choice of a vocation and of a husband or wife. Of the two, I believe the second is even more significant than the first. The man or woman who enjoys a happy marriage can, if necessary, adjust to the unavoidable difficulties of his or her vocation or can even change a job. Husbands or wives who are trapped in the wrong kind of marriage may drive themselves mercilessly to compensate with satisfactions elsewhere but will almost certainly fail to find them. No matter how immersed you may eventually be in your vocation, it will occupy and challenge only a part of you. Your marriage, on the contrary, will involve the whole of your personality—your physical being, your intellect, your emotions, your spiritual capacities—everything!

There is no other experience or relationship quite like marriage. It can bring us the most exalted happiness—or the most miserable distress—of which we humans are capable. The negative possibilities of marriage are illustrated by the following excerpts from a news story which appeared several years ago in the *Miami Herald:*

I GOT A TELEGRAM SAYING HE DIED

Edward Hallenbeck spoke in broken cadences of grief:
"All I know is I got a telegram saying he died. I don't know what happened. They said she inflicted the wounds." His son, Terry, 23, an Air Force enlisted man, was stabbed to death Wednesday in Sunnyvale, Calif. The young airman's bride of four days, Mary Ann, 21, was arrested and charged with murder. . . .

Police said young Hallenbeck was stabbed as he unpacked in the couple's honeymoon apartment. The weapon was a seven-inch carving knife, a wedding present.

He died two hours later in a hospital.

Police said Mrs. Hallenbeck told them after her arrest, "I just had to do it."

How can we account for this unspeakable tragedy? Did Terry reveal himself to be a cruel and sadistic groom? Was the young bride unable to face the responsibilities of marriage? Did she find her first sexual encounter with her husband intolerable? We have no way of knowing.

It could have been any of these answers, or a hundred others. What we do know is that, though this is an extreme and fortunately a rare kind of occurrence, it does occasionally happen, and it demonstrates the abysmal misery which some couples find in marriage. Not all marriage failures are as horrifying as that of Mary Ann and Terry. Many couples remain married for life, but one or the other partner comes to feel that he or she was trapped, that with a wiser choice of mate life could have been completely different and happier.

The husband and wife who are divorced after some years of marriage, or who maintain the appearance of a successful marriage despite the fact that both are miserable, constitute a truer and more common example of marital failure than do the Hallenbecks. They—and their children—also suffer a good deal more, even if less dramatically. There is probably no greater cause of unhappiness and emotional distress among children than parents whose marriage has failed.

Others find sublime happiness in marriage. One man said on his thirtieth wedding anniversary: "The luckiest event in my whole life was marrying my wife. Sure, we have had plenty of problems. There have been times when we quarreled and perhaps even acted momentarily in unloving ways toward each other. But neither of us could have become what we are today without the love and encouragement of the other. God's greatest blessing to us has been our love for each other and the opportunity to express this love in our marriage." His wife—too choked up with emotion at the moment to risk any verbal comment—expressed her agreement with the silent eloquence of her eyes.

Most marriages probably fall in the large middle area between the extremes symbolically represented by heaven and hell. Often a mediocre marriage—or even what might appear to be a bad one—will survive for life. With all its inadequacies, it just may be the best kind of marriage the husband and wife are capable of experiencing. My hope is that the pages to follow will help you eventually to enjoy a much richer and happier marriage than you might otherwise have known.

There is a peculiar paradox here. Though marriage is the most crucial decision we face, though it has the potential of bringing us so much happiness or sorrow, it is one of the few important choices in life for which no preparation is required by law. To become skilled at a craft, one must first serve as an apprentice. To qualify as a physician or rabbi, an attorney or accountant, one must go through a rigorous course of preparation. To obtain employment as a beautician or barber, one must demonstrate ability and receive a franchise from the city or state. To drive an automobile one must qualify by taking a test. But to secure a marriage license, all one needs is the required amount of money and, in most states, a blood test. We can only speculate on how much of the unhappiness which some couples experience could be avoided with proper education before marriage.

Both science and Judaism have something to say about the circumstances and conditions which can increase the probability of success in marriage. The purpose of this book is to transmit to you the insights of both science and Judaism, to stimulate your own best thinking on marriage, and to provide the kind of knowledge which Terry and his bride apparently lacked.

Why now?

This, of course, is not the beginning of your education about marriage and sex. In actual fact that education began long before you were aware of it. When your mother first held you in her arms as an infant, you were learning something about love and the pleasures which physical contact can bring to people who love each other. When you observed from earliest childhood the manner in which your parents acted toward each other in your home, you were learning many things—perhaps some good, some bad—about love. When you first discovered that certain parts of your body were more sensitive and pleasurable than others, you were beginning to learn important lessons about sex. Your education in this area has been going on since the moment of your birth.

Unfortunately, not all of it has been good. Your parents and teachers may have been reluctant to transmit the information and attitudes you need; you may thus have been forced to obtain at least some of your information from friends, never fully knowing whether or not that information is accurate. Of the men and women who responded to the famous Kinsey Report, only 5 percent cited their parents as the principal source of their information on sex. Studies indicate that no more than 30 percent to 40 percent of high school youths received most of their sex education from their parents.

A majority of both boys and girls had received most of their sex facts from friends their own age. Needless to say, too often such "education" amounts to little more than the blind leading the blind. College freshmen were asked which topics they found most difficult to discuss with their parents. Eighty-five percent answered sex—80 percent petting—almost as many listed love, courtship and marriage. Even at this level, between a third and a half admitted that most of their information in these areas had come from friends.[1] Intelligent decisions are possible—concerning both marriage and the sex problems you face now—only when based on knowledge which is reliable and accurate.

If you are among the fortunate few whose parents have felt comfortable enough in their own family and sex lives to discuss these subjects with you fully and freely, you have a head start toward acquiring such knowledge. In any event, however, it is possible that there are areas not covered, misconceptions which await correction and questions which remain unanswered. Some parents—much as they would like to help their sons and daughters—find themselves unable to do so because they themselves were not adequately informed in their own youth.

There is a further reason why this is precisely the time in your life when questions of love, sex, marriage and the family must be faced. It is during the high school and early college years that most young people begin to feel most urgently a whole host of sensations, desires, needs and fears growing out of their sexual development. A great many marriages take place at this early age. And even for those who postpone any serious thought of marriage until later, there is evidence that very few men or women later change the type of sex behavior they establish for themselves at this stage of their lives. The kind of relationship you develop now with the opposite sex, your dating habits, your attitudes and conduct with regard to sex—all these will have a direct bearing on the success of your marriage. In short, enough is at stake—in terms of your present needs and doubts as well as your eventual happiness as a husband or wife—to make the concerns of this book among the most important you face.

All too often when sex education courses are proposed for public or religious schools there is a hue and cry of opposition. Many people are afraid of sex education, probably because they fear their own sex drives. Their most frequently expressed reason is that open discussion of sex will lead to an increase in sexual experimentation by the students.

Our most reliable current information indicates that quite the opposite is true. The sex knowledge and behavior of women students were compared recently at a large state university. Among those who had been sexually active, not one answered every question on sex accurately; 9 percent of those who were less active sexually had perfect scores. The following table is additionally instructive:

	100% Knowledge	50% Knowledge	No Knowledge
Sexually active students	0	59%	25% +
Sexually less active students	9%	80%	0

A similar relationship exists between knowledge of sex and the incidence of venereal disease. Two public schools were studied in the same area. In one, where information was given about gonorrhea, the number of cases declined by 50 percent over a period of two school years. During the same time span, gonorrhea cases increased in the school where no such information had been given. Subsequently, when sex education was introduced in the second school, gonorrhea victims decreased there too, by about 50 percent.[2]

Clearly, then, the fears of those who oppose sex education are groundless. What few studies have been made of the relationship between sex knowledge and successful marriages show that a positive relationship does indeed exist. It is in the hopeful expectation of helping you achieve a happy marriage that these chapters will deal—openly and honestly—with sex as well as with other factors which will affect your married future.

Before concluding this chapter, a definition is needed. The verb *pet* is rarely used any more, but to my knowledge there is no adequate synonym. A generation ago *to pet* meant the fondling by either sex of those parts of the other's body which are most sexually excitable. It is with this meaning that I shall use the word from time to time.

For instance

The purpose of this book is not only to deal with theory but also to help you face and solve the kinds of problems people actually encounter in marriage and family life. For this reason, at the end of each chapter you will find several cases illustrating the points of that particular chapter. In your class or discussion group these cases will be explored in depth. In order to arrive at an intelligent opinion of your own, it is essential that you read the entire chapter carefully and also think about it before the discussion. While all these cases are fictional, there is no problem or situation described in them with which I have not actually been confronted in my professional career.

A. David and Doris have known each other since their freshman year of high school. For several years they were only casual friends; for the past two years they have dated only each other. David, who is twenty-two, is eight months older than Doris. Both are now seniors at the same college. When they graduate in June, David hopes to enter medical school, while Doris anticipates a teaching career. David's parents, who are wealthy, are prepared to finance his medical education but they are unhappy over the couple's desire to be married at the end of the year. Their principal objections are that Doris's parents are divorced and that she is a Protestant while they are Catholics. Both young people are convinced they can handle the religious disparity without too much trouble. They feel their love is sufficiently strong so that when they have children they will then be able to agree on the religion the children will follow.

Because they attend the same college, David and Doris have been able to see each other almost daily. They enjoy skiing together in the winter, swimming and golfing in the summer. Both love opera and symphonic music, neither cares very much for museums. They agree on having a family of about three or four children and on spending more money for books, records and travel than on clothing and social pursuits.

What positive factors do you see which would point to probable success for David and Doris in their marriage?

What negative factors which might lead to failure? Would you recommend that they proceed as they have planned? Why? How would you feel if you were their parents?

B. Bill and Frances fell madly in love the very first time they met on a blind date four months ago. They have been together practically every evening since. Frances's mother is worried over their interest in each other, chiefly because Bill is thirty-four while Frances is only twenty. She is trying not to be selfish, however, realizing that her view could be colored by the fact that since her husband died eight years ago Frances has been the focus of all her attention and love at home; there are no other children. Bill has tried to reassure Mrs. Ames by promising that after they are married she will be welcome to live with them.

Before meeting Bill, Frances enjoyed nothing more than curling up before the fireplace with a good book. She has done little reading recently; Bill prefers to spend their evenings together bowling or dancing, and in order to please him she has raised no serious objection. She feels very safe and secure when with him. He seems to know the right answer whenever she herself is in doubt. He is able and willing to make decisions without troubling her.

The one thing in their relationship which bothers Frances considerably is the matter of sex. Whenever they pet, she finds the experience exciting, pleasurable . . . but also frightening. She is afraid of her own strong sexual desires and is worried that if she says no to Bill too often she may lose him.

What positive factors do you see which would point to probable success for Bill and Frances in their marriage? What negative factors which might lead to failure? Would you recommend that they proceed as they have planned? Why? Which of the two couples described in these cases has the better chance for a happy marriage? Why?

2

MISS PEACH   by Mell

What
is
love?

"I love my school . . ." "I love my wife . . ." "I love oranges . . ." "I love my brother . . ." You have probably heard each of these statements made, though in each the word *love* is obviously used in quite a different sense. This illustrates how many varied meanings the word is given and how very difficult it is to define. For our purpose, we are interested chiefly in one special kind of love: that which unites a man and a woman in marriage. This

kind of love, to be sure, is closely connected with other kinds. Indeed, it is doubtful whether a person who did not receive adequate love from parents and did not learn to give love to brothers or sisters or friends is capable of fully loving a husband or wife. But we shall limit ourselves here to the *man-woman-marriage* kind of love.

Even when thus simplified, a definition is difficult. There is a story of a teacher who asked her children to draw pictures of what they wanted to be when they became adults. As they busily followed her instructions, she walked up and down the aisles to examine their work. Coming to one little girl who sat before a blank piece of paper, she said: "Mary, I guess you don't know what you want to be." To which Mary at once replied: "O yes, Miss Martin, I do know. I want to be married, but I don't know how to draw it!" Similarly, even individuals who have experienced love as the most wonderfully compelling reality of their lives often find it impossible to describe it in words.

Many attempts have been made. Professor F. Alexander Magoun, who pioneered in teaching college marriage courses, suggested two possible definitions which are worth our consideration. After first rejecting the humorous definition that love is "an itchy feeling around the heart that you can't scratch," he offers the following alternatives:

1. Love is a feeling of tenderness and devotion toward someone, so profound that to share that individual's joys, anticipations, sorrows and pain is the very essence of living.

2. Love is the . . . desire on the part of two or more people to produce together the conditions under which each can be and spontaneously express his real self; to produce together an intellectual soil and an emotional climate in which each can flourish far superior to what either could achieve alone.[1]

David Frost once defined love on a television program as follows: "Love is when each person is more concerned for the other than he is for himself."

In their book, *Is Sex Necessary?*, James Thurber and E.B. White give this definition: "Love is the strange bewilderment which overtakes one person on account of another person."

Here is the definition suggested by John Ciardi, a poet: "Love is the word used to label the sexual excitement of the young, the habituation of the middle-aged and the mutual dependence of the old."

How do you react to these proposed definitions? Which, in your judgment, is better? Why? Which do you think are serious and which facetious? What, if anything, needs to be added to complete our definitions of love? Judged by these statements, do you think your parents have had a good love relationship? The parents of your friends? Have you yourself ever experienced for someone feelings which meet the requirements of any of these definitions? Do any of Professor Magoun's words or ideas surprise you?

If any do, it might well be the thought that persons in love want to share each other's *sorrows* and *pains* as well as the joys. Yet this is truly an important aspect of mature love. People who expect to share only the happiness of others, while receiving from them strength to surmount their own weaknesses and fears, possess a most immature concept of love.

It is important to note the implication in the second definition that neither partner in a genuine love relationship is expected to surrender personal individuality or needs. Given two normal people, it is seldom, if ever, possible to have a good marriage when one partner is constantly sacrificing for the other. A martyr is not likely to be a successful husband or wife. (Or, for that matter, a good parent.) Paradoxical as it may at first seem, the person who habitually and fully submits to a mate does not demonstrate true love. To be sure, each partner in marriage will often sacrifice something he or she very much wants in order that a mate might achieve satisfaction. But in a good marriage both will be making such sacrifices—probably with about equal frequency—and the one who renounces personal desires at a given moment will feel that in the long run far more is gained than lost.

Dr. Eric Fromm, an eminent psychoanalyst, has written

wisely about mistaking exaggerated dependency needs for love: ". . . irrational love is love which enhances the person's dependency, hence anxiety and hostility. Rational love is love which relates a person intimately to another, at the same time preserving his independence and integrity."[2] And, "Most people see the problem of love primarily as that of *being loved*, rather than that of *loving*, of one's capacity to love. Hence, the problem to them is how to be loved, how to be lovable."[3] Also, "Infantile love follows the principle: *'I love because I am loved.'* Mature love follows the principle: *'I am loved because I love.'* Immature love says: *'I love you because I need you.'* Mature love says: *'I need you because I love you.'* "[4]

Which comes first: loving or being loved? Which comes first in marriage? What is the difference between liking and loving a person? Is it necessary to like someone in order to love him? To love in order to like her? Number the following in the order of your love for them:

_____ Mother   _____ Neighbor
_____ Father   _____ Sweetheart or steady
                                date, if any
_____ Yourself   _____ Favorite teacher or camp
                                counselor
_____ Siblings   _____ Rabbi
_____ Best friend   _____ Doctor

True or false?
The less I love myself, the more I can love others.
Give reasons for your answer to the above statement.

Love is largely a matter of right emotional relationships. Perhaps an analogy or two will help. Hydrogen and oxygen must exist in the right relationship to each other in order to form water. If, instead of two hydrogen atoms and one oxygen atom, we had one hydrogen atom and two oxygen atoms, the result would not be water. Similarly, the various parts of a watch must be located and operating in the right relationship for one to have a timepiece which functions. If the spring is too large or too small, too strong or too weak, in comparison to the other parts, the watch will not work. If all the parts, though they be of the proper size, are thrown into an envelope but not installed in the right interrelationship, everything physically necessary for a watch will be in the envelope, yet there will be no watch. In each of these analogies, the sum total of the parts in right relationship to each other is more than the sum total of unorganized parts.

Water is more than just hydrogen plus oxygen. A watch is more than just the parts of which it consists. And a couple in love becomes more than one man plus one woman. The man becomes a better man, the woman becomes a happier woman —because of their loving relationship—than either could have become without the other.

A common mistake

Very often love is confused with romance or infatuation. You know the usual Hollywood pattern: gorgeous, glamorous female meets handsome, heroic male . . . they dance to soft music under the stars . . . know at once that each is meant for the other . . . it's love at first sight and they live happily ever after. Or do they? That depends on whether the question applies to an imaginary role or the real life of the movie stars.

There is no such thing as love at first sight. There can indeed be romance at first sight, attraction or infatuation at first sight, but not love! Infatuation is a lower level of experience than love. It can sometimes develop into love, though more often it does not. Even when it does, only the passage of a considerable amount of time can prove this conclusively. Meanwhile, the problem becomes frustrating and dangerous because, for a young person especially, it is so very difficult to distinguish the two; the early manifestations and sensations of infatuation and love are exasperatingly similar. The overwhelming probability is that whatever strong emotional bonds a high school boy or girl has felt toward a contemporary of the opposite sex have been infatuation, rather than love. Because far too many couples fail to distinguish between the two feelings in time to avert disappointment and tragedy, it is vital for us to think about the differences. There are primarily four:

1. The first is the test of time. Love has an enduring quality which infatuation lacks. Infatuation is like a match touched to a pile of combustible brush. The flame catches at once, bursts immediately into frightening fullness which gives the appearance of lasting forever, then quickly subsides and dies. Love is more like a fire built from small beginnings; first, a few pieces of kindling, then larger logs to build the flame, steady replenishment when needed, glowing coals to warm oneself for many hours.

The following diagram may help indicate the difference. Except for the rare instance where infatuation leads to love, it begins more dramatically, develops far more rapidly and expires while love may still be incubating.

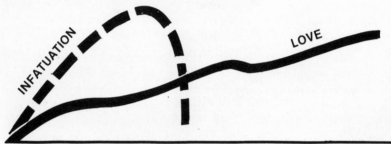

The dips in the line representing love are meant to indicate that love is seldom uncomplicated or smooth. It has its moments of crisis, of conflict, of doubt. But it is likely to be far more enduring than infatuation.

2. A second way of distinguishing infatuation from love is to see whether the emphasis is on the self or the other person, on getting or on giving. The man who is infatuated, for example, is really mostly interested in himself; the object of his infatuation is important only for what she can give him. The frame of reference is: *how–much–pleasure–it–gives–me–to–be–with–you.* The man who is truly in love is at least as interested in his mate as in himself; he becomes more important to himself in proportion to what he is able to give to or do for her. All this is equally true if "woman" is substituted for "man" and "she" for "he" in each of these sentences. In true love, the frame of reference is: *how–much–more–adequate–and–secure–each–of–us–feels–because–of–the–other.*

Dr. Harry Stack Sullivan, a well-known psychoanalyst, has said that love begins when one feels another person's needs to be as important as his own—not *more* important, but *as* important.

3. Couples who are infatuated are interested exclusively in themselves. They prefer to spend most of their time alone. While of course those who are in love also like to spend some time only in each other's company, they enjoy being with others, too. Psychologists have helped us understand that there is no such thing as loving only one person in the world. To be sure, the love of husband and wife for each other differs considerably from their love of others, but the fact remains that neither is capable of loving a mate unless he or she can also love a great many other people.

To love one person in a very special and wonderful way means that, together with that person, I must also want to interest myself in others and do whatever I can for them. Infatuation can be compared to a couple who use a magnifying glass to focus the rays of the sun only on themselves; sooner or later they are likely to be burned. A couple in love tries to direct the sun's rays so that warmth and comfort can be diffused to others, too. Here is the interesting observation of a French philosopher, Antoine de Saint Exupéry: "Life has taught us that love does not consist of gazing at each other but in looking outward together in the same direction."·

Some of the most beautiful love relationships in history have been between two people whose love for each other prompted them to do generous work for others. Elizabeth and Robert Browning wrote exquisite poetry—individually, yet each stimulated and encouraged by the other. Marie and Pierre Curie together discovered radium, and with it brought blessing and healing to multitudes. Louise and Stephen Wise established a great synagogue and labored for those less fortunate than themselves. Not all of us possess the genius of couples such as these. But even ordinary husbands and wives—if each is mature and if they truly love each other—bring blessings of warmth and strength into the lives of those who surround them. Apparently, our ancient rabbis understood this special quality of love. They incorporated this story into midrashic literature:

There once lived a pious man who was childless. He prayed for a son, vowing to invite to his wedding feast every poor person in the city. A son was eventually born to him, and he gave him the name of Mattaniah, namely, a gift from God. The boy grew up and his wedding day approached. The father invited all the students of the Torah and all the poor, who together filled six rooms.

God wished to test the bridegroom, and He sent the Angel of Death, in the guise of a man attired in soiled raiment, to beg for a place at the wedding. The bridegroom refused on the plea that all who could be accommodated had been invited. Moreover, the man's garments were objectionable.

In the night the Angel of Death revealed himself, declaring that he was about to take away the bridegroom's soul, since he had failed in the test. The bride gave voice to this prayer: "O Lord of the Universe, Thou hast said in Thy Torah that, when a man takes unto himself a wife, he shall bring her cheer for a full year and not leave her. May it be Thy will that my husband live before Thee, and I shall teach him to practice lovingkindness to everyone without discrimination."

Her prayer was heard on High, and the Angel of Death was commanded to leave.

What was the nature of this young woman? Her mother was accustomed to draw cool water from a spring for school children. When she became old, her daughter said: "You need not abandon your good deed. I shall lend you the strength of my arm and carry most of the weight so that you may continue to perform the *mitzvah*."

It was this consideration for her mother that made her deserving in the eyes of the Lord.[5]

4. Finally, infatuation is a purely physical experience, while love is both physical and spiritual. By *spiritual* here we mean that two people are together interested in creating or appreciating beauty, in discovering or understanding truth and in improving themselves ethically. True, infatuation involves emotions too, but they are less stable and mature than the emotions of love. It is important to note that love is no less physical than infatuation, but where the one is physical *only*, the other is

physical *plus*. If the primary or sole interest two people have in each other is physical, if their principal joint activity is petting, we can be sure it is an instance of infatuation, not of love.

The statement, "I love oranges," comes closer to infatuation than to love. It obviously bespeaks an attraction which is purely physical and in which the "lover" intends to destroy the orange and use it for his own benefit. Far too frequently men and women mean this when they mistakenly and immaturely believe themselves to be in love. To say that love is a spiritual as well as a physical experience is to say that there is something sacred in the love of a man and a woman for each other. We shall see in subsequent chapters that this sacredness is precisely what Judaism has always taught.

Meanwhile, there are several fascinating assertions in rabbinic literature which bear on this discussion. One is the talmudic statement: "When love was strong, we could lie, as it were, on the edge of a sword; but now, when love is diminished, a bed sixty ells wide is not broad enough for us."[6]

What were the rabbis attempting to tell us here? Were they in fact speaking of love or of infatuation? Is it possible for true love to become diminished? What is the relationship between love and hate?

Here are two rabbinic views on the meaning of love which apparently contradict each other:

a. "Love without admonition is not love."[7]
b. "Love is blind to defects."[8]

Which of these statements is more realistic or accurate? Why? Can the two be reconciled?

Another ancient rabbinic comment on love is worth pondering:

If love depends on some selfish end, when the end fails, love fails; but if it does not depend on a selfish end, it will never fail. An example of love which depended on a selfish end? That was the love of Amnon for Tamar. An example of love which did not depend on a selfish end? That was the love of David and Jonathan.[9]

Compare this statement to the views of Eric Fromm, quoted a few pages back. Do you agree that Amnon and Tamar exemplify a selfish, hence temporary relationship (see II Samuel 13:1–17), while the love of David and Jonathan was unselfish and lasting (see I Samuel, Chapters 19 and 20)? Why did the rabbis call Amnon's love for Tamar selfish? Because it was sexual? What is the difference between love and friendship?

It is possible to arrange a neat list of the four principal differences between infatuation and love, as we have done in this chapter. To distinguish one from the other in actual experience, however, is far more difficult. The feelings which inundate a person who is infatuated and sexually attracted to another are among the most powerful, indeed at times overwhelming, in human experience. They are so strong that it often becomes almost impossible to think clearly or judge objectively. It is easy to think that one is primarily interested in another rather than oneself, that the emotion one feels is broad enough to encompass many others, and that the relationship is spiritual as well as physical—even when, in fact, none of these suppositions is true. This is why the first test of love—the test of time—becomes in a way the most important test of all. Hasty marriages are almost never a good idea. As we shall see in a later chapter, couples who wait patiently, who give themselves opportunity to apply the test of time, have a much better chance for marital happiness than those who marry in haste.

A rebellious seventeen-year-old girl was determined to marry her boyfriend despite the warnings of her parents. They were worried by the fact that he was a high school dropout with a minor prison record. The girl wrote in her diary: "Love can blot out reality."

Do you agree? Why? Can infatuation blot out reality? Romance?

End of story: the two were married and, after several years of turbulence and two children, were divorced.

Further help in the difficult task of distinguishing love from infatuation comes from Dr. Fromm, whom we have already quoted several times. He suggests that the four elements necessary for genuine love are: care, responsibility, respect and knowledge.[10]

> What does it mean for people to *care* for each other? To feel *responsible* for each other? To *respect* each other? To *know* each other? Try to think of a specific person with whom you share these four kinds of relationships. Specifically, how does each trait manifest itself in behavior?

Rabbi Eugene B. Borowitz expresses his understanding of love as follows:

> Our beloved is so concerned with our welfare, he will struggle to provide us with whatever we need or desire. He will do anything to prevent harm from befalling us. More, he cares not only for what we are but for what we yet will be. He recognizes our potential and helps us try to reach it. Love thus validates our existence as nothing else can and, with an unparalleled immediacy, helps turn us into the people we always were meant to be.[11]

> Is it possible to be infatuated with two people simultaneously? To love two people at the same time?

Adding up

To summarize, perhaps the closest we can come to a valid definition of love is something like the following: Love is a consuming desire to share one's whole life both physically and spiritually with another person of the opposite sex. It means sharing one another's sorrows and pains no less than one's pleasures and joys. In love one is at least as anxious to give as to receive. Love is a relationship in which both partners are able to develop their own abilities and fulfill their own hopes in far greater measure than either could have done alone.

A few pages back, you were asked to mark the following statement true or false: *The less I love myself, the more I can love others.* One who accurately understands the meaning of love knows the statement is false. Only a person who realistically accepts and respects himself or herself is capable of loving another. Wholesome love of self means precisely such acceptance and respect, not vainglorious egotism! Men or women who lack it —far from loving others more—will most probably project their own insecurity and destructive criticism against other people.

The kind of love described in this chapter makes it desirable and possible for two people to marry and establish a family. Recognizing the supreme importance of this kind of experience, Judaism has had, from its beginnings, many things to say about love, marriage and the family. You have already become acquainted with a few of these Jewish emphases in foregoing pages; in the next chapter we shall encounter more of them.

Through the centuries, writers and poets have probably devoted more of their time to love than to any other single theme. What, if anything, can we learn about love from each of the following selections? Do you agree with the writer's concept of love? Why? Feel free to add any other literary expression of love which is especially meaningful to you.

Genesis, Chapter 24

And Isaac went out to meditate in the field in the evening; and he lifted up his eyes and looked, and behold, there were camels coming. And Rebekah lifted up her eyes, and when she saw Isaac, she alighted from the camel and said to the servant, 'Who is the man yonder, walking in the field to meet us?' The servant said, 'It is my master.' So she took her veil and covered herself. And the servant told Isaac all the things that he had done. Then Isaac brought her into the tent of his mother Sarah and took Rebekah as his wife; and he loved her. So Isaac was comforted after his mother's death.

Sonnet 116   WILLIAM SHAKESPEARE

Let me not to the marriage of true minds
Admit impediments. Love is not love
Which alters when it alteration finds,
Or bends with the remover to remove.
O no! it is an ever–fixed mark
That looks on tempests and is never shaken;
It is the star to every wand'ring bark
Whose worth's unknown, although his height be taken.
Love's not Time's fool, though rosy lips and cheeks
Within his bending sickle's compass come;
Love alters not with his brief hours and weeks,
But bears it out even to the edge of doom.
    If this be error and upon me proved,
    I never writ, nor no man ever loved.

How Do I Love Thee?   ELIZABETH BARRETT BROWNING

How do I love thee? Let me count the ways.
I love thee to the depth and breadth and height
My soul can reach, when feeling out of sight
For the ends of Being and ideal Grace.
I love thee to the level of everyday's
Most quiet need, by sun and candle-light.
I love thee freely, as men strive for Right;
I love thee purely, as they turn from Praise.
I love thee with the passion put to use
In my old griefs, and with my childhood's faith.
I love thee with a love I seemed to lose
With my lost saints—I love thee with the breath,
Smiles, tears, of all my life!—and, if God choose,
I shall but love thee better after death.

True Love   JUDITH VIORST

It's true love because
I put on eyeliner and a concerto and make pungent
    observations about the great issues of the day
Even when there's no one here but him,
And because
I do not resent watching the Green Bay Packers

Even though I am philosophically opposed to football,
And because
When he is late for dinner and I know he must be
  either having an affair or lying dead in the middle of a
  street,
I always hope he's dead.
It's true love because
If he said quit drinking martinis but I kept drinking them
  and
  the next morning I couldn't get out of bed,
He wouldn't tell me he told me,
And because
He is willing to wear unironed undershorts
Out of respect for the fact that I am philosophically
  opposed
  to ironing,
And because
If his mother was drowning and I was drowning and he
  had to
  choose one of us to save,
He says he'd save me.
It's true love because
When he went to San Francisco on business while I
  had to stay home with the painters and the exterminator
  and the baby who was getting the chicken pox,
He understood why I hated him,
And because
When I said that playing the stock market was
  juvenile and irresponsible and then the stock I
  wouldn't let him buy went up twenty-six points,
I understood why he hated me,
And because
Despite cigarette cough, tooth decay, acid indigestion,
  dandruff, and other features of married life that tend
  to dampen the fires of passion,
We still feel something
We can call
True love.

For instance

A. Grace is in no hurry to marry. She is a very attractive woman and has been popular since her early high school days. Now twenty-six, she receives many calls for dates, and enjoys her social life a great deal. She has politely rejected four proposals of marriage, saying each time that her father is the most wonderful man she has ever known and she does not expect to marry until she finds a man as superb as he. Her parents are pleased with her attitude. They agree that their family relationship is an exceptionally close one and that they are able to give Grace a warm and satisfying kind of love. They see no reason for her to risk giving up something she knows and needs for something of which she cannot, after all, be sure.

What do you think of Grace's attitude and that of her parents? When do you think she might be ready for marriage? Does she seem to be more or less secure than the average person in her circumstances? How great is her capacity for the kind of love discussed in this chapter?

B. Do you recall the case of Frances and Bill, described in Chapter 1? Mention was made there of the security Frances felt whenever she was with Bill. Bill encourages her to feel this way. He remembers that when he was a child his mother, who had to carry most of the family burdens because his father was a weak person, lived an unhappy life. And he does not want his wife to face a similar situation. He feels that a man who truly loves his wife will protect her as far as possible from all difficulty. Because of his strong conviction on this, he makes nearly all the important decisions for the two of them. When they are married, he expects to handle all the details of their budget and checking account, giving Frances a generous allowance and sparing her the trouble of managing any money matters. When he faces business reverses or worries, he does not mention them to her; he wants her to be happy. These are some of the reasons Frances feels confident and secure. She is sure they will have a happy life together.

What would you say appears to be the prognosis for this marriage? How valid is the love between these two people? Does it meet the requirements set forth in this chapter? To what degree do Frances and Bill seem to meet each other's needs?

C. Karl and Jennie had experienced twenty years of happy married life together before she was stricken with a serious and presumably incurable disease. Though there is no danger of imminent death, Jennie is almost completely incapacitated, spending most of her time in bed. On the rare occasions that she is able to leave her bed for a few hours, she must be helped into a wheelchair and then back to bed. It is five years since they have been able to share any kind of sex life. Karl has been so attentive to her, so solicitous of her needs, that their friends call him a saint. He has given up golf, cards and everything else he formerly enjoyed. Hurrying home from work at the earliest possible moment each day, he sends the nurse away and hovers over Jennie with tender care. Whenever she voices her guilt over the heavy burdens her illness has placed upon him, he interrupts to tell her over and over how much he loves her and how happy he is to care for her.

Is it possible for two people to remain in love under these circumstances? Does their relationship fulfill the requirements of love discussed in this chapter? Are they mutually meeting each other's needs? Are they each helping the other develop their own highest capacities? How would you judge their relationship in the light of what this chapter says about martyrdom?

D. To all the facts about Karl and Jennie described above, add this: Jennie has deteriorated to the point of having to be placed in a nursing home, where she will have to spend the rest of her life. She is virtually an infant; all her needs must be met by nurses. She no longer even recognizes Karl or anyone else who visits her.

Do these facts change any of your answers to Case C above? Can we still speak of love between Karl and Jennie? What are Karl's obligations to Jennie? To himself? Does he have the right to divorce her? To marry someone else?

E. Donald and Jo are so "madly in love" they can scarcely bear being apart. All day long on the job he thinks of her and can barely wait for the evening when they can be together again. They used to date with one or two other couples but recently find they are spending their evenings more and more alone. Other people just seem to distract their attention and to delay the hour they really desire—the time when they can curl up together in the comfortable livingroom chair. The physical attraction between them becomes stronger and stronger. They have petted a lot and have had intercourse which they find mutually exciting and pleasurable. While both have some doubts as to the propriety of their behavior, somehow they seem unable to resist intimate physical contact when they are together. This desire, far from subsiding in the six months they have been in love, grows stronger from day to day. It is this fact more than anything else which convinces both of them that their love is genuine; they wish they could marry now, but financial conditions make this impossible for at least another year.

Is this a case of love or infatuation? Why? Of what significance is the fact that they have felt this way for six months and that their feelings toward each other grow stronger and stronger? Would their situation be better if they were able to marry now?

3

"I'm afraid your mother is right, Miss Collins; it says, 'No one is good enough for you.'"

Love
and
the family

Most of us probably take our families for granted, precisely because we have always lived as part of them—much as we take the oxygen in our atmosphere for granted because we have breathed it from the instant of birth. But a moment's reflection will convince us that the family is not only one of humankind's most important institutions, it is a uniquely human invention. There is nothing like the family in animal life. There are, perhaps, prototypes for the clan or tribe in the herds found among certain species of animals, but there is nothing even resembling the family!

One reason for this is that it is only the human infant that remains dependent on its parents for so long a time. In animal life, the newborn needs one or both parents for a matter of weeks, sometimes months, rarely as long as a year or two. Usually the male parent is not aware of his offspring, while the female parent remains with them only so long as she is biologically needed. Human children need parents at least through the years of adolescence, sometimes longer. A strong and durable family is the only means of insuring them the prolonged attention they require.

One of the most impressive pieces of sculpture in London's Tate Gallery is *Family Group* by Henry Moore. It depicts a mother and father holding their child in such delicate and graceful balance that, if either one should let go, the child would fall. This is a true representation of the fact that children require the active interest and support of both parents. If either one is absent—by virtue of divorce or death—the other must exert extra effort to compensate for this absence.

This is, however, only part of the story. We observed in the last chapter that a distinguishing feature of love is its spiritual as well as physical dimension. The capacity for spiritual experience is exclusively human. Animals are capable only of physical relationships. True, we can see, in the more highly developed of them, certain incipient emotions, loyalties and attachments. We observe in some animals the ability to accept discipline and other traits which are the beginnings of what later becomes spiritual experience on the human level. But only in us are these potentialities sufficiently developed to be called spiritual; only in us, therefore, is the family possible.

The human family is a product of the kind of love with which we became acquainted in Chapter 2. It results when a man and woman feel so strong a desire to share all aspects of life that they wish to establish an environment in which such sharing will be permanently possible. Hence the family at its best is both a consequence of love and the best means we know of fostering its further development.

The Jewish family

In no culture or group has the family been so important as in ours. One of the earliest idyllic descriptions of wholesome family life, encompassing three generations, is found in Psalm 128:

> Happy are all who revere the Lord,
>   who follow His ways.
> You shall enjoy the fruit of your labors;
>   you shall be happy and you shall prosper.
> Your wife shall be like a fruitful vine within your house;
>   your sons, like olive saplings around your table.
> So shall the man who reveres the Lord be blessed.
>
> May the Lord bless you from Zion;
>   may you share the prosperity of Jerusalem
> all the days of your life,
>   and live to see your children's children.

For many centuries this beautiful ideal was the goal of most Jewish families and was in fact realized by many of them. You may have read *New Atlantis*, the account by Francis Bacon of a fictitious perfect community. In it there was only one Jewish family. They had been invited to the community to teach the rest of the inhabitants the qualities of family devotion and love for which the Jewish people has long been famous.

Sociologists have marveled at the strength and beauty of Jewish family life. To this, more than anything else, they have attributed the fact that rates of juvenile delinquency, intoxication, drug addiction, sexual immorality, and divorce have been substantially lower among Jews than in any other group. Some have asserted that the exceptional quality of the Jewish family is due to the many privations and persecutions our people has suffered. It is suggested that, because Jews were not accepted in the larger society, because their lives were insecure and so many satisfactions outside the family were denied them, they turned to their own families for compensation.

While this was undeniably a factor, it is far from the full explanation. The excellence of the Jewish family was also created by factors from within our heritage, by the ideals of family life which developed as part of the ethical code of

Judaism. Modern Jews who are unaware of these ideals are impoverished persons; doubly impoverished, because they have forfeited a legitimate source of pride in being Jews, and have neglected a possible stimulus to added happiness in their marriage. One of the tragedies of Jewish life in the United States today is that, because our knowledge of Jewish teaching in this area is less thorough than it once was, the superiority of Jewish family life is now being threatened.

Experts are agreed that in recent years the differences between Jewish and non-Jewish families have decreased. If this were due to improvement in the quality of non-Jewish family life, it would be cause for rejoicing. Unfortunately, the opposite is true. The number of broken families, the rates of delinquency, drug addiction and divorce among American Jews have increased alarmingly. The superiority of Jewish family life—while still existent—is not nearly as dramatic as it was half a century ago. This represents a great loss both to us and to society at large.

In the summer of 1964, Louis Z. Grant, a Chicago Jewish attorney who has specialized in matrimonial law, declared that there had been a tenfold increase in divorces among Jews during the preceding decade. The greatest proportion of these divorces, he said, were to be found in "the lost generation of Jews, without a proper Jewish education." Unfortunately, this trend has continued. The principal purpose of this chapter is to review some of our Jewish precepts on marriage and the family, in the hope that they may increase the probability of happiness some day in your own marriage.

Ancient wisdom

There are numerous indications in Jewish tradition that, long before the advent of modern psychology and marriage counseling, our ancestors were aware of the truths we have already discussed regarding love. They knew that love means a full sharing of life between the lovers, that it provides a fulfillment together for each that would be impossible for either alone. Thus one of our ancient rabbis said: "He who has no wife remains without good, without a helper, without joy, without a blessing. . . ." To which a colleague added: "He is not a whole man." And still other rabbis said: "The unmarried man diminishes the likeness of God." In much the same spirit, one of the medieval Jewish mystics declared: "The שְׁכִינָה *Shechinah* (God's Spirit) can rest only upon a married man, because an unmarried man is but half a man, and the שְׁכִינָה does not rest upon that which is imperfect."[1]

What would you regard as the distinction between a whole man and a half man? Can it be said that every married man is a whole man, while every unmarried man is half a man? What might the rabbis have had in mind when they suggested that the unmarried man "diminishes the likeness of God"? Is an unmarried woman necessarily half a woman? Can a woman have a creative, fulfilled life without ever marrying? Without having children?

The completeness and fulfillment which husband and wife can bring to each other was further emphasized by our ancient teachers in their comments on the sadness of either mate's losing the other. Thus the Talmud proclaims: "The widower lives in a darkened world."[2] It adds that when a man's wife dies, his steps are shortened, his spine becomes bent and it is as if the Temple had been destroyed in his time. To which Rabbi Samuel bar Nachman added: "For everything there is a substitute except for the wife of one's youth."[3]

The association of God with love, already noted, is of special consequence to Judaism. One legend relates that God creates each soul in two parts. One half He places in the body of a male, the other in the body of a female. And love means that the two halves of one soul, created together and originally meant for each other, are reunited in accordance with God's plan. In another rabbinic legend we are told that God thought His creation of the universe had been completed after he had formed Adam. He was disturbed, however, by a note of discord which marred the harmony of the spheres. An angel whom He sent to investigate reported back that the disturbing sound was Adam's sigh of loneliness. Then God created Eve to be Adam's partner, the discord disappeared and the work of Creation was really finished. In the same vein, when asked by a Roman woman what God has been doing to keep Himself occupied since Creation was completed, one of the ancient rabbis answered that He spends His time matching couples for marriage.

These are some of the quaint, poetic ways in which the teachers of ancient Judaism expressed their conviction that love is part of the very plan of the universe—not merely an incidental relationship conjured up by us on our own. The same truth can be seen and expressed in modern scientific terms. We tend to think of nature as being harsh and cruel, as indeed it often is. What we too frequently forget is that the beginnings of love may be seen in nature, too. Protons, neutrons and electrons must all remain in the proper proportion and relationship with each other for atoms to exist. Atoms must follow a similar pattern if there are to be molecules. Molecules, in turn, must relate to each other in a manner which could almost be called cooperative if there are to be cells, cells if there are to be whole organisms, individuals if there are to be tribes and nations, nations if a peaceful world is to survive.

We see this most dramatically in the relationship between cells. Originally there were only single-celled forms of life on the earth. In the course of time, two cells "learned" to remain together in a larger whole; then four, then eight—until, finally, we have organisms which contain many millions of cells. When cells developed a way of remaining together, they also began the process of specialization. At the risk of minor over-simplification, it may be said that one group of cells undertook the responsibility of digestion for the entire organism, freeing another group to assume the responsibility of locomotion, another of reproduction, another of elimination, and so on. Despite the fact that all this took place automatically, with no conscious intent on the part of the cells—what was really occurring is that cells were "learning" to do things for each other. With this ability each individual cell was able to realize itself and its potentialities to a greater degree than any of them could have done alone.

Here, on the crudest, most elementary level of simple biology is nature's pattern for what later became human love. It would be stretching the truth to call the relationship between cells—or, for that matter, even between animals—love. Yet the fact is that, long before the appearance of the first human being on earth, nature demonstrated that it already possessed the potentiality for love and was moving through evolution in the direction of love. Human love developed out of these earlier relationships just as truly as the human arm and hand developed from the foreleg and paw of earlier animals.

This is a modern way of understanding what our Jewish ancestors meant when they associated human love with God. Love—though experienced in its fullest dimension only on the human level—is part of the dynamic purpose or thrust of the universe itself.

"By this ring"

Through the centuries, Jewish law underscored the importance of marriage. One talmudic passage rules that the only purpose for which one is permitted to sell a Torah scroll is to make marriage possible for a poor girl who would otherwise be unable to marry for lack of a dowry. Another passage states explicitly: "A man shall first take unto himself a wife and then study Torah." We can appreciate these two statements only when we realize that Torah and its study constituted the most precious possession and sacred obligation of the Jew. In ancient Temple days the High Priest was not permitted to perform the most sacred rites of the year, those of atonement on Yom Kippur, unless he was married.[4] It was decreed also that, if a marriage and a funeral processional approached an intersection simultaneously, priority was to be given to the former.

Occasionally you may have heard a person say, either facetiously or in earnest, that he or she preferred to remain single because marriage would mean relinquishing a certain amount of freedom. Evidently some people were of this opinion in talmudic times, too. The rabbis answered them by telling the story of an emperor who said one day to Rabbi Gamaliel:

> Your God is a thief, because it is written (in Genesis): "The Lord God caused a deep sleep to fall upon Adam, and he slept; and He took one of his ribs (to create Eve)." Rabbi Gamaliel's daughter, who had overheard the conversation, asked her father to let her handle the matter. The next day she entered a complaint with the emperor that thieves had broken into her home the night before,

taking a silver vessel and leaving a gold one. "Would that such a thief visited me every day!" exclaimed the emperor. The rabbi's daughter at once continued: "Was it not, then, a splendid thing for the first man when a single rib was taken from him and a wife was supplied in its stead?"[5]

There are, indeed, certain restrictions which one voluntarily takes upon oneself in marriage; we would be wise to perceive, however—as our rabbis did—that, in the right kind of marriage, what each partner gains is far greater than the loss.

No reward of marriage is greater than parenthood. This, too, is a truth long recognized by Judaism. We are reminded by our rabbis that the very first positive commandment given by God was: "Be fruitful and multiply and replenish the earth!" (Gen. 1:28) No marriage is considered complete until the couple is blessed with offspring. Among the many sayings that have come down to us are these: "A man is not a complete man if he has no son and daughter. . . . A man without children is like a piece of wood, which though kindled does not burn or give out light. . . . A man with children eats his bread in joy; a man without children eats it in sadness."[6]

If these statements were being phrased today, they would no doubt each commence with "A man or woman. . . ." The ancients were regrettably less sensitive to sexual equality than we are today. You will notice again and again—as you read the many quotations in these pages taken from either the Bible or the Talmud—how frequently they are expressed from a masculine point of view. We must remember that they were written by men in a patriarchal society. Even though they often sound sexist to us, they must be quoted accurately, as written. Later in this volume we shall turn our attention to the role of woman in the Jewish family and to changes in both vocabulary and ideas which must be made today if we are to avoid blatant sexism.

Meanwhile, with reference to the quotations given above, ask yourself these questions:

Does a married couple have a responsibility to bear children? What are the advantages and disadvantages of having children? Would your parents have been better off without children? With more children than they have? Do you want to be a parent some day? Why?

Because our rabbis realized the enormous importance of love, they created a marriage ceremony by which men and women could formally declare their feelings for each other and, with the sanction of God and society, begin to establish a family. This ceremony they called קִדּוּשִׁין kiddushin, a word you will immediately recognize as coming from the same root as the words קַדִּישׁ kaddish and קִדּוּשׁ kiddush, hence expressing sanctity or holiness. The blessings recited as part of this ceremony acknowledge God as the Source of Love. The couple drinks from one or two glasses of wine, symbolizing the fact that henceforth they will taste together both the happiness and the sorrow of life. In an Orthodox or Conservative ceremony a כְּתוּבָּה ketubah is read—a kind of contract in which the groom accepts certain legal obligations toward his bride. In addition to his promise that she will be compensated financially if their union should ever be dissolved, he vows that he will "worship, esteem and treat her kindly, as is the custom of Jewish husbands." Traditionally the groom placed a gold ring on the bride's finger. As he did this, he declared: "By this ring you are consecrated unto me (as my wife), in accordance with the faith of Moses and of Israel."

הֲרֵי אַתְּ מְקֻדֶּשֶׁת לִי בְּטַבַּעַת זוֹ כְּדַת מֹשֶׁה וְיִשְׂרָאֵל

Harei at mekudeshet li betabaat zo, kedat Mosheh veYisrael.

In many modern ceremonies the bride also places a ring on her groom's finger. The Hebrew formula which the Talmud suggested for her to recite seems never to have been adopted as common practice. Some rabbis today ask the bride simply to repeat the groom's declaration with a change of gender: "By this ring you are consecrated unto me (as my husband), in accordance with the faith of Moses and of Israel." Other rabbis direct the bride to address her groom in the words of Song of Songs: "My beloved is mine and I am his."

דּוֹדִי לִי וַאֲנִי לוֹ Dodi li va'ani lo.

Thus from the beginning husband and wife understand that they partake of precious Jewish tradition, that Jewish survival depends on the kind of home they establish and that they in turn are dependent on Judaism if they are to fulfill the richest potential of their marriage.

The Jewish marriage ceremony is one of simple dignity. In this, as in all other respects, our rabbis resented ostentation and attempted to forbid it. Whenever wealthy parents were inclined to indulge in extravagant wedding ceremonies, the rabbis reminded them that the real religious significance of the occasion must not be obliterated by gaudy tinsel. If a prospective bride lacked the means for a respectable wedding gown, it became the responsibility of the community to provide one. In American Jewish life today this emphasis is needed even more than in the past. Rabbis generally agree that the most appropriate places for a marriage ceremony are one's home or temple. The reception following the ceremony should be dignified and simple. In place of an expensive and ornate celebration, how much better it is for the bride's parents either to help the young couple with the money saved or, if such help is not needed, to contribute to an important philanthropy in honor of their happiness.

Can you think of places as appropriate for a wedding as your temple or home? How about outdoor weddings? What should a bride and groom respectively promise each other at their wedding ceremony? Try to write a declaration which they could recite jointly or to each other.

No guarantee

One of the most common mistakes made by young people today is the assumption that, merely because they love each other and have participated in a wedding ceremony, a happy life together will follow automatically. The founders and teachers of Judaism were too wise to make that error. They knew that marriage is a priceless opportunity, not a guarantee; that each couple must earn its own happiness. And in order that Jewish husbands and wives might realize the promise of their love and establish together families that would achieve happiness, our tradition contains a number of important directives.

Here are a few of the injunctions which our rabbinic fore-bears promulgated:

- Your wife has been given to you in order that you may realize with her life's great plan; she is not yours to vex or grieve. Vex her not, for God notes her tears.
- A wife is the joy of man's heart.
- A man should eat less than he can afford and should honor his wife and children more than he can afford.
- A man should be careful not to irritate his wife and cause her to weep.[7]
- If your wife is short, bend down and whisper to her.[8]
- He who loves his wife as himself who honors her more than himself who rears his children in the right path and who marries them off at the proper time of their life, concerning him it is written: And thou wilt know that thy home is peace.[9]
- Man should ever be mindful of the honor of his wife for she is responsible for all the blessings found in his household.
- A man must not cause his wife to weep for God counts her tears.
- Strive to fulfill your wife's wishes for it is equivalent to doing God's will.[10]

How can we account for the fact that all these instructions are directed to the husband? Does this mean only he must act considerately in order for the marriage to succeed? How about the wife's meeting his needs? Does a weeping wife always mean a bad marriage? Why does one of these quotations stipulate that a man should love his wife "as himself"? Should he not love her more than himself? What do you think of this same statement's apparent implication that a man should honor his wife even more than he loves her?

The following additional rabbinic comments may help you answer some of these questions:

- When the husband is blessed, his wife is also blessed thereby.

- A wife who receives love gives love in return; if she receives anger, she returns anger in equal measure.[11]

In the same category is the talmudic dictum that the choice of a new place of residence or of a different profession must be made jointly by husband and wife. Significantly enough, the only circumstance in which this did not hold was if one of them wished to live in the Holy Land and the other did not. In that event, the desire of the one who wanted to live in the land of Israel received priority.

Finally, Jewish tradition has long recognized that husband and wife must be sensitive to each other's moods and needs, must be able to perceive them, even without a word from the other. Thus a chasidic rabbi related this incident:

> A commander-in-chief received a message telling him that his main line of defense had been broken by the enemy. He was greatly distressed and his emotions showed plainly on his countenance. His wife heard the nature of the message and, entering her husband's room, she said: "I too at this very moment have received tidings worse than yours."
>
> "And what are they?" inquired the commander with agitation.
>
> "I have read discouragement on your face," replied the wife. "Loss of courage is worse than loss of defense."[12]

The teachings of Judaism about marriage have not been just theoretical. That they have actually influenced behavior is indicated by studies which reveal that among Jews in the United States marriages occur at a later age than in other groups and that Jews are likely to have more stable marriages than others.[13]

In spite of all

Our account of traditional and historic Jewish attitudes would be incomplete were we not to say something about the Jewish view of divorce. After all, men and women are not perfect.

Despite the high ideals of Judaism and the best efforts of individual husbands and wives, not every marriage has succeeded—either in the past or in our own time. Some religions are unalterably opposed to divorce. They decree that marriage is a permanent covenant which must never be broken. No matter how unhappy two people may be in their marriage, it must be maintained. In certain faiths divorce is prohibited; in others, a couple may be divorced but neither may subsequently marry again.

Judaism agrees that marriage is a sacred enterprise, one into which we should not enter lightly nor with the idea that it can be easily dissolved. The Talmud stipulates that "a man should not marry a woman with the thought in mind that he may divorce her."[14] In our tradition divorce has always been looked upon as a pathetic tragedy. "He who puts away the wife of his youth, for him God's very altar weeps."[15]

A beautifully poignant and poetic story is told concerning the proposed divorce of one couple. It is based on the talmudic law that a husband whose wife has given him no children in a decade of married life may divorce her.

> There was a woman in Sidon who lived ten years with her husband and had borne no children. They went to R. Simeon b.Yohai and asked to be divorced. He said to them: "As your coming together was with a banquet, so let your separation be with a banquet." They agreed and prepared a large banquet at which the wife made her husband drink more than enough. Before he fell asleep he said to her: "Pick out what is most precious to you in my house, and take it with you to your father's house." What did she do? When he had gone to sleep, she beckoned to her servants and said to them: "Carry him on his mattress to my father's house." In the middle of the night he awakened and said to her: "Whither have I been brought?" She said: "To my father's house." He said to her: "Why have I been brought here?" She replied: "Did you not tell me last night to take what was most precious to me in your house and to go with it to my father's house? There is nothing in the world more precious to me than you."[16]

What does this story intend to convey to us? What does it demonstrate about Jewish law? Do you think that the inability to have children was a valid ground for divorce? Is it today?

It is clear, then that in Judaism marriage has always been deemed a permanent, sacred bond, not to be disturbed or upset for slim cause. Yet our tradition does not prohibit divorce. It recognizes that even more tragic than the separation of husband and wife is their living a life of pretense and deceit. Often couples who have reached the end of the road remain together nonetheless in order to spare their children the consequences of a divorce. Now Judaism is aware of how tragic such consequences can be; children need a unified home, with discipline and love from both parents, to maximize their chance for wholesome development.

Malcolm Boyd, an Episcopal priest, has described in a poignant passage his recollection of the conversation in which his parents first told him of their impending divorce. He was a young child at the time.

My father's voice had an infinite tiredness. "Malcolm. Your mother and I both love you. We both want you to be safe and happy and secure. . . ."

I sat there on the hassock, trembling on the verge of nowhere.

Another silence.

I never heard my mother's voice more even, more controlled. "What we need to know, Malcolm, is whether you'd rather stay with me or go with your father. It's not going to be easy, either way. I'm going to have to move into a small apartment, and I'm going to try to find a job. Your father will have his own place."

Another silence. I looked from one to the other and hoped I was just having a bad dream. But I knew I wasn't. This was happening.

I didn't say anything. I had no idea which one I wanted to be with. I wanted to stay with both of them. I looked at my father's face, impassive there on the couch, so worn and somber. What would I do? Where would I go? I was afraid. Things were going on all around me that I didn't understand, and Daddy and Mother were a part of those things; however, just as I was, they also were hurt by them, angered by them. And I knew there wasn't anything I could do about those things. . . . I had a vision of racing down strange city streets, yelling, Daddy help me, the monster's after me, and knowing that Daddy couldn't.

But *why?* Why did things have to be like this?

I shriveled inside me. I didn't know. And how could I ask them to explain? And how could I make them stop? I felt helpless. I was desperately afraid of the plight in which I found the persons that meant more to me than anyone else in the world—that archetypal man against whom all other men in my life would be measured; that archetypal woman who had given me birth and would soon provide my home and sole source of familial love.[17]

If your parents are divorced, you can well identify with Malcolm Boyd's plaintive cry. You know how he felt. It isn't easy to divide your allegiance and time between two parents who unfortunately no longer love each other but both of whom still love you. And, if either of your parents has married again, you are aware of additional complications caused by your relationship to a new family which simultaneously is and isn't yours. Even if you haven't experienced this kind of trauma yourself, you may have friends who have and through whom you know how real Boyd's pain was.

In some instances the children of a divorced couple are given a choice as to the parent with whom they will live; in other cases the choice is made for them. Where the decision is left to the children, they should try to make it on the basis of where they themselves will be more comfortable, without feeling guilty toward the parent who is not selected.

Unfortunately, a divorced parent will sometimes try to influence a child against the other parent. This is grossly and inexcusably unfair to the child. A son or daughter who is thus "used" should avoid expressing favoritism toward one parent or the other.

It is most important to remember that, however unpleasant or difficult the separation of one's parents undeniably is, it need not blight the lives or damage the eventual marriages of their children. Quite to the contrary, many young men and women who have lived through parental divorces have used this experience to learn from their parents' mistakes and thereby, in due course, have had better and stronger marriages themselves.

As difficult as divorce may be, a home which is intact physically while broken spiritually, a home which is maintained though husband and wife no longer love each other, perhaps have even come to hate each other, can harm children even more drastically than divorce.

This is more than just theory. My daughter was divorced. The effect on her two children was serious. But I was eyewitness to the fact that they were far more deeply disturbed by the years in which their parents lived together unhappily than by the final separation. My family's experience is typical. A study of schoolboys in the state of Washington revealed that intact but quarreling families were more likely to produce delinquents than broken families.[18] Judaism, understanding this, has provided the conditions under which two people whose marriage has failed may seek a separation.

Before examining these conditions, it would be wise to pause for a further word about marriages that have failed. From time to time every rabbi hears of a couple who are not happy in their marriage but think that if they have a child it might help. It almost never does. A successful marriage is a precondition for having children, not a consequence. A child has the right to be born into a happy home. Later we shall see that the time for troubled people to straighten themselves out is before marriage, not afterward. And the time for a shaky marriage to be repaired is before the arrival of children. The appearance of children does not remove troublesome problems; it very often adds new ones.

Now let us turn to the conditions under which Jewish tradition approves divorce. They are first described in the Bible: "A man takes a wife and possesses her. She fails to please him because he finds something obnoxious about her, and he writes her a bill of divorcement, hands it to her and sends her away from his house." (Deut. 24:1) The first thing that will strike you in these words is that they give the privilege of divorce only to the husband. A complicated structure of talmudic law based on this biblical passage shows the same tendency; no direct right of divorce is provided for the wife. The rabbis seem to have been aware of this inequity. Therefore they provided that, in certain circumstances, a wife could petition the court to ask her husband for a divorce, and, if right were on her side and he refused, the court was authorized to pressure him until it obtained his assent. Maimonides expressed this principle of Jewish law as follows: "If a woman says, 'My husband is distasteful to me, I cannot live with him,' the court compels the husband to divorce her, because a wife is not a captive."[19] So the possibilities for a woman to obtain a divorce were not quite so one-sided as they first appear.

In Jewish law a woman was entitled to a divorce if her husband refused to have sexual intercourse with her, if he contracted a loathsome disease which she was unable to endure or if his occupation caused an odor about his person which she could not stand. Also if he treated her cruelly, prohibited her from visiting her parents, changed his religion or was notoriously immoral.

A husband could obtain a divorce if his wife was guilty of adultery, insulted him or his father in his presence, was morally indecent in public, disregarded the ritual laws pertaining to women or refused to have sexual intercourse with him. If husband and wife agreed mutually that they did not wish to remain married any longer, no further justification was needed; the court was compelled to grant their request. In all cases, however, the rights of the wife to adequate support, stipulated in the כְּתוּבָּה ketubah (marriage contract) which was read during the wedding ceremony, had to be respected.[20]

In Orthodox and Conservative Judaism it is necessary for a couple to obtain a religious as well as a civil divorce. The religious divorce, called a גֵּט get, is issued by a rabbi or rabbinical court. In Reform Judaism the civil divorce is considered sufficient.

Judaism accepts divorce, but only as a last resort. Every possible effort must first be made to correct whatever may be faulty in a marriage, in the hope that it can be preserved. Indeed, reconciling a quarreling couple is considered a great virtue. The story is told of Rabbi Meir, who lectured to the public each Friday evening. A certain woman attended these lectures regularly. Her husband, who was not interested in them himself, objected to the fact that she returned home later than he wished. Finally he banished her from the house in a temper and said she could not return until she had spat in Rabbi Meir's eye. She spent the week with a neighbor and returned the following Friday to hear the rabbi's lecture again. In the meantime, the rabbi had heard of her husband's unreasonable demand. He called the woman to him before the assembled audience and said: "My eye gives me pain. Spit into it and it will be relieved." It took considerable persuasion before the woman was willing to comply, but she finally did and her husband, when he heard of it, took her back again. We are not told whether she attended subsequent lectures, or, if she did, how her husband reacted. The point of the story is clear: a great rabbi estimated his own dignity and position to be less important than repairing a broken marriage.[21] We need not approve the behavior of a husband who obviously tried to dominate his wife's interests and activities.

Future of the family

Like our sexual mores, like marriage itself, the institution of the family has been exposed to many changes and there are differences of opinion even among experts as to whether families as we have known them will endure. Psychoanalyst William Wolf has written: "The family is dead except for the first year or two of child raising. This will be its only function."

Dr. Irwin Greenberg, professor of psychiatry at Albert Einstein College of Medicine, disagrees. He insists that the more turbulent and uncertain life becomes the more "people will marry for stable structure." The family, he adds, will serve as our "portable roots," anchoring us against the winds of bewildering and threatening change.

Sociologist Alvin Toffler chooses the middle ground between these extremes. He suggests that "the family may neither vanish nor enter upon a new golden age. It may . . . break up, shatter, only to come together again in weird and novel ways."

Which of these men is right? Will people continue to live in organized families? Judging from your own experience, what are the advantages and disadvantages of family life?

It will help you approach these questions intelligently if you consider the specific changes which have occurred in American family structure and life during the past generation or two. For one thing, our families are on the average much smaller than they once were. Instead of the extended family—in which there were many children, where often three and sometimes four generations lived together—we now live, most of us, in nuclear families, that is to say, just parents and one or two children. In the past there was much interaction among individuals and generations in the same household. Children learned—for better or worse—by observing how persons related to each other, by experiencing how tensions were resolved, by living through such family crises as illness, death, marriages, funerals, economic distress in their own homes. The resolution of these and similar crises, at best, offered a living laboratory which created knowledge and sensitivity to the needs of others. With small family units, with the illness and death of grandparents more often removed to hospitals and nursing homes, opportunities for family learning are restricted.

Concurrent with this kind of change, the family is no longer the natural economic unit it once was. In the rural environment previously so typical for Americans, every member of the family, of every age, had to accept financial or occupational responsibilities to insure survival. We now assign most of our economic functions to agencies and individuals outside the family. Many young children today relate milk to cartons rather than cows and cereals to convenient packages rather than the fields in which they grow. Families formerly worked together naturally and inevitably. Now we must devise artificial and sometimes silly projects in what may be a losing battle to give parents and their children responsibilities and activities to confront together.

Even when we are together in our homes, it is often in the passive sense of watching a television program—if, indeed, not several programs on a variety of sets—not in the active performance of essential tasks which unite us. To an alarming degree, our homes are no longer places of cooperative living; they have become service stations where each of us stops from time to time for food, changes of clothing and rest. It would be foolishly naive to ignore the inevitable effect of changes such as these on our families.

Are the family ideals of Judaism still valid in the light of these changed circumstances? Is it possible, or even desirable, to return to the kind of families our grandparents knew? How typical of your family is the description given above? Do you enjoy your family life? Would you be satisfied with the same kind of home when you marry?

Families can be good or bad, wholesome or sick. This is because people can be healthy or neurotic. Emotionally unbalanced or immature individuals sometimes use their families as an arena in which they attack, threaten, and tyrannize each other. For people who are mature and well, the family offers an environment of love, of trust, of learning and growing together. Fathers and mothers give their sons and daughters models of adequate sex roles. Brothers and sisters learn to recognize and satisfy another person's needs and thereby to fulfill themselves. As against the corrosive impersonality and mechanism so characteristic of society at large, the family can bless us with people who really care.

On a spectrum of families at their best and worst, where would you place your family? Does your home cramp your development or encourage it? If you were a parent, what would you do differently? What could your parents do to improve your family life? What could you do?

For instance

A. Fred and Lisa were married eleven years ago. Things seemed to be going well with them for the first few years. Since their financial circumstances made it necessary for both to work, they planned not to have children too soon. By the time of their fifth anniversary, however, Fred had received a substantial raise in salary, Lisa was able to think of resigning her position and they decided it was time to have their first child. Despite their desire and effort, Lisa has not conceived. With the passing of time, both have become tense and anxious over the situation, with the result that their sex life together isn't good and they are picking and nagging at each other more than before. Fred appears to be even more disappointed than Lisa over their inability to have a child. He feels that the whole purpose of their marriage is being frustrated. The idea of adopting a child is repugnant to him; he says that if he cannot have a child of his own, he will not take someone else's.

Things have finally reached a climax with Fred's request for a divorce. He blames his wife for her failure to conceive, says he is being cheated out of life's greatest privilege and cites the provision of talmudic law that, if a wife fails to become pregnant in ten years of marriage, the husband may ask for a divorce. It is his contention that our rabbis were wise, that they foresaw a situation such as this and made provision for divorce under these circumstances because they knew such a marriage was no good.

> What advice would you give this couple? Whose fault is it that Lisa has not conceived? Is there anything they could do about it? Can you feel toward an adopted child as you would toward your own? Is it possible for a childless marriage to be a good one? Is Fred right in invoking Jewish law to resolve this situation? Why?

B. Joan bitterly resents the statements from Jewish tradition given in this chapter to the effect that no one who has not married can be a whole person. She was once in love in her youth, but, when that didn't work out successfully, she invested her emotional life in other directions. Now in her fifties, she has become a successful psychiatric social worker, specializing with children. She has written and lectured widely, is recognized as a leader in her profession, derives great satisfaction from the work she has been able to do for deprived and unfortunate children. She insists that she is a more complete person, that she lives a richer, more rewarding life than some of her married friends who are chained to their husbands and homes.

> Is Joan right? Can an unmarried man or woman be a whole person? If so, does this prove that Jewish tradition is in this respect wrong? Is it possible or desirable for a woman to combine marriage with a career?

C. Norman is in his senior year at college, majoring in psychology and planning to get a graduate degree in that field after receiving his diploma in June. He has heard and read a great deal about the alleged superiority of the Jewish family but is frankly not impressed despite the fact that he is himself Jewish. In the first place, he points to the fact that his own family life wasn't anything to brag about. He recalls from early childhood that his parents never did get along very well, that the atmosphere of their home had been one of tension and stress. His father had studied Bible and Talmud extensively and attended synagogue services regularly. Yet his knowledge of Jewish family ideals didn't seem to have much effect on his life.

Norman does not deny that the average Jewish family life has been superior to his own. To the extent that this is true, however, he credits it all to compensation. He says that because Jews were restricted to ghettos, prevented from following certain occupations or entering into the larger social life of the community, they had to seek in their homes the satisfactions and gratifications denied them elsewhere. He is convinced that in the free society of America it is only a question of time until the apparent superiority of the Jewish family disappears.

Do you agree with Norman? Are his conclusions rational or emotional? Is it possible for a person to know Jewish tradition thoroughly, yet not apply it to his own life? Would the experience of Norman's father be a valid reason not to study Bible and Talmud? Is Norman's prognosis for the future of the American Jewish family sound? Why?

D. This chapter contains a great many quotations from Jewish tradition on marriage and the family. After studying them carefully, select three which you think are the most important and three which, in your judgment, are no longer valid and should be rejected. In each case, be prepared to explain your choices.

4

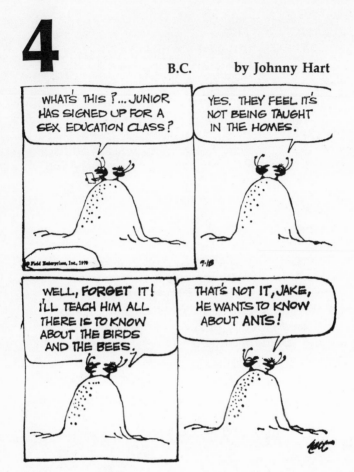

A family
is more than two

Our rabbis knew, of course, that a family consists of more than
two people. If they stressed the need for love and consideration
between husband and wife so emphatically and repeatedly, it
is because they were aware that only on such a foundation
could the proper atmosphere be established, which would enable children to grow healthfully. Having established the
foundation, they then gave equal thought to the relationship

between parents and children, recognizing that mutual obligations must be met if the family is to be firm. Above all, they understood what too many modern parents tend to forget: that unless mother and father speak with one voice to their children, agreeing in their presence on all major family matters, there is little chance for happiness in the home. A chasidic rabbi voiced this thought perceptively when he said: "If husband and wife quarrel, they cannot raise good children."[1] Perhaps, as happened from time to time with the rabbis of old, he somewhat overstated the case; good children do sometimes result from a home in which there is dissension. But bickering between parents is an obstacle which is at best difficult to overcome.

In addition to establishing an atmosphere of concord and peace, what more specific obligations has Jewish tradition assigned to parents in relationship to their children? First, to discipline them firmly. The Book of Proverbs contains a number of injunctions along this line, among them:

- Train up a child in the way he should go,
  And even when he is old, he will not depart from it.
- Withhold not correction from the child;
  For though thou beat him with the rod, he will not die.

In similar vein the Midrash says: "He who rebukes not his son leads him into delinquency."[2]

Lest you get the impression that Jewish tradition approves unreasoning harshness and sadistic cruelty on the part of parents, we hasten to assure you that the discipline referred to above was to be based on compassion and love. The mood between husband and wife was presumed to overflow, as it were, into their relationship to their children. Discipline tempered by tenderness and compassion was the Jewish ideal. The Midrash helps us appreciate this when it tells us that when God spoke to Moses from the burning bush, fearing that he might be frightened, He spoke to him in the voice of his father!

Discipline is a sore spot in many modern families. Some parents feel that imposing restrictions and punishment on their children hampers their development. Others see it as their obligation to lay down rather rigid rules of behavior and to insist that their children abide by them.

Most experts in the psychology of childhood and adolescence have concluded that children and even young people your age need and ultimately want discipline. Without it, they are sometimes afraid of their own impulses and never learn to control them. As a religious leader, I would agree and would add that only by learning to understand and accept fair parental discipline in their homes can our sons and daughters be prepared for the fact that the world itself imposes many disciplines upon us. This is true throughout our lives. An individual who scorns nature's rules for good health will in all probability become ill. One who consistently cheats others or abuses them will in the end, not only be unpopular, but will in all likelihood be unhappy or even emotionally sick.

Children can resent or repudiate their parents' discipline. No one can, over the long run, ignore the disciplines of nature and life. They are inescapable. Individuals who are led to believe in their earliest years that they can live happily by always doing whatever they feel like doing will be unprepared for adult life in the real world.

This doesn't mean that all parental discipline is proper. To be effective, it must be (1) fair, (2) loving, (3) consistent and, so far as possible, (4) a natural consequence of the behavior it is meant to regulate. In most cases children who know they have done wrong will accept the punishment imposed by their parents if it is not excessive; if, even while being deprived, they know their parents love them; and if they can depend upon their parents' reactions to be consistent from situation to situation. Discipline is resented when the behavior of parents becomes primarily a means of ventilating their own hostilities. Or when it is way out of proportion to the offense. Or when a specific kind of conduct is ruthlessly punished one day and indulgently ignored the next. Or when there is no apparent connection between what a child has done and the disapproval he or she receives in consequence. For example: after several futile warnings, it is far more effective to let a favorite toy be stolen or ruined by rain once than to nag constantly about putting it away.

Perhaps there has been too much emphasis on punishment in the paragraphs above. Discipline should involve approval and reward even more than it does punitive measures. If parents respond only to misdeeds, never to good behavior, the atmosphere of their home becomes poisoned.

Why have we included this rather extended discussion of discipline in a book on Judaism and marriage? First, in the hope that it might aid you to understand your own parents and family, hence also yourself. Later we shall have occasion to note how closely your present family situation is related to your future marriage. Second, a few simple insights about discipline can be extremely useful to you after your marriage in helping you and your spouse to establish a healthy, happy home for your own children.

When that time comes, it will be important for you to realize that parents too are human, hence can and do make mistakes. A parent who has erred in either judgment or deed should honestly admit it to his or her child. This can have two advantages: (a) children who know their mothers and fathers do not pretend to be perfect will be less likely to expect perfection of themselves; and (b) they will be encouraged to follow the example of honesty set by their parents. As you grew from infancy and childhood through adolescence into your early adult years, you probably became aware of the fact that being a parent is no simple or easy accomplishment, that parents too often face serious problems which are necessarily reflected in the lives of their families. Sometimes what appears to be neglect or hostility in the behavior of a mother or father may actually be an echo of tension or worry which has little to do with that parent's feelings toward a child, but makes it difficult to give maximum attention and consideration to the child's needs. Parents too are human. Like their sons and daughters, at times they feel so oppressed by burdens and worries that they fail to act out effectively the very real love they feel for their families.

On a spectrum extending from extreme discipline to extreme permissiveness, where would you place your parents? Is the discipline of your home fair? Loving? Consistent? Suitably proportioned to your conduct? Can you give specific examples to support your answers? Have you or can you discuss discipline with your parents? How do you feel when you have been rewarded or complimented for good behavior? When you have been punished? When you have done something you knew was wrong without in any way being disciplined? What is the difference between being disciplined by someone else or by yourself? Are you capable of self-discipline? How can we account for the fact that often the very young people who complain most bitterly about their parents' discipline impose the same measures on their own children a generation later?

The greatest responsibility of Jewish parents by far was to teach their children the Torah; not only the five books of Moses as such, but all of Jewish tradition, knowledge, literature and faith. It would be easy to fill the rest of this chapter and several more with quotations which illustrate this truth. Here are just a few:

- A home where Torah is not heard will not endure.
- If a man does not teach his son Torah, it is as if he had merely created an image.
- He who teaches his sons and grandsons Torah is as if he had received it himself at Mount Sinai.
- R. Hiyya b. Abba saw R. Joshua b. Levi hurrying one morning to take his grandson to school. He asked him: "Why the haste?" and R. Joshua answered: "Is it a small thing to stand at Mount Sinai?"
- He who teaches Torah to children abides with the שְׁכִינָה   Shechinah. [3]
- R. Huna ate no breakfast until he had taken a boy to school.
- Jerusalem was destroyed only because the children did not attend school and loitered in the streets.[4]
- One is immortal if his descendants study the Torah.[5]

The preeminence of Jews throughout the world in every field of advanced study is often attributed to the emphasis of our ancestors on learning and knowledge. Even in the Soviet Union, where many obstacles are placed in the way of Jewish intellectuals, the number of our people engaged in graduate study has been far beyond their proportion of the population.

Does the prominence of Jewish scholars in such areas as philosophy, sociology and science fulfill the urgings of ancient Judaism that we study Torah? Are these fields of general study a modern way of saying *Torah?* Would it be better if Jews limited their advanced studies to specifically Jewish disciplines?

More than words

Our ancestors were perfectly aware of the fact that parents could give their children no more effective lesson than the example of their own lives. A mother who is contemptuous of her children's dignity can scarcely succeed in teaching them to respect the rights of others. A father who is dishonest in either his personal or business life cannot impress upon his children the importance of integrity. Parents who do not take their adult religious responsibilities seriously, who do not strive to learn more about Judaism, cannot hope to achieve much in this direction with their sons and daughters. Our teachers understood and attempted to express all this when they said: "Every Jew should so conduct himself that his sons will rejoice to say: 'The God of my father.' "

Perhaps no one has expressed this truth more eloquently than several of the chasidic rabbis. For example:

The Belzer Rabbi commented on the verse in Exodus 10:2 —"And that you may tell in the ears of your son, and of your son's son, what I have wrought upon Egypt, and My signs which I have done among them; that you may know that I am the Lord." It may be remarked that the end of the verse would have seemed more correct if it had been expressed thus: "that *they* shall know that I am the Lord." But the verse was intentionally worded "you" instead of "they" in order to furnish us a lesson. Recount to your sons the wonders of the Lord, but remember that this will have a beneficent influence upon them only if you yourselves recognize that He is the Lord.

A man asked the Kotzker Rabbi to pray for him in order that his sons might study the Torah diligently. He replied: "If your sons will see that you are a diligent student, they will imitate you. But if you neglect your own studies, and merely wish your sons to study, the result will be that they will do likewise when they grow up. They will neglect the Torah themselves and desire that their sons do the studying."

These rabbis were not without a sense of humor as they sought to emphasize the importance of parents setting an example for their children. One of them is reported to have seen a man and his son, both drunk, reeling together in the gutter. He said to his own son: "I envy that father. He has succeeded in his ambition to have a son like himself. But I do not yet know whether you will be like me. See to it that the drunkard does not have better success with his son than I with you."[6]

Ahead of their time

One of the most astounding things about the ancient and medieval teachers of Judaism, as we have already had occasion to observe, is the degree to which they anticipated the wisdom of modern psychology on the subject of good family relationships. They knew, for example, how dangerous and destructive it is for parents to play favorites among their children. Several of them noted that this was one of the major causes of the jealousy which Joseph's brothers felt toward him—the fact that he was obviously their father's favorite. The Talmud states quite categorically: "Show no partiality among your sons. Treat all of them alike."[7]

Our ancestors understood, too, that it is primarily the mother who sets the religious tone of the home. According to the Zohar, a medieval book expressive of Jewish mysticism, "The chief influence transforming a man's house into his home is his wife. The שְׁכִינָה Shechinah will not forsake his house if his wife keeps it according to the ways of Israel."[8]

Many centuries earlier the Talmud had given an effective illustration of this truth:

A pious couple lived together for ten years and, having no children, were divorced. The man married an impious woman and she transformed him into a man of wickedness. The pious woman married a man of wickedness and she transformed him into a man of goodness. Therefore the sages declare: "Woman determines man's behavior."[9]

Another remarkable insight of a chasidic rabbi seems almost to anticipate conditions today, when so many young couples are married before they are able fully to support themselves, as a consequence of which their parents often provide financial aid. He said:

A passenger on a ship patiently awaited the day when it would reach port. When the ship was nearing the harbor, a storm drove it back to sea, much to the chagrin of the traveler.

Likewise a man is afflicted with anxiety for his sons and daughters until he succeeds in rearing them to maturity. Then he hopes to be freed from worry regarding their lot. But his oldest son comes with his troubles, seeking paternal counsel, and the father's retirement is delayed. The daughter also comes with her problems, and once more his hope of a quiet life is postponed. Few of us are ever entirely free from worry and the necessity of continuous labor in this world.[10]

Finally, another chasidic rabbi summarized the obligations of parents toward their children and underscored their immense importance in these words: "God treats a man in the same way that the man treats his children. Do not neglect your children, and God will not neglect you."[11]

What is your evaluation of the responsibilities which Jewish tradition placed upon parents? Were they reasonable and fair? Are any of the responsibilities outlined above no longer valid or important in modern life? Are there any which you think should be added to these? Do your parents play favorites among their children? If so, how do you feel about it? How is it manifested? Have you ever discussed this problem with them? What was their reaction? Is there anything further you can do to correct matters?

Other side of the coin

Thus far we have attended only to the responsibilities of parents toward their children. Wholesome family life is impossible however unless a sense of obligation is reciprocal. Children owe something to their parents too, and the teachers of Judaism were no less sensitive to this aspect of family relationships. The same Book of Proverbs which we quoted on parental duties has much to say about those of children. Among its more memorable quotations are these:

- A son who deals shamefully and reproachfully
  Will despoil his father, and chase away his mother.
- Hearken unto your father who begot you,
  And despise not your mother when she is old.

Jewish postbiblical tradition is as specific here as we have already found it to be regarding the proper conduct of parents. The Talmud, for example, asks and at once answers:

In what does reverence for a father consist? In not sitting in his presence and in not speaking in his presence and in not contradicting him. Of what does honor for parents consist? In providing for them food and drink, in clothing them, in giving them shoes for their feet, in helping them to enter or leave the house. R. Eliezer said: "Even if his father ordered him to throw a purse of gold into the sea, he should obey him."[12] In further comment on the prohibition against contradicting one's parents, the same passage of the Talmud goes on to say that, if a father errs on a matter of law, his son should not directly charge him with having made a mistake. Rather let him indirectly and subtly suggest: "Father, in the Law it is written thus"— proceeding to quote the proper biblical or talmudic passage.[13]

A proper respect for one's parents was interpreted as dependent as much on the spirit of one's actions as on the actions themselves. Thus we are told that one who feeds his father on fattened chickens may not be showing him due consideration, while another who orders his father to do the heavy work of treading the mill may be fulfilling his responsibilities. How is this possible? In the first instance, if the father asks whence the chickens were obtained, the son may impatiently reply: "Eat, old man, eat and be silent!" In the second case, the government may have issued a decree that all millers report at once to the capital. And the son, out of love for his father, directs him to remain at home, doing the relatively safe work there, while he—the son—responds to the greater danger of government labor.[14]

The great devotion due one's parents is manifest in the rabbinic comment that father and mother are partners of God in the proper rearing of a child.[15] It was said that, since God knew He would be unable to attend to the needs of each individual child, He created parents to act in His stead. One rabbi proposed that parents are entitled to even more honor than is God. He deduced this from two biblical verses. One stipulates: "Honor God with your substance" (Proverbs 3:9)—which he interpreted to mean that if one possesses substance one is to honor God with it, otherwise not. A different Bible verse, however (Exodus 20:12), says: "Honor your father and your mother." There are no qualifications or exceptions here; children are to honor parents regardless of whether they own anything.[16]

In commenting on the obligations of both parents and children, our rabbis exhibited a profound understanding of the family. They were aware of the fact that if individual members of a household merely try to get everything possible for themselves, without consideration for the others, the result will be a jungle, not a family. A wholesome family is possible only when all those who are a part of it attempt to find solutions for the problems and meet the needs of all, not just themselves.

Do you agree with all the statements from Jewish tradition here quoted on the obligations of children to their parents? Are there any obligations which should be added to these? In what ways do you think you succeed in honoring your parents? Where is there room for improvement?

Not just theory

Many examples are given of famous rabbis whose behavior toward their parents was considered exemplary. Abimi, for example, was said to have had five sons, all ordained as rabbis. Yet whenever Abimi's father would call him, he would run to open the door, crying out: "Yes, yes, I am coming to you." One day his father asked him for some water. By the time Abimi had come with it his father had fallen asleep. So he stood there patiently until his father awakened and then gave him the water.

One day the mother of Rabbi Tarfon broke her sandal as she walked through the courtyard. In order to save her from walking barefoot, Rabbi Tarfon bent down, putting his hands on the pavement ahead of each step so she could walk on them instead of the cold stones. When he later became ill, his mother asked his colleagues to pray for him, saying: "Pray for my son, Tarfon, for he honors me more than I deserve." When she told them what he had done, their reaction was: "If he had done a thousand times more for you, he would not have shown half the honor for a parent which is commanded in the law!"

In this, as in all other respects, our rabbis were emphatic in asserting that laws and principles are significant only if they be carried out in action. A chasidic student is said to have observed, in the midst of studying, that his rabbi was deeply engrossed in trying to understand a certain verse he wanted to teach. Knowing from experience that such concentration was usually of long duration, he ran home for his lunch, expecting that he could return before the rabbi would be ready to continue the lesson. As he finished eating, his mother asked him to run an errand for her. The boy refused, giving as his excuse that he did not want to delay to the point of missing part of the lesson. On his way back to the school, however, it occurred to him that the whole purpose of studying was to perform good deeds and that helping his mother in fulfillment of a lesson he already knew was more important than hastening to learn another. So he reversed his direction, performed the errand for his mother, and only then returned for his studies. As he entered the room, his rabbi said at once: "You must have done a good deed, for the moment you entered a complicated matter I had not previously understood became clear to me."

The Talmud also tells of a Gentile whose respect for his mother was extreme, particularly in view of the fact that she seems to have been demented and hence very unreasonable and demanding. Once, when he was conducting an important public meeting, she hit him in the face for no reason. When the slipper with which she had struck him fell to the ground, he bent down to pick it up for her. On another occasion she is said to have torn his silken robe, hit him on the head and spat in his face—all in the presence of others. But he neither retaliated nor answered her, in order not to put her to shame.[17]

> How do you react to these directives of Jewish tradition on the responsibilities of children toward their parents? Are they reasonable? Balanced? Fair? Can they serve as a guide for us today? If followed literally, would they improve the quality of our family life? Try to summarize in one paragraph of your own words the responsibilities of children toward their parents as you see them; in another paragraph, those of parents to their children.

There was one important qualification to the high degree of honor and respect which children were enjoined to give their parents. It was conditioned upon the parents themselves fulfilling the requirements of an ethical life. It was deemed to be their most sacred responsibility, as we have already seen, to teach their children the ethical values of Judaism. Only if they did so, were they entitled to all the deference described above. And what if they acted in contradiction to these ethical values? A passage in the Talmud is quite clear on this point:

> It is possible to think that even if the father ordered his son to defile himself or not to restore a lost article which he had found, he is to obey him; consequently there is a text to teach, "Ye shall fear every man his mother, and his

father, and ye shall keep My Sabbaths." (Lev. 19:3) All of you alike are bound to honor Me.[18]

Small wonder, then, that Jewish family life existed on so high a level throughout most of our people's history. Our ancestors were not willing to let the matter rest on general statements, however pious and poetic. They said much on the importance of love and marriage, on the duties which members of the family should fulfill for each other. And they crystallized their eloquent principles into specific directives and laws which every Jew was expected to observe.

A factor which contributed enormously to the success of the Jewish family in the past was the joy with which Jewish parents and their children together celebrated our Jewish holidays. All were involved in preparing for and observing *Shabbat, Sukot, Pesach* and every other occasion of special Jewish significance. Parents did not send their youngsters off to a special school where they were taught about festivals and customs which were never recognized at home. Each such occasion, by being part of the family's life style, became a special opportunity for two or three generations to establish firm and joyous ties with each other. This, coupled with our ideals of family life as we have reviewed them here, made of the Jewish home what our ancestors called a   מִקְדָּשׁ מְעַט   *mikdash me'at,* a small sanctuary.

Is your home a *mikdash me'at*? Which Jewish holidays and festivals are observed by your family? How? Are they happy occasions? Do your parents take the synagogue as seriously as they expect you to? Can you discuss this subject with them?

Now that we are aware of Jewish tradition, in our next chapter we shall be ready to inquire into the age at which one is ready for marriage. First, however, a discussion of the following cases will reinforce our understanding of Judaism and enable us to apply its teachings to practical problems.

For instance

A. When his temple bulletin reprinted the quotation of the Belzer Rabbi given in this chapter, Dr. Allen called his rabbi to object. He felt the implied criticism of himself was unwarranted and that it put him in a bad light with his son who is a member of the Confirmation class. "It happens," he said to the rabbi, "that I myself do not believe in God and do not practice any of the rituals of Judaism. I have arrived at this position after many years of careful thought. I attend religious services just on the High Holy Days, if my medical practice permits, and even then only to please my wife.

"I have joined the congregation and enrolled my children in the religious school," he continued, "because I want them to know enough about Judaism to accept or reject it on their own when they are old enough. But you have no right to expect me to do anything in which I do not honestly believe. So long as my son and daughter are willing to attend your classes, I shall send them. Should they ever seriously object, however, I tell you right now that I will not jeopardize our happy and peaceful family life by forcing them. Either you accept us on this basis or we shall have to resign from the congregation!"

> Had you been the rabbi, how would you have answered Dr. Allen? Do you think the doctor applies similar standards to all other areas of his relationship to his children? To matters of health, for example? Would it not be hypocritical for him to attend religious services? How would Jewish tradition answer him? How would modern psychology answer him?

B. "It's all very well to stress the importance of studying Torah," says Mrs. Arkberg, "but we have to be practical and realistic. In ancient and medieval times that was just about all a Jewish student had to study. My own grandfather has told me that in his European boyhood he attended a חֶדֶר *cheder* (Hebrew elementary school) six days a week, learning every phase of Jewish history, literature and religion. That was the entire content of his education until he came to this country at the age of nineteen.

"But today our children have to study many other things. They need time to do their school work adequately if they are to gain admittance to a good college. They should be acquainted with music and the arts even beyond the formal lessons of school. They must prepare properly for whatever vocation or profession they are to follow. It seems to me that we have to establish priorities and decide just how much time our overly busy youngsters can afford to give to their religious education. My own feeling is that two hours a week in class is just about the limit and that it is unreasonable to expect them to do homework as well."

Has Mrs. Arkberg exaggerated the demands made upon children and young people today? Is it true that each person and family must establish educational priorities? Is it impossible for us in modern times to take the emphasis our ancestors placed on Jewish education seriously? Other than knowledge for its own sake, can Jewish education contribute anything substantial to the welfare of Jewish adolescents and adults? Can it in any way increase the probability of a happy marriage?

C. Jim Starker doesn't argue about the importance of religious education or the responsibility of parents in this direction. He agrees with everything Jewish tradition emphasizes on this subject but says that modern life is so complicated that parents have to divide their responsibilities, with each specializing, so to speak, in certain areas. Religious education he believes to be his wife's department. He travels on business most of the week, comes home Friday evening exhausted and feels he should be entitled to spend the weekend relaxing and enjoying himself. He assumes the obligation of earning a living and managing family finances, without imposing any of this on his wife, and he sees no reason why she should expect him to share a responsibility which is properly hers.

Is it true that parental responsibilities are more complicated and difficult than they were in the past? That some of these responsibilities must be carried primarily by one parent or the other? Does Jewish tradition agree that religion is more the field of mothers than of fathers? Would it justify the attitude of Mr. Starker? Who assumes the major part of parental religious responsibility in your home?

D. A feud has been raging for many months between Mr. Bernstein and his college-junior son. It is time for Larry to prepare his application for graduate school. He feels a very strong desire to study engineering. His father, who is a prominent attorney, insists that Larry's field should be law. "After all," says Mr. Bernstein, "you can't deny that I have had many more years of experience than you. I know life better and may even know *you* better than you do. I am therefore in a better position to know where you could lead the most successful kind of life."

Larry's father has also asserted that he is entitled to honor and respect, neither of which his son seems anxious to give him in this matter. He has often cited some of the quotations and examples given in this chapter and has said that what he asks of Larry—for his own good, actually—is less than many great Jews were willing to do for their parents in the past.

The situation has become critical. The two are equally adamant. Larry will not apply for law school. His father told him last night that, if he changes his mind, his tuition will be covered by his parents; if he insists on studying engineering, he'll have to be on his own.

What is your evaluation of this impasse? Who is right? Is it true that Mr. Bernstein has more experience than Larry on which to base a decision? What guidance can either of them receive from Jewish tradition?

5

Old enough to love?

There is an interesting cycle involving the age at which marriage takes place. In ancient times it was customary for marriages to occur quite early. According to the Talmud, "he who reaches the age of twenty and does not marry spends all his days in the thought of sin." In post-talmudic times, however, marriage was consistently postponed to a later age, due largely, no doubt, to the fact that life became more complicated. After

World War II there was a reversal of this trend, so that again there were many brides and grooms in their early twenties or even late teens. According to United States government statistics, 49.3 percent of brides marrying for the first time in the 1950s were less than twenty years of age; 40.2 percent of grooms marrying for the first time were twenty-one or under.[1] There is reason to believe now that another swing is occurring; again the age of marriage seems to be going up. This may be because of changes in our premarital sexual standards, about which we shall have more to say later, or because more young couples today are living together without being married. Whatever the cause, another shift seems to be on the scene.

By and large, however, marriage still takes place in this country earlier than it did a generation or two ago. At a time when a longer period of education or training is required before beginning a career and when average young people reach financial independence later than their parents did, how can we account for earlier marriage?

There are several valid explanations. For one thing, boys and girls begin to date at an earlier age. Many of them therefore start to feel bored with casual social contacts and are anxious for more advanced and sophisticated relationships with the opposite sex. Home pressure is another explanation. In some instances parents—mothers in particular—push their adolescent youngsters—daughters especially—in the direction of marriage faster than they might otherwise be inclined to move. A third possibility is that we live in a time of intense anxiety and tension. The threat of nuclear war, the struggle over human rights domestically, the many bewildering changes which seem to be imminent in our social and economic structures—all these make our age a challenging but also a threatening time in which to live. Some young people no doubt look toward marriage as a means of reaching for security and assurance.

Fourth among possible explanations is the increased willingness of many parents to subsidize their children in marriage. Only a generation or so ago it was unusual for a young man to think of proposing to a girl until he could reasonably expect to support her. Today a great many couples are married while one or both are still students, with parents assuming a measure of financial obligation until the couple can make it on their own. In other instances, either the wife or both partners work to support themselves until they are finished with school. A fifth possibility is the increased tendency of high school boys and girls to go steady. We shall have more to say about this a little later; for the time being, we simply note it as another factor in the large number of marriages at an early age.

Sixth, and finally, mention must be made of the fact that standards of sexual conduct among college and high school young people have changed. As a consequence, a certain number of girls become pregnant and find or feel it necessary to marry for that reason. No one can really weigh these several factors in order to determine which are of the greatest importance. Nor is it necessary that we do so. Together they account for the many weddings in which both bride and groom are very young.

There have been enough of these marriages so that a number of jokes are already being told about them. One is about the Christian church wedding of an eighteen-year-old groom and a seventeen-year-old bride. When the groom declared to the bride: "With all my worldly goods I thee endow"—his mother turned to his father and said: "There goes Junior's bicycle!"

Before proceeding, a word is in order concerning the prolongation of adolescence in our culture. I have already mentioned the fact that young people today must complete a longer period of preparation before they can enter a profession or even certain complicated businesses. Instead of emerging from the partial dependence of adolescence into the independence of adulthood at age eighteen to twenty-one, as was once the case, many of us now do not complete this transition until we are twenty-five or older. This obviously delays the achievement of maturity. It also makes it more difficult for young people to defer sexual intercourse until they are ready for marriage. We shall have more to say on this a bit later.

And then?

How successful are such marriages? The record is not very encouraging. One authority tells us there are six times as many divorces in marriages where both spouses were under twenty-one at the time of their wedding as when both were over thirty-one.[2] Another survey reveals that three of five teenage marriages end in divorce within three years.[3]

Parade Magazine published a survey of several hundred men and women who had graduated from high school six years earlier. Almost half were married, and almost half of these had married before both partners had reached the age of twenty. Regardless of whether or not they were married at the time of the interview, seven out of ten said they were opposed to early marriages. This even included some who reported themselves to be happy in their wedded life. Barbara McIntyre Gross, who had three children and was separated from her husband, said: "At eighteen you're pretty stupid. Maybe I was trying to prove I was grown up. I thought I knew better than my parents, better than everyone."

Samuel R. Porter, who dropped out of college one year after his wedding in 1958, said: "It's the biggest mistake of my life, and I'll regret it for the rest of my life. We should have waited. When I was eighteen, I wouldn't listen. I'm sorry I didn't."

Not all of those interviewed felt this way. Garlynn Rodriguez, who also became a wife at eighteen, said: "I think that marriage matured me more than anything else. Learning to live with someone else and sharing his life—that makes you grow up much faster."

Two leading experts have summarized their conclusions as follows: "It is our conviction that many persons marry when they are too young, not necessarily in years but in maturity, in experience and in the ability to meet the many responsibilities of family living. Such marriages are 'bad' marriages, not perhaps because the couple is unsuited to each other, not because of any deficiencies in the persons concerned other than those which time can erase, but because they have assumed life's major responsibility before they were ready to do so. It injures a young horse to do heavy work too soon, the best automobile should not be overtaxed when it is new, a plank breaks when it is overloaded. . . . A child should not undertake an adult's job. Marriage means much more than the legality of sharing a common bed."[4]

What do you feel is the proper age for love and marriage? Is it the same for everyone? Should marriage or a career come first for boys? For girls? Do you think you yourself are old enough to experience genuine love for someone of the opposite sex who is approximately your own age? Have you ever been in love? What do people often refer to as "puppy love"? How does it differ from real love? Should a couple be financially self-sufficient before they marry? In answering these questions consider the following quotations from rabbinic literature and decide how valid they are for today.

- A man should build himself a home, plant himself a vineyard and then bring into the home a bride. Fools are they who marry while they have no secure livelihood.
- In olden times the pious Sages were willing to go about hungry, to see their wives and children go hungry and to devote all their attention to Torah and *mitzvot.* God came to their succor and aided them on their way. In our times, however, there are no such sincere scholars, and they must not rely upon the aid of God if they do nothing for themselves. Nowadays no one should marry until his livelihood is secure.[5]

We need a definition

Our discussions thus far on the meaning of love and the importance of marriage must surely have convinced you that only emotionally mature individuals can confidently expect to achieve happiness in wedlock. This brings us face to face with one of the most difficult tasks we shall encounter all through these pages: the attempt to define the word *maturity.* Most of us tend to consider ourselves mature and others immature, without actually pinning down what we mean. Students of human behavior have devoted many hours and innumerable volumes to the subject. Most of them would agree that the following traits distinguish mature people:

1. They learn from experience and grow as a result of their errors. Being imperfect human beings, they will probably continue to make mistakes the rest of their lives but will, on the

whole, successfully avoid repeating the same ones over and over.

2. They willingly assume responsibility. A child must be repeatedly reminded of obligations and duties. Mature adults have developed an inner monitor which tells them these things on their own. Although Judith Viorst speaks from a woman's point of view in the following passage, boys and men should have no difficulty transposing her comments into a male key:

> An adult rinses out her pantyhose and writes thank-you notes even when no one's around to tell her she should. She doesn't spend the gas-bill money on earrings even when no one's around to tell her she shouldn't. A girl relies on other people to define, and remind her of, her obligations, but a grownup has to be her own grownup.
>
> "Judy," my mother would say when I was a teenager, "did you make your bed?"
>
> "Yes, Mom, I did."
>
> "And did you hang your jacket in the closet?"
>
> "Yes, Mom, I did."
>
> "And what about your wastebasket—have you emptied it?"
>
> "Gee, Mom, I can't remember *everything.*"
>
> Now, this little routine isn't strictly the province of 18-year-olds. There are 30-year-olds who want somebody else taking charge. Indeed, with a cooperative, daddylike husband a wife can spend her whole lifetime playing child-bride, never having to decide when to put on the roast beef or go to the dentist or blow her nose.
>
> A lot of husbands, however, refuse to cooperate.
>
> Six months after she got married, my friend Allison told me, there was a terrible water leak in her apartment. She rushed next door, phoned her husband and told him he'd better come running home right away. "You've got to move the furniture and you've got to call the plumber," she wailed, "or everything will be destroyed!" Her husband's reply was icy and inelegant. "Get your ass back over there and do what has to be done." And that's what being a grownup is all about.[6]

Mature people accept responsibility in another sense too. When the consequences of their conduct are unpleasant, they accept the blame—without destroying themselves and without requiring a scapegoat.

3. There is purpose to their lives. They project important goals for themselves and plan their activities as progressive steps toward the attainment of these goals. Thus they feel fulfilled through growth. They avoid just living each day and making each decision as if it were unrelated to any larger objective.

4. They learn to live with unhappy situations which they can neither change nor honorably avoid. Recognizing that life cannot always be exactly the way they want it, they distinguish between those circumstances within their power to improve and those to which they must become reconciled.

5. They accept themselves—their virtues as well as their faults. Since they do not expect to achieve perfection, they need not castigate themselves for falling short of it. They are able to evaluate realistically both their abilities and their deficiencies, trying to enhance the former and avoiding excessive guilt over the latter. They can accept criticism and disappointment because these are balanced by achievement and success. So long as they have done their best, they do not deem failure a disgrace.

6. Because they don't expect perfection of themselves, they have no need to demand perfection from others. This applies especially to their parents. Adolescence can be a time of great turbulence between young people and their parents. You may have heard of the twenty-four-year-old who was amazed at how much his father had learned in the past seven years. It is quite likely that more change had occurred in him than in his parents.

It is common knowledge that some of our own faults and a good deal of our emotional distress are due to our parents' mistakes in relating to us when we were very young. One mark of immature people is that even in adulthood they use these parental mistakes—real or imaginary—as an excuse for their own deficiencies. I know people in their sixties and seventies who still do this. Maturity means, among other things, accepting our parents for what they are, forgiving their errors and attempting to improve ourselves, no matter how much we may have been wronged in the past.

7. They do not need to dominate or control others. There is enough satisfaction for them in improving themselves, in exercising their own freedom, so that they gladly extend the same freedom of choice to those whose lives touch theirs.

8. They are able to defer a pleasure they would like to have now for the sake of a greater joy which cannot come until later and which depends on renouncing the enjoyment which is immediately available.

Emotionally mature people, then, are those who . . . learn from experience . . . assume responsibility for their own acts . . . move each day toward fulfilling the larger purposes of their lives . . . reconcile themselves to even the most unpleasant circumstances and conditions if they are beyond their power, or anyone's, to change . . . accept themselves, their successes as well as their failures . . . are at peace with their parents . . . feel no need to dominate others . . . are able to postpone something desired now in favor of greater happiness later.

No one is mature in all these respects and under all circumstances. We all sometimes act childishly, immaturely. Judith Viorst has expressed it very well:

> So it's clear I can't flatly declare, Yes, I'm there, I'm mature, I am now a grown woman. The best I can do is to say that I'm there in part. And just some of the time. And not under all conditions. And not with everyone.[7]

The best each of us can hope for is to improve, to exhibit greater maturity in these directions with each passing year. Obviously, the more mature two people are, the greater will be the probability of happiness in their marriage.

> Can you think of criteria which have not been included in our list here? Judged by these standards, how mature do you measure yourself to be? How mature are your closest friends? It could be interesting for three or four friends to rate each other and themselves. Use 3 for great maturity, 2 for average and 1 for little maturity on each of the traits we have given; then add up your total and do the same for each of your friends. Each person can learn a lot by comparing a self-rating on maturity to friends' opinions of him or her. Don't attempt this, however, if

you are too thin-skinned to take honest criticism. No one prerequisite for a happy marriage is more essential than emotional maturity. Hence the extreme importance of understanding this part of our discussion, as well as the next section in which we try to trace the steps through which such maturity is achieved.

Couples who marry at too early an age often get into trouble because of a failure to measure up very well in maturity. Another source of difficulty is that both are still growing and groping at the time they marry. Neither has really reached full maturity or defined permanent goals in life. If, after they are married, the bride and groom continue their maturation in the same direction, a good marriage is possible. If, however, they mature away from rather than toward each other, their chance for happiness is not very great. The closer they are to full development and maximum maturity at the time of the wedding, the more probable is their happiness together.

The road to love

Every normal human being is born with the capacity to love and a need for love. We do not achieve the kind of love required for marriage, however, until we have grown successfully through a number of earlier stages. Each stage is typical and adequate at the age at which it appears. Each is dangerous if it persists much beyond its proper time. Here are the levels through which we must grow on the road to mature love:

1. *I Love Myself Only.* Tiny infants are at first aware only of themselves. Their universe extends only as far as their own fingers and toes. Others gradually become important only insofar as they can satisfy personal needs. They want what they want when they want it—or else! This stage shouldn't last beyond the age of two years at most.

2. *I Love My Parents.* At a fairly early point in life, infants begin to be aware of others as existing in their own right. This process begins with their parents. Mother and father become individuals they are able to love for themselves, not just for what they give them. This is normal up to the age of six or seven, is unusual beyond eight.

3. *I Love My Gang Too.* Somewhere along the line children reach out for meaningful relationships that go beyond their own home. They become part of a group, usually made up of others who are their own age and sex. At this point in their lives they are likely to evidence strong antipathy to members of the opposite sex. Their personal importance and self-esteem are reinforced by belonging to a group. Such an attitude as this is characteristic of the early teens, seldom lasts beyond eighteen.

4. *I Like Girls/Boys.* The strong aversion to the opposite sex becomes strangely transformed into an equally strong attraction. We suddenly discover that boys or girls aren't really as abominable as we had supposed. Therefore we like the opposite sex quite generally—any and all of them.

5. *I Like One Girl/One Boy.* The general, diffuse attraction for the opposite sex is narrowed down, after a time, to one particular person at a time. This is the stage of violent "crushes"— with the object of one's affections probably changing quite frequently.

6. *I Love the Only One.* In due course the field becomes narrowed to one. Having been attracted to all of the opposite sex, then to one at a time, we reach the point of choosing a permanent partner for life.

Now the interesting and significant thing about all this is that each stage is normal and healthy at a given point in our lives. Each, moreover, contributes something to the richness of the next. The more fully we experience the earlier levels of love, the readier we are at the proper time to know the meaning of full marital love. The person who has not yet grown through the first five steps is less likely to be ready for marriage. The danger in early marriages is that one or both of the partners may still be in that category. Then trouble is on the horizon.

Most of us never entirely outgrow these earlier stages. From time to time we may be able to detect some trace of an earlier level, usually in something irrational or inappropriate that we have done. This is nothing to worry about, if it happens only on rare occasions. If, however, a person's general behavior is arrested on a level which should have been outgrown, there is reason to believe that thoughts of marriage are premature.

How much can you remember in your own life of each stage described above? At which level would you place yourself now? Can you give one example from each period through which you have already passed—to show how you have said or felt or done something within recent months which indicates a residue from that previous period? If you are unable to find illustrations from your own recent experience, try to do so from the behavior of your friends.

One author has summarized the growth from infant self-love to the capacity for mature love and has at the same time reminded us of our earlier conclusion that real love must encompass more than one's husband or wife. Her words are worth remembering:

> The adult who has successfully come up the ladder of love development eventually reaches a kind of love that affects not only his own dear ones with whom he is in closest contact but in addition many people whom he has never met. He is concerned with his responsibility to mankind. He does things to promote human welfare. He feels warmly toward the men and women and children whom he meets. He has faith in the power of love that can operate through the life of a really mature person in many ways. While inevitably leading one into hard work and some difficult trials, this kind of love builds character. Its strength comes from an inner peace that enables one to weather life's storms. It can be attained not in a single step but only through the mastery of the other steps of love development that lead to it.[8]

In Jewish tradition the Bar Mitzvah ceremony—more recently Bat Mitzvah too—has been a formal, public means of recognizing that a young person has reached a significant stage of maturity.

> Do you think it's a good idea for the community to encourage such a public ceremony? Should it be retained, discarded, or changed to a different age? Why? Would it

be a good idea, if Bar and Bat Mitzvah are continued, to hold the ceremony not at the same age for everyone, but for each child when he or she gives evidence of sufficient maturity? Are we Jews the only ones who have practiced such a ceremony? In what respects was a thirteen-year-old mature several centuries ago? Now? Using the criteria of maturity listed in this chapter, how mature were you on your thirteenth birthday? Now?

Two dangers

There are two further possibilities which young couples must guard against as carefully as they can. It happens frequently that—consciously or unconsciously—the prospect of marriage represents an escape hatch from some situation which appears to be intolerable. Sometimes it's an unhappy home or unpleasant parental pressure. Or it may be a frustrating job—or an inability to decide which of several vocations to follow—or envy of friends who are already married.

Under any of these circumstances, marriage can be not only a means of escape but perhaps also a weapon with which to strike back at the offending party. If a young person knows that a parent is strongly opposed to a marriage, what a wonderful opportunity it may be to assert independence, to get back at the parent for all the abuse—real or alleged—suffered at his or her hands. One expert describes what sometimes happens:

> How often is this "love," which some feel, merely the desire to get away from a quarrelsome, bickering family, a dominating mother or a tight little office in which one feels stifled? It is understandable that people should strive to get away from that which annoys them, although the basic reasons for the annoyance may be in themselves. When you marry you *assume* responsibilities; you do not *escape* them. A good marriage will mean that life will be much richer and more worthwhile, but it will not be easier. Marriage creates as many problems as it solves. The success of your marriage will depend upon what you are getting into, not what you "get away from."[9]

In this connection, let us understand that sometimes young people who are suffering from emotional problems look upon marriage as a possible cure. But people who are having difficulty handling themselves and their problems while single will nearly always experience still greater trouble in marriage. The time to straighten oneself out emotionally is before the wedding, not afterward. Though it is true that the responsibilities of marriage can sometimes contribute to an individual's maturity, it is even truer that maturity already achieved increases the probability of a happy marriage.

A second, related danger is that of falling into a bad marriage "on the rebound." Men and women who have just been rejected by someone to whom they had been engaged or with whom they had an agreement are often ripe for an unfortunate partnership with someone else. It isn't easy to live through such an experience; to lose a relationship on which one has depended can be very damaging to one's self-esteem and pride. What could be more natural than wanting to fill the void as speedily as possible? Natural, yes—but, for that very reason, dangerous! Such individuals are apt to be so anxious to compensate for their recent loss that they fail to consider whether the proposed partner is or is not really the right one for a lifelong relationship. We have expert testimony on this point too:

> While you are still somewhat emotionally sore from the last breakup, be unusually careful not to go steady again too soon. It is easy to get caught in the trap of your own feelings at a time like this. You may find yourself hurrying things with some newfound friend, just to prove to yourself that you can win and hold a person of the other sex. This is your pride crying for a little support. You have felt rejected by your old love, so you let yourself in for anything that will comfort your deflated ego.
>
> You have heard about people who marry for spite. When something happens to break up an old affair, one or the other of the pair rushes into a new union just to show the other that "it did not matter after all." An effort to show your lost lover that you don't care lies back of these plunges into a new affair. What your actions really

say is that you did care very much, or you wouldn't be rushing off to prove otherwise. Unfortunately, such hasty unions on the rebound rarely work out. They tend to be grossly unfair to the new partner, and they certainly are no help to either of the persons who have recently stopped going together.[10]

Either of these dangers can be formidable, even when the individuals involved are aware of their motivations. What makes them devilishly difficult—at times even cruelly tragic— is the frequency with which the real dynamics of the behavior are unconscious. When this occurs, it is possible to convince oneself that one is genuinely in love, though such may not be the case at all.

Good rules to follow, therefore, are these: 1. When on the rebound, go slowly. Try not to become emotionally involved again too soon; if you find you are, don't rush into a permanent alliance. Give the old, dependable time-test a chance to work. 2. If you have been generally unhappy about your relationship with parents or others or yourself, be suspicious of any overwhelming emotional attachment to someone of the opposite sex. Be as sure as you can that you are moving *toward* something desirable, not *away from* something unpleasant.

The question remains

There is no simple or easy answer to the question this chapter has approached, no one way of determining who is old enough for love. What we do know beyond the slightest doubt is that marriage is serious business, not child's play. We know also that marriage demands emotional maturity and that maturity is not just a matter of age in years and months. One person may be ready for marriage at nineteen, another not ready at thirty-nine. Each must do the most honest, objective job he or she can of evaluating personal maturity and judging whether they have successfully emerged from the necessary earlier stages of development. Only then have they the right to give serious consideration to marriage.

For instance

A. "I refuse to be alarmed about youthful marriages or to take too seriously the statistics of divorce in this age group." These were the words of one parent who had read the manuscript of this chapter. She continued: "I married at nineteen and will admit that my husband and I faced pretty rough sledding for a while. But I think I would have confronted the same problems no matter when I married. We have to remember that young people today are biologically ready for marriage long before social conditions permit them to marry. It isn't fair to expect them to live with all their sexual tensions for five or six years; it's better for them to marry than to become promiscuous. Anyway, it seems to me that most students do better after they are married than before. So far as my own children are concerned—though they are now only seven and ten years old —when the time comes, I'm willing for them to marry when young."

What do you think of this woman's comments? Is it probably true that she herself would have faced the same problems in marriage even at an older age? Is she wise in ignoring the statistics of divorce among young couples? Do you think she would feel differently if her children were ten years older? How do your parents feel on this matter?

B. Rabbi K. was on the spot. Leah and Philip, two of his favorite young congregants, had appealed to him for support. At the ages of eighteen and twenty-one respectively, they wanted very much to marry. Leah was a freshman in college, Philip a senior. They had known each other for five years and had been going steady for two. As you may already have suspected, their parents were vigorously opposed to their being married. But they had agreed to invite the rabbi for dinner and listen to his advice.

The young couple argued that each set of parents was prepared to continue supporting their son or daughter through graduate study anyway and that with little more than that they could get along all right. The parents expressed great fear that

Leah especially wasn't old enough for marriage. They were concerned, moreover, about what would happen if she became pregnant. That might well mean dropping all their study plans and changing the whole course of their lives. When confronted with the divorce statistics mentioned in this chapter, Philip and Leah said they were aware of the risks but felt sure they would be among the successful couples; they were confident they loved each other enough to surmount all difficulties and problems.

What advice would you give if you were Rabbi K.? Were the parents realistic in fearing the possibility of pregnancy? If Leah did in fact become pregnant and either or both of them had to drop out of school as a consequence, what effect do you think this might have on their marriage? How much weight should be given to the couple's confidence that they would be different, that they could avoid the risks involved?

C. When Lilli was shown the criteria of maturity described in this chapter, she studied them for a while thoughtfully then, much to her parents' surprise, admitted that she didn't consider herself to be very mature. That, however, did not deter her from being eager to marry Frank at once. For one thing, she said, he was very much more mature than she and therefore could be expected to overcome some of the problems she might be unable to handle. She relied on his strength a great deal. When her parents continued their opposition, she became angry and said that, to be perfectly honest, she didn't think they rated too high on these maturity items either, yet they seemed to have remained together all right for twenty-two years. So she was willing to take a chance on being no worse than they. "Anyway," she added, "how do I know I'll be very much more mature in another two or three years; and you certainly wouldn't expect me to wait longer than that, would you?"

Do you think one partner's maturity can compensate for the other's lack of it? Which of the following would present the best possibility of a happy marriage: 1. two immature individuals; 2. one immature, the other very mature? Had you been one of Lilli's parents, how would you have answered her? What effect do you guess your response would have on her?

D. Irene was an awkward, rather homely, girl who had never been popular with boys. As a matter of fact, she didn't have many girlfriends either. She had seldom been asked out on dates; this bothered her a great deal. When she did go out, she felt insecure and unsure of herself.

Last summer Tommy asked her for a date. It took a lot of courage on his part, for he too had experienced difficulty in social adjustment. He hated to ask a girl for a date because every refusal was a bitter pill to swallow. He and Irene seemed to hit it off well from the start. They dated regularly through the summer and fall, and by spring Tommy had "popped the question." Irene's parents were of course delighted at the favorable turn in her life, but they felt that at nineteen she wasn't yet ready for marriage. To tell the truth, Irene had some doubts herself, though she wouldn't admit them to anyone else. She was afraid, however, that if she turned Tommy down he would stop dating her and she might never have another chance to marry.

How can you explain the fact that these two got along so well as dating partners? Wouldn't that fact seem to indicate they would probably have a successful marriage? What would your advice to Irene be? To Tommy? Were her fears about never having another chance realistic? Is it better for a girl to accept an offer of marriage despite her doubts, or to remain unmarried and possibly alone?

6

"Believe me, there's nothing like a blind date to make you appreciate a lonely evening at home."

How to make the right choice

After "how can I tell whether I'm really in love?" the question most often addressed to experts in marriage is "How can I choose the right husband or wife?" This is of far greater urgency to us now than it was at a time when parents arranged matches for their children. In some cultures, marriages are still arranged by elders; families couple their respective daughters and sons. The bride and groom have nothing to say in the matter; sometimes they don't even see each other until all the plans have been completed.

It has been argued in some quarters that, on the whole, this kind of social structure makes for better marriages than our way of doing things. This is, we are told, due to the fact that parents are apt to be more sensitive to such factors as similarity of background and taste and the financial competence of the groom. They are also less likely to permit a daughter to remain permanently unmarried. And finally, being themselves free of romantic attraction in the matter, they can view the two young people in question with greater objectivity than the prospective bride and groom are able to see themselves.

Despite the logic and validity of this contention, there are also obvious advantages to *our* system of self-selection. In any event, it is not probable that in a democratic, humanistic society such as ours, there will be a change in the way we select our mates. Consequently, young people must choose with all the care they can. It would be wise for them to follow the advice of the Talmud: "You may make haste to buy property but you must pause and consider before taking a wife."[1]

Where parents once had everything to say about the selection of their children's mates, today we have swung very nearly full circle to the point where they frequently have nothing to say. Many young people in our culture are notoriously disinclined to follow their parents' advice in this respect. And many a parent has had to learn the lesson our ancient rabbis attributed to King Solomon. They said that he had a beautiful daughter about whose future he was extremely anxious. He asked once to see in a dream who her husband would be. When his dream revealed that her mate would be one of the poorest lads in the kingdom, Solomon was perturbed. He disapproved of this match and was determined to prevent it.

So he built a palace on an inaccessible island, surrounded it with an impregnable stone wall and locked his beautiful daughter and her servants in to protect her from her prospective groom.

Sometime thereafter, the young man in question was wandering one cold night in the forest. Lacking enough clothing to keep from freezing, he came upon the carcass of a bull and climbed into it for warmth. As he slept, a huge bird snatched up the carcass, flew with it many miles, and dropped it on the roof of the palace. When the princess went to the roof the following morning, she beheld the handsome young man and at once they fell in love. After a time they were married in the presence of her servants.[2] It would seem that our rabbis were attempting to tell us that not even the heroic efforts of a strong-minded king could prevent his daughter from marrying whomever she would.

In an earlier chapter, we mentioned the rabbinic statement that since God completed the work of Creation He has been matching couples. Here is the full passage embodying that belief—it will help you realize how important the choice of a mate was to our ancestors.

A matron once asked Rabbi Jose ben Halafta: "What has your God been doing since He finished making the world?" "He has been matching couples in marriage," was the reply. . . . The matron declared that she could do as much herself; nothing was easier than to couple any number of slaves with as many slave-girls.

"You may think it easy," said Rabbi Jose, "but it is as difficult for God as dividing the Red Sea."

The matron accordingly tried the experiment with a thousand males and as many female slaves, setting them in rows and bidding this man take this woman, etc. The next morning they came to her, one with a broken head, another with gouged-out eyes, a third with a broken leg; one man saying: "I don't want her," and a girl saying: "I don't want him." Thus was the matron constrained to say that the mating of man and woman was a task not unworthy of the intelligence of God.[3]

While we cannot pretend to be God, it is our hope that this chapter may offer wisdom enough to allow you to achieve greater success than the Roman matron. What, then, are some of the things to be remembered in the selection of a mate? We do not suggest that one should walk about with a rating sheet and pencil in hand, scrupulously interviewing each prospect before asking for or accepting a date. The urges which impel young people toward each other are mostly sexual and emotional, not calculating and intellectual. But there is a place for reason and good sense even in emotional relationships. Many a marriage has been wrecked on the rocks of failure because the couple concerned never bothered to check their hearts with their heads. The easiest time to think rationally about the qualities in a mate which make for a good marriage is now, before a romantic attachment makes it more complicated to think clearly.

A difficult word

What must we look for in the selection of a mate? Much of the answer may be summed up in a single word: compatibility. Unfortunately, however, this is far from an easy word to define. The dictionary defines *compatible* as "capable of existing together" or "congenial." Fire and water are not compatible: fire is extinguished by water; water is evaporated by heat. Some people have as much trouble existing together—especially in the same household—as fire and water. If this is the case, it is imperative that it be discovered before marriage, rather than after.

Usually when a man and a woman are described as being incompatible, it is assumed they are uncongenial sexually. We shall have more to say about this in a later chapter. Meanwhile, there are many other kinds of compatibility on which a good marriage must depend.

1. There is, for example, *intellectual compatibility*. All other things being equal, it is not good for a very bright man to be married to a rather dull girl, or an intelligent girl to be coupled with a stupid boy. Such a match may be exciting for a short while, but it will soon become insufferable. Our rabbis knew this centuries ago. Addressing themselves presumably to one who is himself intelligent, they said:

> A man should sell all he possesses with the object of marrying the daughter of a scholar or giving his daughter in marriage to a scholar. That is like uniting grapes of the vine to grapes of the vine, which is good and acceptable. But let him not marry the daughter of an ignoramus,

because that is like uniting grapes of the vine to berries of the bush, which is something ugly and unacceptable.[4]

The *Shulchan Aruch,* sixteenth-century code of traditional Jewish law, suggests a hierarchy of values in choosing a mate which reflects the enormous stress put on intelligence.

A man ought always to strive to win in marriage the daughter of a Torah scholar and to give his daughter in marriage to a Torah scholar. If he cannot find the daughter of a Torah scholar, let him seek to marry the daughter of renowned communal leaders; if he cannot find one of these, let his choice be the daughter of a congregational leader; if not one of these, then the trustee of a charitable fund; if not one of these, let him select the daughter of an elementary Hebrew teacher, but let him not marry off his daughter to an ignorant man.[5]

2. There is *social compatibility.* It is not snobbery we speak of here, but rather the undeniable fact that, all else being equal, two persons who come from similar social backgrounds stand a better chance for happiness in their marriage than if there is a vast gap between them in this respect. Despite all the fascinating Cinderella-type stories in print and on film, serious studies of marriage show this to be true. With similar social backgrounds, it is more probable that the values and aspirations of two people will also be alike and that the adjustments to be made after the wedding will be less serious than they might otherwise be.

The Talmud seems to have recognized this point, but makes a rather curious comment with regard to it: "It is not wise to take a wife of superior rank—rather go down a step in choosing a wife."[6]

Do you agree that if there is to be a disparity in social standing between husband and wife, it is better for the male to be somewhat above the female? Why? Would this be as valid today as in talmudic times? Why? Would you call this talmudic comment sexist?

3. *Economic compatibility* is important too. We have in mind here not the financial background and standing of the two families, which would actually be a part of the preceding point, but rather the *attitudes* and *ambitions* of bride and groom regarding financial matters. If one is a compulsive buyer and the other a habitual saver, this does not augur well—not merely because of the probable dissension between them on money matters, but also because one's feelings about the saving or spending of money disclose a great deal about one's general personality.

Related to this type of compatibility is the question of marrying for money. You may have heard the familiar quip that it's just as easy to fall in love with a rich girl or boy as with a poor one. While this may be true, it introduces other complicating factors. It is certainly questionable whether a good marriage is likely to result if a man deliberately sets out to fall in love with a wealthy girl. And while there is nothing wrong with a girl's being concerned about the ability of her future husband to earn a respectable living, if this becomes the overriding factor in her choice, there is reason to doubt the outcome.

Here again, the wisdom of the ancient rabbis was remarkable. The Talmud contains at least two admonitions bearing on this: "He who weds for money will have delinquent offspring." Also: "He who looks for the earnings of his wife sees never a sign of blessing."[7]

> Do you think either the writer of this book or the Talmud exaggerates this aspect of choosing a mate? Would there be a serious problem if one marriage partner was perfectly willing to let the other spend money as extravagantly as he or she pleased, while remaining frugal personally? If there is to be a wide financial disparity between groom and bride, would it make any difference which was the wealthy one? Does financial subsidy from parents help or hinder in making a good marital adjustment? Why? Would it make any difference from which set of parents the help comes?

4. There is a wide variety of *character traits* in which it is important for groom and bride to be compatible. For example, if one

is very rigid while the other is permissive and lax, there is probably trouble ahead. If one is punctual and the other careless of time, if one is neat and the other sloppy, if one is an extreme introvert and the other an enthusiastic extrovert, it is easy to anticipate some of the difficulties they almost certainly will have to face.

5. *Cultural tastes* are of equal importance. It would be difficult for a music lover to share life meaningfully with one who hated music—or perhaps even for an opera lover to be happy with one whose musical tastes run to jazz and rock. The future would appear to be bleak if an avid reader married one who never opens a book, or a vigorous athlete were paired with a shrinking, fearful recluse, or a connoisseur of art were attracted to one who hates museums.

> If opposites like those described here were sufficiently attracted to each other to enjoy dating, would that not of itself seem to indicate they have enough in common to make good marriage partners? How could we account for such individuals finding each other interesting for dating in the first place? How about the old adage, "opposites attract"?

6. *Similar interests in children* are also important. Since one of the most important aspects of marriage is rearing a family, it is essential for the two prospective mates to agree on whether they are to have children, how many to have, and in general, to agree on methods of disciplining the children. If you yourself are the product of a home in which your parents frequently disagreed on matters pertaining to your behavior, you will understand how frustrating—even agonizing—this can be from the child's point of view and how vital it is, therefore, to have as much agreement as possible between parents. We have already touched briefly on the importance of husbands and wives speaking with a single voice on all matters related to their children. What we have in mind here is agreement on the *attitudes* toward children which underlie their specific statements or actions.

Two individuals who love children appear to have a better

outlook for a happy marriage than if one loves children and the other does not. Even two people who both dislike children would seem to have better prospects in this regard than two who strongly disagree—though they would be removing from their lives one of the most exquisite joys of marriage, that of having and loving children.

7. *The more similar two people are in their leisure-time interests, the better for their marriage.* Two of the earliest experts on marriage estimated that couples who share and enjoy all their outside activities together have fifteen times as much chance for happiness in marriage as do couples who lack such agreement.[8] Would you like, incidentally, to test yourself on this with the next person you date? Pick up the current issue of any magazine or newspaper, go through it together, and find out how many items there are in which both of you are deeply interested—items about which you would like to enter upon a serious discussion.

8. *Compatibility of age* is important, too. While it is impossible to establish an exact mathematical formula, we know that too great an age disparity is not good. A girl who wishes to marry a man fifteen years her senior is apt to be unconsciously searching for a father substitute, not a husband. A man in that relationship may well be anxious to find a daughter-substitute rather than a wife. Similar unconscious motivations may be at work if the woman is appreciably older than the man. Marriages based on such needs are fraught with danger.

How can one tell whether such explosive unconscious factors are operating in the choice of a mate? It is far from easy to do so. The only reasonably certain way to discover this is through psychotherapy in depth. If there are other reasons which suggest the need for such therapy, it should certainly be sought. If this seems to be the only problem of a serious emotional nature you experience, it would be wise to discuss the problem with someone you can trust, someone who knows you and your family well, and who is professionally competent to help you think through the complicated problems involved. That someone could be your rabbi, your physician, a camp counselor, or teacher. Any of these would probably be in a position to consider the matter a little more objectively than your parents who are, after all, emotionally involved with you.

It shouldn't surprise you by this time to learn that our ancient rabbis were aware of this problem too. According to the Talmud, "he who weds his daughter to an old man, and he who gives a wife unto his minor son, commits a wrong."[9] The Torah, as you probably already know, directs that, if a man dies without a child, his brother is obliged to marry the widow and to give her a child to carry on the dead man's name. Chapter 25 of Deuteronomy, verses 5 through 10, describes the procedure to be followed. We read that, if a man is reluctant to fulfill this obligation, "the elders of his city shall call him and speak to him." In commenting on this passage, the Talmud says:

> This teaches that they gave him advice suitable for him. If he was young and she old, or vice versa, they would say to him, "What sense is there in your marrying one much younger than yourself?" or "What sense is there in your marrying one much older than yourself? Go, marry one who is about your own age and do not introduce strife into your house."[10]

In addition to the unconscious motivations involved, there are two very important practical problems to be considered when the bride is very much younger than the groom. The life expectancy of women in the United States is considerably longer than that of men. This means that, even when husband and wife are of approximately the same age, the man is likely to die first and the woman will face a certain number of years toward the end of her life as a widow. Where an age disparity exists, with the husband much older than his wife, this probability is obviously increased. While this is not a very pleasant or happy prospect to consider at the time of one's choice of a marriage partner, long-range possibilities must be faced in making a decision one hopes will last for life.

The other practical difficulty pertains to the future sex life of the couple. There is no reason for a woman twenty and a man thirty-five to face any trouble in this regard. When she is fifty, however, and he sixty-five, serious problems of sexual adjustment may develop.

Some men and women continue to enjoy intercourse into their seventies or even eighties, but there can be a great gap in the frequency with which a woman of fifty and a man of sixty–five desire or can repeat it.

9. *Interest in other people* is also an area where compatibility is to be tested. As with attitudes toward the saving or spending of money, the kind of people one likes indicates much about one's own personality. Everything else being equal, two people who like each other's friends, who react similarly to a third person whom they have both met for the first time, are likely to face a brighter future together than two who normally disagree about other people. It is worth observing here that individuals who have many friends of their own sex usually make better marriages than those with few friends.

10. *It would be difficult to exaggerate the importance of religious compatibility.* This includes not only the advantage of coming from the same general religious faith, but also the attitudes of the two toward religious belief and practice even when they share a common religious background. Since we intend to comment on this at greater length later, it is merely mentioned here briefly as one of the important areas of life in which compatibility is essential.

11. It would not surprise me at all to hear a howl of dissension when I mention *compatibility between the two families involved in a prospective match.* I can almost hear many of my readers protesting with vehemence: "But I'm not marrying a family! I'm marrying an individual, and that's all that counts!"

True, one marries an individual. But it would be a disastrous error to assume that the family of the individual can therefore be ignored. Most young couples live in the same community with the parents of one or both of the partners. Unless they can get along well together, there is trouble lurking in the not-too-distant future. A wife whose husband is at odds with her parents becomes the rope in an emotional tug-of-war. A husband whose wife is at war with his parents is in no less lamentable a position. Many a marriage has floundered catastrophically on the rocks of in-law trouble. I have discovered, in many years of counseling engaged and married couples, that the in-law problem is the one most frequently raised as a barrier to happiness. While it is undeniably true that sometimes this is just a convenient distraction to camouflage serious deficiencies on the part of husband or wife, the fact remains that one is wise to give the most serious kind of thought to the family of one's fiancé or fiancée.

Aside from everything else, the family of your mate will be important in determining the heredity of your children. Remember: half your children's chromosomes and genes will come from your family, the other half from the family of your mate. It is entirely possible that some trait—physical or emotional—which you find extremely objectionable in your future father-in-law or mother-in-law may show up conspicuously in your own child.

Our tradition scores high in recognizing the importance of this factor too. The Talmud enjoins: "Before taking a wife, investigate her brothers, for most children resemble their mother's brothers."[11]

Is it true genetically that most children resemble their maternal uncles? If so, what would this mean for us in anticipating our prospects for marital happiness? If this is not true, would it justify our forgetting the talmudic injunction altogether? Why?

Transferring the major love relationship of grown children from their parents to their mates is sometimes a painful problem. It is not easy for parents to let go, to stop after so many years of directing their children's lives and to accept them as mature adults. On the other hand, there are young people who have become too closely attached to one or both parents and fail to make the necessary adjustment toward husband or wife as the most important recipient of love in their lives. In either event, the result can be disastrous.

It is important, however, to be aware not only of your future mate's family but also of his or her relationships with others in the family as well as of your relationships within your own family. Does there seem to be too much emotional dependence of either on the other? Too much resentment or rebellion? Any apparent attempt to dominate? What kind of marriage do your parents and the parents of your fiancé or fiancée have? Would you be content to have a similar marriage?

Our relationships with parents are often complicated and ambivalent. At times we love, at other times we seem to hate the same person. It is possible, in selecting a mate, unconsciously to seek someone to whom we can transfer all or part of our emotional feelings toward either parent. It is even possible to be searching for someone against whom to shift a resentment of one or the other parent which, though pervasive and strong, we haven't been able consciously to recognize in ourselves.

That is why it is so important to recognize how you relate to your family and how your prospective partner relates to his or hers. Does your future spouse in any way resemble—physically or emotionally—either of your parents? Is the resemblance in a trait you admire or dislike? This kind of question should be raised as soon as your relationship begins to seem serious. The longer it is delayed, the more seriously you become emotionally and sexually involved, the more difficult it will be to achieve honest, objective answers. All else being equal, people who have a warm, loving, mature relationship with parents who themselves have a good marriage are the best candidates to enjoy such a marriage themselves.

Jewish tradition has long recognized the nature of this problem. Immediately after the Bible tells of Eve's being created as Adam's partner in life, it adds: "Therefore shall a man leave his father and mother, and shall cleave unto his wife, and they shall be one flesh." One of the postbiblical rabbis added: "Before a man marries, his love goes to his parents; after he marries, his love goes to his wife."[12]

Do you agree with the statement made by this rabbi? What was he trying to say? Could he have said it better?

In this connection, there is also the question of whether a young married couple should live in the household of either set of parents. Jewish tradition has a number of things to say about this. The Talmud, for example, asks: "Can a goat live in the same barn as a tiger? In the same fashion, a daughter-in-law cannot live with her mother-in-law under the same roof." Without inquiring too specifically into which of the two is to be identified with the goat and which the tiger, the point our rabbis meant to emphasize is clear.

Two very interesting comments on this matter come from the Apocrypha. In your judgment, are they consistent or in disagreement? The first goes: "I have carried iron and removed stones, and they were not heavier than for a man to settle in his father-in-law's house." The other reads: "Honor your father-in-law and mother-in-law, because henceforth they are your parents."[13]

Recognizing the need for practical guidance in facing the problem of in-laws, the *Shulchan Aruch* stipulates that if either husband or wife finds the visits of parents–in–law or other relatives disturbing to the peace of the household, such visits are to be prohibited. Neither mate, however, can deny the other the right to visit his or her parents in their home.[14]

Is this sound advice? Is a happy marriage possible where either partner insists that the other may visit his parents in their home but not invite them as guests?

12. Though we began this section by stating that incompatibility does not always mean sexual uncongeniality, there is no denying that it sometimes does. Sex is very important in marriage—so important that we plan shortly to devote several chapters to it. For that reason, we merely list here *the need for sexual compatibility,* deferring our discussion to a later section.

In general

Several summary comments are needed here on the general subject of compatibility. First, it would be foolish to suppose that any two people can or should be identical in all respects. Indeed, their household would likely be a dull and boring place if this were so. What is important is not that bride and groom be carbon copies of one another, but that they resemble each other in most respects and do not differ too widely in the rest.

It is a dreadful mistake to marry someone with whom one knows there is serious incompatibility, in the expectation that after marriage things will change. True, two people who live lovingly in a good marriage do have an effect on each other; it has been said that sometimes husbands and wives come not only to think alike but almost seem to resemble each other. But this is true only if there was sufficient compatibility to begin with. A home is not a reform school. If you don't love your prospective mate as he or she is, quit before you become too deeply involved!

Professor F. Alexander Magoun, whom we have quoted earlier in these pages, has made a wise and eloquent comment on this subject:

> The only person one ever has the right to try to change is one's self. Immaturity often manifests itself in an attempt to reform the betrothed. A mature person sees faults, balances them against virtues, and accepts another individual for what he is.[15]

Incidentally, beware, if you find no faults in your spouse-to-be! There never has been and never will be a perfect human being. If you can identify no faults, it means you don't know the other person nearly as well as you think you do. You may be sure of one thing: sooner or later after the wedding, faults will become evident—in you and in your mate. To know them in advance means to be prepared for the adjustments you will later have to make. There is another reason it is important to recognize faults in the person you intend to marry. To love means to fulfill the needs of the loved one. If you are unaware of that person's faults, how can you possibly know—far less, fulfill—his or her needs?

It is essential that you like your mate as well as love him or her. Actually, we are begging the question in this statement, because if you do not truly like and respect a mate, it isn't love at all but at best, only infatuation. A good question to ask is whether the person you think you might want to marry is one whom you would find interesting, with whom you would want to spend a great deal of time, from whose companionship you could learn and grow, even if there were no sexual attraction involved. This is not an easy question to answer, but it is an essential one to ask.

Other people with whom we become emotionally involved can have a variety of effects on us. They can make us feel

a. Inferior, or
b. Superior, flattered, possessing an inflated ego, or
c. Satisfied with ourselves as we are, or
d. Acceptable to ourselves as we are but eager to improve.

Neither the first nor the second kind of reaction is a promising one for marriage. The third is acceptable; only the fourth is really good.

Some years ago, I visited an elderly man who had lost his wife the day before. They had been married more than fifty years. As the old man talked to me, he kept nodding his head sadly from side to side, saying: "Did I lose a friend! I lost the most wonderful friend a man could have!" He came eloquently and pathetically close to summarizing what we are trying to convey here. If, in addition to everything else which binds them together, a man and woman can feel they are solid friends to each other, theirs is apt to be a superb marriage.

The Talmud contains the following rather curious statement: "Every man receives the wife he deserves."[16]

Do you agree? If so, why? If not, is there some element of truth in this assertion?

On reaching a decision

A number of tests have been devised to evaluate the personalities of two individuals who are contemplating marriage and to anticipate their probable compatibility. While no such test is infallible, and life's most important decisions cannot be made entirely on the basis of psychological evaluations, such tests can nevertheless be helpful, particularly where there is reason to doubt how well any two people are matched. Most rabbis and marriage counselors are aware of these tests and can arrange to administer them to couples who want to know more about themselves, both individually and together.

Since it is likely to be several years until most of you will be ready for this kind of intensive test, we offer you here a brief chart with which two people may attempt to evaluate themselves and the relationship between them. It is adapted from a similar list originally published in Crawford and Woodward's book, *Better Ways of Growing Up,* published by the Muhlenberg Press. To be justified in considering themselves compatible, any two individuals should be much alike on at least half these items, somewhat alike on many of the rest, and without major discrepancies on more than four or five. When a dating relationship begins to grow toward permanency, it should be both interesting and instructive for you and your partner to rate yourselves by these criteria. Two steps are recommended:

1. Let each of you rate your individual compatibility.
2. Compare your separate evaluations and discuss them.

The extent to which you agree can in itself be a measure of your being well matched.

HOW COMPATIBLE ARE WE?

1. Very different
2. Mildly different
3. Somewhat alike
4. Much alike

☐ Home background.

☐ Personal standards of right and wrong.

☐ Ideals regarding home and family.

☐ Desires for and feelings toward children.

☐ Educational background and interests.

☐ Intelligence.

☐ Religious interests and preferences.

☐ Vocational preferences and attitudes.

☐ Ambition for money and social standing.

☐ Spending and saving habits.

☐ Relative emphasis on home and outside activities.

☐ Cultural tastes: art, music, drama, books, etc.

☐ Personal habits: eating, sleeping, smoking, etc.

☐ Circle of friends.

☐ Recreational and social interests.

☐ Temperament and mood.

☐ Punctuality and neatness.

☐ Attitudes toward parents of both.

☐ Tendency to be critical.

☐ Tendency to praise and reassure.

For instance

A. Bob is one of the most intelligent young men in his college class. He was elected to the National Honor Society in high school and became a member of Phi Beta Kappa in his junior year at the university. He loves people, is warm and outgoing in personality, makes friends easily and quickly becomes the center of conversation in any crowd. Laura is quite the opposite. While not stupid by any means, she had to work very hard in both high school and college; one year she had to attend summer session to make up a course she had flunked. She did manage to graduate with slightly lower than average grades. Socially she is shy and retiring, generally uncomfortable in the presence of people she has met for the first time. In a gathering she likes to sit back and listen to others, rarely offering to contribute anything herself.

Bob and Laura are aware of these differences between them but feel that, far from being liabilities, they enhance their relationship. Laura glows with pride whenever she listens to Bob holding forth on any subject. He, on his part, seems to want and need the adulation she gives him. "We complement each other perfectly," they have often said. "Each of us supplies what the other needs."

What do you think this couple's chances are for a happy and successful marriage? Are they likely to feel this way permanently about the differences between them? Why?

B. Harry thinks Phyllis is a spendthrift; this is the most serious fault he can find in her. He himself has come from an impoverished family and has had to work hard for everything he possesses. With diligent work and careful saving, he has built up a comfortable amount of reserves and is very careful about how he spends his money. He attributes the fact that Phyllis doesn't know the value of a dollar to the wealth of her parents who have always given her everything she ever wanted.

They have discussed this difference a number of times and think they can overcome it. Harry has made it clear that he will marry Phyllis only on condition that he is to be the manager of all their financial matters. He will give Phyllis an allowance, reviewing it with her from time to time, but the final decisions are to be his. This is the only area in which he insists on being the boss. Phyllis is willing to accept such an arrangement because she is confident her parents will continue to give her whatever she may want but is unable to purchase from her allowance.

It should be added that Harry is also much neater than Phyllis. He is willing, however, to let her keep the house in the way she wishes, so long as he can be in charge of his own closets and dresser.

How important is it that Phyllis and Harry have faced this problem and arrived at a solution? Do you foresee any great difficulty between them after they are married? Should Phyllis tell Harry of her expectations from her family or leave well enough alone in order not to create unnecessary premarital disagreement?

C. When Justin comes home in the evening from a hard day's work he wants nothing so much as to sit down after dinner at the television set and spend a relaxed few hours watching. Brenda doesn't care much for television; an hour or two on Sunday is enough for her. She is, however, extremely fond of bridge, finding it the most relaxing diversion she knows. They have agreed that Justin will watch television as often and as long as he likes, while she is to feel free to join three of her bridge-playing girl friends. They have, as a matter of fact, followed this kind of schedule several nights a week throughout their engagement and it seems to have worked out well. The only serious disagreements between them have taken place on Sunday afternoons when they have from time to time watched TV together. Then Justin invariably wants to see a football or baseball game and Brenda, who doesn't care for athletics at all, would prefer an entertainment program. They have had a few unpleasant arguments over this but aren't particularly worried because they plan to have two television sets after their marriage so they can watch what they want without annoying one another.

How successful do you think this marriage will be? Are Justin and Brenda likely to have other problems of disagreement? Do you think their arrangements will be as successful in married life as they seem to have been during their engagement? Why?

D. What do you think is the point of the following rabbinic story? "Three years had passed since the day Abraham had sent Ishmael away. He longed to see him and sought out his camp in the pasture-country of Paran. When Abraham came to his son's tent, he found Ishmael absent from home. He asked Ishmael's wife for a little water, but the ill-natured woman refused to give it to him. Abraham said: 'When thy husband returns, pray tell him that an old man from Philistia came to visit him and, not finding him home, offered this advice: the pegs of your tent should be changed.'

"Ishmael understood this allusion to his wicked wife and divorced her. He wedded another woman, named Fatima.

"The following year Abraham again wished to visit his son and again found him away from home. Without waiting for a request, Fatima offered him hospitality and urged him to partake of food and drink. Abraham said: 'When thy husband returns, tell him: his pegs are excellent and he should retain them.'

"Ishmael thanked his gracious wife and blessed the Lord who had sent him so admirable a mate."[17]

Did Abraham have the right to interfere in this way in his married son's life? Was he entirely fair to Ishmael's first wife? What do you think is the point of this story? In the light of what had occurred earlier in the life of Abraham and Ishmael (see Genesis 16:1–16 and 21:1–21), is any light shed on the failure of the young man's first marriage? In view of past events, is there anything surprising in the outcome of the story?

E. Iris's mother is angry and bitter. She feels that her son-in-law, Craig, has poisoned her daughter's mind against her own parents. Before Iris's marriage, she and her parents had been very close. At first Iris phoned her mother every day and consulted with her frequently over recipes and other household matters. Then Craig began to interfere. He resented the amount of time his wife was spending with her mother and the fact that she was still so dependent on her. Where once the couple would visit Iris's parents every Sunday, Craig now insists that they visit his parents as often as hers and that they spend some Sundays away from all four parents. Iris tells her mother that she agrees with her but her husband is so unreasonable on this subject that she doesn't dare risk an open break with him. Things have reached the point now where her mother feels most uncomfortable when the four of them are together. She and Craig barely acknowledge each other. The atmosphere is almost like one of armed neutrality.

> Judging by the facts presented here, where does the fault lie for this sad situation? Is Iris's mother being reasonable? Is Craig? Has Iris handled the problem wisely? What could be done to improve matters? Could Iris's father do anything to help? If things go on as they thus far have, do you think Iris and Craig will be drawn closer together?

F. As far back as Claire can remember, her father has been "master" of their house. All important decisions are made by him. Neither her mother, her sister, nor she herself would think of taking a major step without seeking and following his advice. True, there were occasions, especially during her early adolescent years, when she resented her father's authority, but he has been wise in his decisions for the family and she likes the idea of a strong man on whom she can depend.

Quite the opposite has been true in Vic's family. His father is a kind, soft-spoken man who has never been decisive. Each week he hands his paycheck to his wife, who proceeds to pay the bills and manage the family's funds. She has been a rock to all of them, keeping calm under stress, resolving every indecision for her husband and children. While Vic's sister has often bitterly resented her mother's strength, he has enormous respect for that strength and has learned to rely on it in every crisis.

Claire and Vic have just announced their engagement. They

and their families are excited in anticipation of the wedding, which has been scheduled for next summer.

If you were a rabbi or marriage counselor, what advice would you give Claire and Vic? Why? Do you foresee any particular problems in their marriage? Could you—by pointing out such problems to them—eliminate them as dangers to the couple's happiness?

G. Gerry's mother is a strong and rather brutal person who has always dominated their family life. She is also a perfectionist, insisting that Gerry and her other child keep themselves impeccably clean, make the honor roll at school and behave with perfect manners in the presence of company. Gerry both loves and strongly resents her mother. She has discovered, without actually verbalizing it even to herself, that the only time her mother becomes soft, compassionate, and loving is when Gerry is ill.

Gerry is in love with Bert. He is a very strong, decisive person, unlike Gerry's father, who is sweet, tender and somewhat withdrawn. While sometimes Gerry feels that Bert is making too many demands on her, generally she enjoys being with him and tries to meet his expectations.

How would you rate the prospect of their marriage? What do you think is likely to be the future of their relationship? Of that between Gerry and her mother? Between Bert and Gerry's mother?

7

Recipe
for
success

By now we know that the first ingredient of a happy marriage
is a wise choice of mate. This, however, is only a beginning.
Even two people who are compatible in most respects can fail
if they do not attend to the rules best calculated to bring them
closer together through the years. The relationship between
husband and wife is so intimate that it cannot be a static one.
In some ways it may be compared to an airplane which must

keep moving forward or fall to the ground. So most couples discover that they either move closer together or farther apart during their years of marriage.

Strange as it may sound, love and hate are very closely related emotions. Infants are born with a nearly insatiable need for love; there is no such thing as an inborn need to hate. Someone has defined hate as love gone sour. When little children fail to receive the kind and amount of love they require, especially from their parents, their innate capacity to give love can turn into a need to hate. Much the same process can occur in a marriage. The need of most adults for one partner in life —to whom they can give and from whom they can receive the most profound kind of love a human being is capable of knowing—is so deep that if it becomes frustrated, the probable consequence is hate. It is always sad to see a husband and wife, who began their life together with such high hopes for continuing love, reach the point of hating each other. But it sometimes happens.

Standing at the marriage altar, almost all couples are convinced that they love each other and confident that they face a happy future. I once officiated at the funeral of a twenty-two-year-old man whose mother and father—still legally married—bitterly refused to speak to each other even under this tragic circumstance. Such a couple is an extreme illustration of the fact that love can be transposed into hate.

The statistics of divorce confirm this. In the United States, between 1870 and 1940, while the population was increasing threefold and the number of marriages fourfold, the number of divorces rose twentyfold. From 1960 to 1971 the annual number of divorces in the United States rose by 80 percent. In the period from 1960 to 1962 there were, on the average, something over four hundred thousand divorces a year.[1] Here are the official statistics since then:

1965—479,000	1975—1,026,000
1973—913,000	1976—1,083,000
1974—970,000	1977—1,097,000

Another way of understanding this phenomenon is in terms of the divorce rate per 1,000 of population. In 1901 it was 0.8; in 1951 it had risen to 2.4; by 1971 it had reached 3.7; in 1977, 5.1.[2]

As alarming as these statistics are, they must not mislead us into assuming that the institution of marriage has failed. While it is undeniably and sadly true that the number of divorces has risen in this country, so has the number of marriages. A higher proportion of the American population than ever has been married at least once. Over two-thirds of the men and women who had been divorced, married again very quickly. We must also bear in mind that the figures for divorce given above include many individuals who had been divorced more than once, thus inflating the total and disguising the number of couples who have been married happily.

It is important to remember two things in considering these statistics. First, not every unsuccessful marriage reaches the point of divorce. Numbers of unhappy couples remain together for a variety of reasons. To borrow the wonderful phrase of Thoreau, they remain under one roof, living together their "lives of quiet desperation." On the other hand, however, it would be a mistake to assume that the entire increase in divorce represents that much additional unhappiness.

The attitude of our society toward divorce has also changed substantially. There was a time when divorce was considered a scandal and a divorced person was looked at askance. Fortunately, this is no longer so. Because divorce is now socially more acceptable than it once was, there is little doubt that a higher proportion of unhappy couples resort to it than did in the past. In whatever way we qualify or interpret these statistics, however, the fact remains that too many couples fail in their efforts to achieve a happy marriage.

We have earlier referred to the fact that in marriage, as in life generally, happiness does not come to us automatically. It results only from understanding the laws of human nature and striving to conform to those laws. Too often couples concentrate only on the benefits they hope to receive from marriage, ignoring the means through which these benefits are possible. Given two individuals who are at least reasonably well matched, what are some of the factors which are instrumental in the making of a good marriage?

Some studies suggest that the three most important determinants are, in order:

1. The happiness of the parents' marriages
2. An adequate time span of acquaintance, courtship and engagement
3. A good sex education.[3]

We have already discussed the third of these; the first two will receive our attention in this chapter. Let us try, however, to be even more specific and detailed in writing our recipe for marital success.

One ingredient is the amount of kindness and consideration each partner in the marriage shows to the other. What a spectacle it is to contrast the thoughtful attention so many couples show during their courtship and engagement to the manner in which they take each other for granted afterward. A Stradivarius violin, abandoned to accumulate dirt and dust, soon loses its purity of tone. A love relationship, taken for granted and neglected, becomes tarnished and marred. No marriage can survive indifference.

A fourteen-year-old girl once told her psychotherapist that she could always identify the married couples in a restaurant; they were the ones who had nothing to say to each other. How sad! And how often true! Yet we may be sure these same couples participated in animated conversation during their courtship.

I sat one day with a man in his mid-seventies whose wife had just died. Though I had known him many years, this was the first time I had seen him shed tears. He said: "I never realized how much she meant to me or how much I loved her until I found out she had cancer."

A midrash relates that Abraham first recognized Sarah's beauty after they had been forced by famine to flee to Egypt. There, you will recall, Pharaoh became enamored of her. One day Abraham, as he noticed Sarah's reflection in a pool, became aware for the first time of her extraordinary beauty. Why did he observe only then what he had previously taken for granted? Because he was in deep trouble, and because there was a threat that he might lose her.

Husbands and wives who appreciate and cherish each other every day, who repeatedly tell each other of their love and demonstrate it, are doing the "work of marriage."

Because Jewish tradition understood this, it adjured husband

and wife always to show by their behavior how much they loved each other. In an earlier context we quoted the *Zohar* as saying: "A wife who receives love gives love in return; if she receives anger, she returns anger in equal measure." A midrash is more explicit on the same point:

> A wise woman said to her daughter who was about to become a bride: "My daughter, if you will respect your husband like a king, he will treat you like a queen. If you will serve him like a slavegirl, he will serve you like a slave. But if you will be too proud to serve him, he will assert his mastership by force and will treat you like a maidservant. If your husband is about to visit his friends, persuade him to bathe and wear fine raiment. If his friends come to his house, welcome them heartily and set before them more than they can eat, so that they will respect your husband. Watch well your home and all of your husband's possessions. He will be delighted with you, and you will be the crown of his head."[4]

> Would you accept this as sound advice for the modern couple? Are there any corrections or improvements you would suggest in it? Does it contain anything which could conceivably do more harm than good in a marriage? Is it sexist?

Often a husband or wife sees marriage primarily as an arrangement for the satisfaction of his or her most urgent needs, period! So long as these needs are reasonably fulfilled, the partnership endures. If they are not, the marriage is quickly dissolved. The element of mutuality is ignored—namely, the fact that *two* people and their needs are involved, that *commitment* and *responsibility* are essential components of marriage.

Some husbands and wives remind me of a bird, alone in its cage, staring at its own image in an attached mirror and enjoying the illusion that it has companionship. Or of a ship which projects a sonar beam to ascertain the location of a second vessel, but only for the purpose of safely guiding itself. The bird is in fact alone. The ship is concerned only with itself; no sense of mutuality exists in either case. Similarly, husbands and wives frequently use each other as mirrors or sonar targets for the benefit of themselves. The marriages of such individuals are not likely to succeed.

When we marry, we assume the responsibility for the fulfillment of our spouse's needs as well as our own. Marriage does not call upon us to be martyrs, to sacrifice our own integrity and wholeness for the sake of another, but it certainly does mean that—come good fortune or ill—husband and wife become responsible to and for each other. The give-and-take will not always be equal. Sometimes one will have to give more than the other because he or she is the stronger person. If the giving is so disproportionate that the giver risks surrendering the self, it may be that the marriage should be terminated. The distinction between a martyr and one who willingly gives more because of love is often excruciatingly difficult to measure. Each couple, each individual, must do the best he or she can to discover it. Yet we miss one of the most important aspects of marriage if we fail to see that it represents a commitment of two people to each other's happiness and welfare.

Root of all evil

Another factor on which the success of a marriage hinges is the ability of the couple to cooperate in handling their financial affairs. True, a failure here often simply reflects a deeper problem, but the fact remains that the economics of marriage must be successfully managed.

How much money two people need depends on their values, their ambitions and the standard of living they hope to achieve. One thing which is certain is that wealth by itself is no guarantee of success. One marriage counselor has reported an interesting study he made in the area of Los Angeles. In an exclusive suburb, he met a family whose income was $100,000 a year but whose home was filled with bickering, worry and angry conflict. In a trailer court, he spoke to a crippled man who lived with his arthritic wife and adolescent daughter. They were supremely happy on the very small income he earned as a part-time watchman. These two couples scored lowest and highest, respectively, of all families studied in Los Angeles County on a marriage adjustment test given by the counselor.[5] This does not mean that all wealthy couples are unhappy and all families of low income are happy. Financial tension is often a problem which jeopardizes the success of a marriage. It is desirable for each couple to have at least a decent minimum of economic security. But money alone will never assure the success of a marriage.

I remember counseling an attractive young couple who were experiencing difficulty during the first year of their marriage. Near the end of an hour's discussion I said to them: "One of your troubles is that you have financial problems." They were startled and protested with vehemence. "Oh no," they both insisted, "that's one area where we have no worries at all. We have both inherited quite a bit of money and stock from our grandparents and can have just about everything we want." This I had known. I proceeded to explain that it is possible to have financial problems because of too much which comes too easily, as well as because of too little.

What helps most in this regard is for husband and wife to have similar economic expectations and desires and to be able to plan and implement their budget together. If both were in the habit of living by carefully planned budgets while single, they have an initial advantage.

A wife whose demands exceed her husband's ability to provide can put severe strain on their partnership. The rabbis were aware of this too. They incorporated the following in the Midrash:

> Once a man engaged in robbery by night, keeping his family in luxury as a consequence. The wife of a neighbor complained to her husband: "What ill-luck is mine that I am married to you. The man across the way keeps his family in every comfort." The husband replied: "But rumor has it that he is a thief. Do you wish me to become like him?" The wife answered: "I care not what your occupation is, provided you give me the luxuries I crave." Being enamored of his wife, the husband begged his neighbor to allow him to participate in his next enterprise. The police were informed and laid a trap for him. The experienced robber succeeded in escaping the snare but the novice was captured and hanged.[6]

Many husbands, in our day too, are impelled to indulge in questionable business practices by the excessive demands of their wives and sometimes, their children. For this reason it is wise for husbands to share with their wives their general financial condition—what they can afford without undue strain, how much is being set aside for insurance, emergency, and retirement, what they can realistically expect their income to be in the future.

How about working wives? A generation or two ago most husbands would probably have considered it a reflection on their own manliness and ability to have their wives help in the support of the household. Today, a substantial proportion of wives continue to work. If the husband is opposed for the reason just described, or the wife resents her need to supplement their income, this can be a serious problem. If both are mature, a working wife can add more to the marriage than just extra income.

Influenced by the women's movement, the roles of husbands and wives respectively have changed greatly in recent years. More and more couples are coming to see the maintenance of their households and care of their children as joint responsibilities, to be shared by both marriage partners. We shall say more about this in a later chapter. For the time being, let it just be noted that a woman who occupies herself with gratifying and meaningful activity, who feels needed and useful as a person, will probably be a better wife to her husband and one day, a better mother to her children. The important thing here is not how much she earns, or indeed, whether she earns anything at all. If there is no need for supplementation to the husband's income, a volunteer job can accomplish as much, provided it offers work which the wife really feels is important and which gives her a sense of fulfilling herself.

Planning ahead

There is another reason why many marriage counselors now advise young wives to work, at least until children begin to arrive, and to resume work, perhaps on a part-time schedule, when their full attention is no longer needed by the family. At the age of menopause or change-of-life, which comes to most women some time between the ages of forty-five and fifty-five, there are often emotional difficulties which can be disturbing. Aside from certain glandular changes which occur in a woman's body at this time of life, a complicating factor is that her husband is still at the peak of his business or professional career, her children are away at college or perhaps already married themselves—and suddenly she becomes aware of the fact that from 8:00 A.M. to 6:00 P.M. there is no one in the world who really needs her, no position of importance and usefulness for her to fill. The woman who has kept her hand on a career may be better able to cope with this period of her life than one who has done nothing but attend to the needs of her family.

Is it possible for a wife to follow this advice without neglecting her family responsibilities? The answer to this must depend largely on the individual; among other things, how much energy and ambition she possesses. Certain studies undertaken at Columbia University seem to indicate that working wives may actually spend more meaningful time with their children than wives who do not work.[7] The important thing is not so much the number of minutes or hours spent in the home by parents and their children, but rather what they do with the time spent together. If a wife seeks a job outside her home as an escape from family responsibilities, her marriage is bound to suffer. If she can fulfill both obligations without ignoring or neglecting her home, this is good.

Two statements in the Talmud appear to be contradictory on this point. The first, which we have already cited in another context, reads: "He who looks for the earnings of his wife sees never a sign of blessing." The second: "It is not seemly for a woman to sit in idleness."[8]

Do these two statements refer to the same thing? Can they be reconciled? How do you suppose the rabbis in talmudic times would have felt about working wives? How appropriate would their attitudes on this be for us today? Why?

The paragraphs just concluded must not be construed to mean that a husband's responsibilities to his marriage and family are less than his wife's. One of my favorite French proverbs reads, in English translation: "He was born a man but died a grocer." Some men allow their careers to usurp nearly the whole of their lives. Their marriages, at best, must be inadequate. In managing their careers, both men and women must reserve major energy and time for their life together and must share the responsibilities of children and home if their marriages are to succeed.

Before we leave the problems of money in marriage, you may be interested in knowing that certain male occupations seem to carry with them a somewhat higher probability of happy marriages than do others. Among these are professors, chemical engineers, and the clergy. Occupations showing a lower degree of success in marriage are laborers, mechanics, and traveling salesmen.

How significant do you think this conclusion is? Should it deter a girl from seriously considering marriage to a man in any of the last-named occupations? Why? Can we account for the differences because of the occupations themselves or because of the types of individuals who would be attracted by them?

A fringe is not enough

Another factor of great consequence in determining the success of a particular marriage is the amount of time the two partners (and ultimately their children) spend together in meaningful ways. The relative ease with which household chores may now be performed, the incessant demands of a man's or woman's business or profession, the shrieking distractions which tempt us both within and outside our homes—these are characteristics of contemporary life which have in some instances corroded the true partnership of marriage.

In Chapter 6 we observed that an important prerequisite for the wise choice of a mate is the capacity of two individuals to share life. This capacity is of little value, however, unless they actually *do* share it. Far too frequently, after the first excitement and flush of the honeymoon have subsided, husband and wife go their separate ways, sharing a roof and a bed, but not truly sharing the most significant aspects of their lives. I recall an occasion some years back when I sat with a shocked and stunned husband whose wife had died that very day. They had been married over thirty years. Yet, when the bereaved husband was asked what his wife's interests were outside her family, and who her closest friends were, the man, after a minute or two of troubled thought, confessed: "Rabbi, I just can't answer that question . . . I don't know." In that pathetic reply he conveyed far more than he had really intended.

We have just referred in passing to the almost irresistible distractions which have made inroads in our family life. There was a time when families did many things together, sometimes things which were essential to the family economy, and sometimes things planned simply for fun. The important thing is that they were done together; often it became impossible even to distinguish the job from the diversion. Today there is almost nothing the members of a family must do together to keep the family going, and, in most of the things we do together for recreation, we have become passive spectators who just happen to be doing things in the same place and the same time, but not really together. A study made in the state of California, even before the wholesale advent of television, showed that 76.4 percent of total leisure time activity there was spent passively watching others do something, rather than actively performing oneself. With television as popular as it now is, the figure would obviously be even higher. A family sitting together in one room watching a TV program (that is, assuming they are not in several rooms, watching different programs on separate sets) is of course preferable to a family scattered to the four winds, but such a family is not forging bonds of unity and love among its members.

Dr. James A. Peterson has expressed this thought with exceptional eloquence:

> Hard physical effort such as scaling a mountain or hiking a great distance or lugging a canoe over a portage or playing a hard fought set of tennis—all of these enable us to release some of the aggressions built up within us. We invest ourselves in these activities and when they are finished there has taken place a kind of catharsis that has value.

There is a type of psychological help for children called play therapy which is based on the definite recognition that creative play enables the child to release feelings hitherto inhibited. In the same way the play of husband and wife releases pent-up feelings and clears the way for more positive feelings.

Recreational events are the sunshine among shadows, the highlights of sometimes gray marital experience. But every experience in the family influences all other experiences. When a couple solves their difficulties in a game they are provided with a new pattern for solving difficulties in other areas. After several such recreational experiences the budget-planning session will be conducted in a little different atmosphere with more gaiety and good humor.[9]

It is unfortunate that so many husbands and wives live the recreational aspects of their lives almost entirely apart from each other. They play tennis or golf or cards with friends of the same sex and are sometimes separated at social gatherings, even for the purpose of after-dinner conversation. During much of the week and year the dictates of economic and communal necessity leave them little choice. But how often—on weekends and at times of leisure—do they rush away from each other, almost as if they feared to learn more about each other! Husbands or wives who put their marriage out on the fringes of experience, giving it only the crumbs of their attention and time, cannot expect much happiness or satisfaction. Members of a family who use their home as a motel—a convenient place to sleep, change clothes and eat—occasionally but not necessarily performing some of these functions together— cannot hope to realize the rich promise of either marriage or love.

Also important

Brief mention must be made of several other factors which affect the success of a marriage. We have already referred to the love relationship which bride and groom have seen between their own respective parents. In ways which are deeply significant, even though mostly on an unconscious level, what children hear and see transpiring between their mothers and fathers makes a permanent imprint on their own lives. It affects their stability and maturity; it offers them a paradigm of what marriage should be. Some years ago Dr. Paul Popenoe completed an interesting study of the relationship between the happiness of married couples and that of the homes from which they came. Over four thousand couples were involved. Of those who grew up in happy homes, 67 percent had achieved happiness in their own marriages. Of those who had emerged from unhappy homes, only 43 percent were happy themselves. This is worth pondering.

It does not mean, however, that if your parents were unhappy and their marriage was unsuccessful, you are thereby doomed to repeat the pattern yourself. In that event, the wise thing for you to do is to find out, if you can, what went wrong in *their* marriage. Why did they fail to fulfill the expectations they harbored on their wedding day? What was there—about themselves as individuals, about their maturity or lack of it, about their understanding of marriage—which derailed them? In short, if your parents were inadequate for marriage or made mistakes, you can learn and even benefit from their mistakes.

A sense of perspective and balance also helps. Married couples confront many annoying practical problems: dishes need washing . . . the roof or a faucet leaks . . . rubbish must be carried out . . . the children bicker or are ill. Responsibilities and chores can corrode the best relationship if they are not met with mutuality and sharing, and if husband or wife fails to realize that their love is more important by far than the petty annoyances which sometimes threaten to divide them.

One day a husband brought a plant to his wife to mark her birthday. Her first remark after opening it was: "You ought to know this color doesn't go well with the furnishings of our home!" A token of love was rejected; the love itself was—perhaps irreparably?—damaged.

Religion plays a large role, too, in determining the success of a marriage. It will interest you to know that couples whose weddings take place in a synagogue or church show a significantly higher probability of happiness than those whose ceremonies are conducted elsewhere. This is not due to any special magic emanating from sanctuaries, but to the fact that the kind of people to whom religion and a religious setting would be important are also apt to be the kind of people whose values and maturity qualify them for happiness in marriage. We say no more at this point about religion as a factor making for marital success, because a later chapter will be entirely devoted to this very topic.

You may have begun to wonder why, in discussing the determinants of happiness in marriage no mention has yet been made of a good sexual relationship. My reason has been the conviction that a good sex adjustment is more likely to be the consequence than the cause of a good marriage. In any event, our next several chapters will be devoted to various aspects of sex, so we shall defer further consideration of this very important topic for the moment. First, however, there is a final consideration which calls for our attention now.

Courtship and engagement

All studies show that the length and kind of engagement experienced by a couple has something to do with the quality of their marriage. At the beginning of this book, when we first tried to distinguish between love and infatuation, we observed that a lasting quality is an important characteristic of love. The proper kind of engagement gives each couple a chance to use the test of time. It affords them an opportunity to know each other better and test their relationship. No one can prescribe the length of time an engagement should last. While it would appear from various investigations that a period of at least a year is best, this varies from couple to couple. What two people do during their engagement, how they use their time of testing, is more important than the actual length of their engagement. Two people who have known each other well for a long time before they become engaged will obviously not need as long a period of engagement as will two who have met recently.

It would be unwise, however, to underestimate the desirability of an engagement which is long enough to perform its proper functions. It is easy for a couple who have known each other for only a few months to say: "Yes, but we have been together almost every evening during that time and have become far more knowledgeable of each other than many couples who have known each other longer." One hundred hours spent together over a period of a few weeks are not nearly as good a barometer of compatibility as the same number spread over a longer span of time. Months of close contact provide a better opportunity than weeks, and a year is a better index than a few months in judging the probability of success for any given couple.

Nothing is more important during courtship and engagement than utter honesty between prospective bride and groom. There is a danger that they may come to know only the best side of each other before marriage, that each may "put on an act" to impress the other. One purpose of the engagement should be to see each other under adverse as well as favorable conditions; to discover how they react to a variety of circumstances, how they handle themselves when they are frustrated and disappointed and grouchy as well as when they are on a high tide of satisfaction. As already mentioned, it is desirable for each to see how the other acts in his or her own family setting and to become acquainted with future in-laws.

The engagement should also be a time for planning the future. In addition to plans for the wedding, the prospective bride and groom should discuss where they are to live, whether in rented quarters or their own home, how many children they want to have and approximately when, the nature and intensity of their religious identification, whether or not the wife is to work, and their feelings toward each other's parents. Careful attention should be given also to their budget, including the proportion of their income to be assigned to insurance and savings. Two people who cannot amicably, intelligently, lovingly make such plans as these during their engagement had better think searchingly about the advisability of marrying.

Dr. Gerald Albert, a psychologist who has specialized in marriage counseling, warns that the following have been found to augur poorly for the marriage of a couple who are courting: ". . . the revelation during courtship that either of the partners cannot confide in the other, or feels persistently disturbed by the other's activities, beliefs or attitudes, a tendency toward dramatic changes of mood, quickness of temper, unwarranted jealousy, a strong need to dominate and frequent feelings of self-blame and remorse."[10]

The sexual relationship between a man and woman during their engagement is of obvious importance too. This will be discussed in a later chapter, after we have considered the role of sex in marriage.

A final word for this chapter regarding engagement: as the wedding itself approaches, some couples find the tension and strain mounting. If this is due to unresolved doubts about their compatibility and love, it should be regarded as a warning signal. It may be caused, however, by the conflicting desires of their two families in planning the wedding. In that event, such pressure doesn't necessarily foretell real trouble. My own strong feeling, incidentally, is that the wedding ceremony and reception should be planned according to the wishes of the couple, not of either set of parents.

Open channels

Our comment about the importance of honesty during courtship and engagement applies no less to marriage itself. The channels of communication between husband and wife must never become clogged. Without being brutal or sadistic, they should be able to tell each other—openly and honestly— how they feel and what they hope. I once tried to help a married couple whose relationship had deteriorated to the point where their only form of communication was to write each other notes! Needless to say, their relationship was too far gone by then for me to save it.

Once, on a long, boring drive between cities I had my car radio tuned to a "Dear Abby" program. A woman had written in to say that she and her husband, married a year, were enjoying a good marriage, loved each other very much, but she faced one vexing problem. Her husband had very rough heels which scraped her legs every night in bed. She had strategically placed skin lotion and a pumice stone in his shower, but he hadn't taken the hint. Question to Abby: how can I—without hurting his feelings—get through to him how much his heels hurt me? This complaint is both comic and pathetic. Surely a couple who had so much difficulty communicating on so simple a problem as this was headed for trouble.

It is particularly important that open communication be maintained on the sexual aspects of marriage. Husbands and wives who do not tell each other honestly where their sex relationship seems to be unsatisfactory deny themselves the opportunity to work together for its improvement. Wives who pretend to have an orgasm during intercourse in order to please their husbands are asking for frustration and disappointment. To achieve success in marriage, honesty must be the rule.

In summary

We have by no means exhausted all the considerations on which the happiness of a married couple depends. Our hope has been to call your attention to the most important of them and to stimulate your own thinking. How happy your marriage will be depends not only on how wisely you choose your wife or husband, but also on the intelligence and care with which the two of you pay attention to the conditions discussed in these past few pages. Among the factors which determine the success of a marriage are the following: the kindness and consideration which husband and wife give each other . . . the degree of agreement between them on money matters . . . the ability of both partners to fulfill themselves through purposeful activity . . . the amount of time they spend together, especially in creative ways . . . the love relationship which bride and groom saw between their parents . . . the quality of their religious life . . . the satisfactions derived through their sex life . . . the extent to which they have wisely used their period of engagement to learn more about each other and to plan their future . . . open and honest channels of communication.

For instance

A. Terry had noticed how irritable Sam had been in the recent past but had no idea of the cause. Whenever she questioned him about his health, he brushed her queries aside and changed the subject. Since she found that further probing only increased his testiness, she soon stopped asking. The real reason for all this was that Sam had been facing serious business reverses. Several deals on which he had counted had fallen through and payments due him were late in arriving.

Sam was worried but did not want to involve his wife in

matters which were his own responsibility. Applications to send both children to camp had already gone in and a mink coat Terry had wanted for years had been ordered. It wouldn't be fair, Sam thought, to deprive the kids of camp or to disappoint Terry who had been so excited over the coat. The chest pains he had experienced over the past few days he attributed to strain and worry; he was confident that as soon as things eased up a little in business he would feel much better. Meanwhile, Terry found that she was responding to Sam's irritability in kind, so that the atmosphere in their home had been deteriorating.

What do you think of Sam's thoughtfulness toward his wife and children? What did it show about Sam himself? About his marriage? Should Terry have been more insistent in ascertaining the cause of her husband's irritability?

B. Read the story of Abraham's way of finding a wife for his son Isaac. You will find it in Genesis 24:1–27. Then be prepared to discuss the following questions, based on this story:

What criteria did Abraham give his servant for selecting Isaac's bride? What criteria did the servant establish for himself? Were they wise? Did Rebecca meet them? Are there any other qualities described in this passage which would suggest Rebecca's desirability as a wife? Can we learn anything here which is applicable to the subject of this chapter?

C. Al has never worked so hard in his life. A few years ago he quit the job he had held for ten years, and together with an old friend, started a business of his own. The two partners invested every dollar they had saved in this new business, plus a considerable amount of money they had borrowed.

For five years now, since their firm was founded, both partners have given it practically every hour of their waking time. Al is at the office daily by 7:00 A.M. and seldom leaves before 7:00 P.M. On Sundays he allows himself the luxury of sleeping until eight, but after breakfast drops by the plant "for a couple of hours." More often than not, it is dinner time Sunday evening before he returns home.

Sue has complained about the almost total absence of her husband from their home. She feels it isn't fair either to her or their three children. Al is very understanding; he says he doesn't blame her for feeling this way but he just can't help himself. "Honey," he keeps saying, "I have no choice. I'm really doing this, you know, for you and the kids. It's your future security and theirs that I want to provide. Once we get this business off the ground I'll try to turn over some of my responsibilities to others and spend more time with the family. But for the time being, it will have to be this way." When Sue protests that "for the time being" has already lasted five years, and asks how much longer it will be, Al can give no answer beyond assuring her he will do the best he can.

> How much does a husband owe his family in terms of providing for their future financial security? In terms of being with them in the present? If the two are in conflict, which should take precedence? What is your guess as to how soon Al will find it possible to spend more time with Sue and his children? What does his conduct reveal about their marriage? What does it portend for its future?

D. Betty has been upset for the past three days, since Ralph suggested that they take their summer vacations separately. "During our engagement," she reminded him, "you were annoyed with my parents because they wouldn't let me go with you on your vacation. Now we've been married only three years and already you don't want me with you. Here at home you spend practically all your time away from me because of business. When we have a chance to spend two weeks together, you don't want to."

Her arguments haven't made much impression on Ralph. "When we were engaged," he answered, "we were new to each other. Now that some of the novelty has worn off, let's act our age. You know I like to play golf on my vacation. I just don't enjoy playing golf with you; there's no competition. So let's go our separate ways for two weeks. I'll go some place where I can play golf with the boys, you go where you can swim, and as a result we'll probably love each other even more when we return home."

Who is right in this argument? Why? Is it wrong for a married man to prefer playing golf with his male friends? Must husbands and wives do everything together? Would you call Betty a nagging wife?

E. Reread the case of Gerry and Bert on page 100. Shortly after the initial excitement of their wedding and honeymoon had passed, Bert began to notice that his wife was making what he considered to be unreasonable demands on him. She insisted that he stop on the way home from the office to do their marketing, that he answer all social correspondence addressed to the two of them, that he assume the total responsibility for managing their finances, and that he do part of the housework. When he objected, she grew angry, accused him of being unfair, and occasionally even threatened to leave him.

With greater and greater frequency, moreover, she spent much time in bed, too sick to care for the house or prepare meals. Once neat and clean almost to a fault, she had become slovenly both in her personal appearance and the care of their home.

Can you explain the changes in Gerry? Might Bert have expected this? Is there anything wrong in a wife's asking her husband to help with marketing and housework? What would you advise Bert to do?

8

"What's to worry about? They'll teach sex like they do the rest of the subjects and the kids will lose interest."

Sex
is here
to stay

You may be inclined to assume that this will be just another routine recital of the so-called "facts of life," which you have heard many times and therefore do not need to hear again. It is true, of course, that some readers will need this chapter less than others, but I hope it will contain information of value for everyone. We have already seen that much of the "knowledge" of sex received even by intelligent young people must be placed in quotation marks because, coming from questionable sources, it is an unreliable—at times almost fantastic—combination of fact and fiction.

In order to test, at least partially, your own level of knowledge about sex, here is a list of fifteen terms which all of us should understand. Right now—before you proceed further with this chapter—write out for yourself one-sentence definitions of these words, numbering them as they are numbered below. Make your definitions as specific as you can. Keep the list; at the end of the chapter go over them again to see how well you did. Here they are:

1. Vagina	6. Intercourse	11. Testicle
2. Womb	7. Petting	12. Scrotum
3. Celibate	8. Masturbation	13. Ovary
4. Virgin	9. Orgasm	14. Hymen
5. Penis	10. Coitus	15. Clitoris

Perhaps you or some of your friends would score higher on this test of sex knowledge if slang terms had been used instead of scientific language. In some instances to follow I shall refer to words by which these sexual organs or functions are described in common conversation. Generally the technical terms are preferable; in many cases the popular expressions which you may have heard more often have acquired emotional overtones which I would rather avoid. Sometimes I can tell how a given individual really feels about sex—whether he or she sees it as something beautiful or ugly, expressing love or a need for power over others—by the language which is used. Let's turn now to the anatomy (body structure) and physiology (body function or performance) of sex in both males and females.

We are about to trace a most thrilling and exciting story. There is much evidence in the universe—in its orderliness and beauty, in the working together of so very many different elements and parts to serve important purposes—which convinces us that it could not be the result of mere happenstance or coincidence. The fact that scientists can learn enough about the laws of the universe, and can depend upon those laws to operate without deviation (and to permit us to land with precision on the moon a quarter of a million miles away), is surely evidence enough for most of us that some kind of Intelligence or Power is responsible for everything that has ever existed.

We call that Intelligence or Power "God."

None of the evidence we find in outer space and on the earth is more wonderfully convincing of this Intelligence than our own bodies. The most highly skilled engineer, using the most ingenious and complicated computer, could not possibly have planned bodies and minds which operate so efficiently and purposefully as ours do. The facts that, regardless of the temperature outside, the internal heat of the human body in normal health always remains within a fraction of a degree of what it should be . . . that no matter how much or how little liquid we drink, the proportion of water in our bodies is maintained at an even level . . . that when we ascend to higher altitudes where less oxygen is available, the red corpuscles in our blood immediately multiply in order to provide enough oxygen to keep us alive . . . that when infection strikes us, our white corpuscles mobilize at once to defend us . . . these and countless other manifestations of intelligence in the planning and operation of the human body impress us with the Intelligence which permeates the entire universe. (Incidentally, if you are interested in detailed descriptions of all this, you will find them in Chapter 3 of the author's *Wings of the Morning,* also published by the Union of American Hebrew Congregations.)

Nowhere, however, is this evidence more compellingly and beautifully illustrated than in the sex life of human beings. Millions of details in structure and function have been so designed that it is possible *through one act* for men and women to propagate their species (that is to say, produce offspring), to enjoy both physical and spiritual delight together, to express and simultaneously enrich their love, and to establish the foundation for families. In observing the truly amazing phenomena of human sex, you come perhaps as close as you ever will to following the way in which God operates in our lives. And some day, in experiencing all this with the man or woman you love, you will come closer than in any other way to God himself.

How sex functions in men

A diagram of the male sexual organs appears below. It shows first of all the penis, which serves the double purpose of conveying from inside to outside the body both urine from the bladder and a liquid substance called semen during sexual excitation. Some slang terms for penis are: *dick, cock, pecker,* and *peter.* Incidentally, a general term for both the male and female sex organs is genitals.

Here is one of the incredible feats of engineering we mentioned. The two functions of the penis could be so incompatible as to make one of them impossible. Urine contains a great deal of acid. Spermatozoa—the microscopic seeds needed to make a woman pregnant—cannot live in the presence of acid. If any acid from urine were to be in the urethra (the tube which extends inside the penis) when spermatozoa are flowing through it, they would immediately be killed and pregnancy could never occur. To prevent this, two things take place when a man becomes sexually excited. First, a muscle closes off the bladder, so that it becomes impossible for a man who is sexually aroused to urinate; second, the prostate gland produces an alkaline fluid which counteracts the effect of any acid which may have remained in the urethra from previous urination, thus making it possible for spermatozoa to remain alive. But we are a bit ahead of our story.

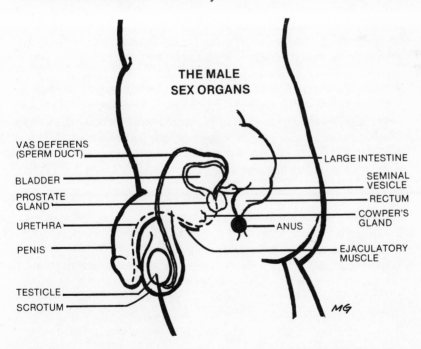

THE MALE
SEX ORGANS

VAS DEFERENS
(SPERM DUCT)

LARGE INTESTINE

SEMINAL
VESICLE

BLADDER

RECTUM

PROSTATE
GLAND

COWPER'S
GLAND

URETHRA

ANUS

PENIS

EJACULATORY
MUSCLE

TESTICLE

SCROTUM

MG

The size of the penis, like that of all other bodily parts, varies greatly from one person to the next. Normally, when a man is not sexually excited, the penis is in the limp position shown in the diagram and is likely to be about 3½ to 4 inches in length. When sexually aroused, it projects itself diagonally upward from the body, assuming a probable length of 5 to 6½ inches. There is no relationship between the size of the penis and the intensity of a man's sexual desires.

Some adolescent boys are very sensitive about the size of their penises. Though fairly common, this is an unnecessary and unwarranted fear. Like any other part of the body—indeed, like the body as a whole—size is in no way related to function. Girls, as we shall soon see, often worry similarly about the size of their breasts. The important thing for both sexes to remember is that your eventual success in marriage will depend upon who *you* are—the *total you* as woman or man —not upon the coincidental size of your genitals or the exact age at which you begin to experience strong sexual desires.

At birth, the tip of the penis is partially covered over with a flap of skin called the foreskin. Circumcision consists of removing this flap, so that the tip of the penis is fully exposed. In addition to the fact that it is a Jewish religious ritual symbolizing the covenant between God and Abraham, circumcision has been found to be healthy for the male and, for some reason which doctors do not yet fully understand, to reduce the probability of uterine cancer in the female.

Beneath the penis is a sack or bag called the scrotum, which contains the testicles, often referred to as *nuts* or *balls.* These are two small oval glands which manufacture spermatozoa (also called sperm). Again we discover magnificent planning. If his testicles were exactly the same size and hung precisely side by side, a man would suffer excruciating pain when they were crushed together. This is for the most part prevented by the fact that the left testicle is usually somewhat larger than the right one and hangs just a little lower, enabling one to slide by the other instead of crushing it. But this is only half the wonder involved in the arrangement of the testicles.

In some male animals the testicles remain permanently within the abdomen. The temperature within the human abdomen, however, is too high to permit the production of sperm. In rare cases where one testicle remains within a man's body, only the one which has descended into the scrotum is able to manufacture human seed. Being housed in the scrotum, the testicles are kept at a temperature which permits them to perform their function. But they would not function if they became too cold. The temperature of the testicles is kept within the narrow range which permits the manufacture of sperm by an intricate arrangement of extraordinary elasticity. In hot weather the scrotum descends farther away from the body to keep cool; in cold weather it contracts, bringing the testicles up closer to the body for warmth. See what we meant by the evidence of purpose and God in the way our bodies function? The most complicated thermostat invented by human intelligence cannot be more wondrous or dependable than this!

The testicles are not capable of producing sperm until a boy reaches the age of puberty, which usually occurs between the ages of ten and sixteen. The fact that in some boys it may come a little sooner or later than the average is of no significance at all in determining either the intensity or normality of their future sex life. As the testicles commence to perform their major function they also produce those physical changes which indicate that the boy is beginning to become a man: hair on his chest, surrounding his scrotum, appearing under his arms, a deepening of his voice, etc.

Once manufactured, the sperm are stored in the testicles and the vasa deferentia. When the supply exceeds the storage capacity, they are automatically released in the form of nocturnal emissions or, as they are more commonly called, "wet dreams." A boy who awakens in the morning to discover that during the night a quantity of liquid was apparently ejected from his penis, perhaps leaving stains on his pajamas and sheet, need not worry; this is nature's perfectly normal way of making room for the storage of more sperm. Often these emissions are accompanied by dreams which are sexually exciting. These too are perfectly normal; they should be the cause of neither fear nor guilt.

Each vas deferens has a seminal vesicle attached to it, the function of which is to supply a yellowish substance which makes the semen thicker, hence better able to carry and preserve the sperm. Ordinarily the seminal vesicles are kept closed by muscles in the prostate gland; it is only during sexual excitement that they open, permitting the secretion to pass into the urethra and become part of the semen.

Finally, there is Cowper's gland—named after the doctor who first discovered it. This gland secretes a slippery fluid which serves the same purpose in sexual intercourse that lubricating oil does in the engine of a car. The upward-downward motion of pistons in their cylinders would create friction which could quickly burn them up if a lubricant were not provided. Similarly, the inward-outward motion of the male penis in the female vagina could cause discomfort and pain if adequate lubrication were missing. It is the function of Cowper's gland and of two glands in the woman's body to furnish such lubrication. The large intestine and anus serve no direct sexual function; they are shown in the diagram just to indicate their relationship to the sex organs.

How sex functions in women

Perhaps even more ingenious than the sexual equipment of men is that of women. It is shown in the next diagram. Mention has already been made of the vagina, the tube or passage through which sperm enter a woman's body; and, if she becomes pregnant, a fully developed child emerges from her body at the end of nine months. Similar to the male penis, the female vagina varies in size—not only from woman to woman but in the same woman, depending on whether or not she is sexually excited. The vagina expands much more slowly than the penis; but, like the penis, it does enlarge when aroused. The entrance to the vagina is called the vulva.

No other part of the body has the automatic elasticity of the female reproductive apparatus. Before sexual intercourse has occurred, for example, the opening of the vagina is only about three-fourths of an inch in width; after some months of intercourse it has stretched to approximately an inch and a quarter; during childbirth it expands to five or six inches, then slowly returns to its normal size.

In a virgin—that is, a woman who has never experienced sexual intercourse—the mouth of the vagina is normally covered by a membrane called the hymen. The thickness and toughness of the hymen vary greatly. In many girls it becomes so stretched, even before intercourse, as to offer no resistance

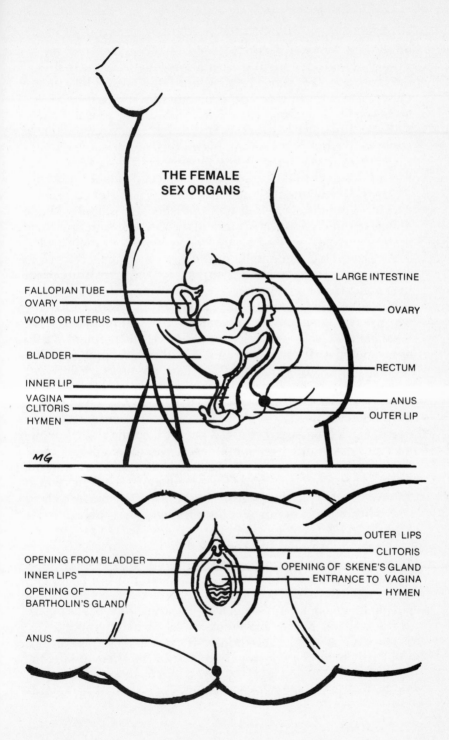

THE FEMALE SEX ORGANS

FALLOPIAN TUBE
OVARY
WOMB OR UTERUS

BLADDER

INNER LIP
VAGINA
CLITORIS
HYMEN

MG

LARGE INTESTINE

OVARY

RECTUM

ANUS
OUTER LIP

OUTER LIPS
CLITORIS
OPENING OF SKENE'S GLAND
ENTRANCE TO VAGINA
HYMEN

OPENING FROM BLADDER
INNER LIPS
OPENING OF
BARTHOLIN'S GLAND

ANUS

at all. If the hymen has not been broken or stretched in advance, it may cause slight pain and some bleeding the first time intercourse is experienced; this is nothing to fear. Only in rare instances does the hymen pose a major obstacle to intercourse, and even then medical help can alleviate any serious difficulty.

Ancient peoples believed that, if the hymen was broken or stretched before her wedding night, this was certain evidence that the bride was not a virgin. In some cultures a white sheet was placed in the marriage bed, and unless it was stained with blood the following morning, the bride was assumed to have had intercourse before and was punished accordingly. While no one in our civilization is quite that crude, there are still some men who expect to find an unbroken hymen in their brides. They need to be reminded that the hymen can be stretched in several ways; the fact that it is broken does not constitute proof that a girl is not a virgin.

Near the outer lips of the vagina is an organ called the clitoris. This is apparently a woman's vestigial remnant of the male penis. Exactly why she should have this remnant we do not know. Perhaps it is a reminder of the interesting fact that in some of the earliest forms of life there was no sharp differentiation between sexes; each organism carried the characteristics and performed the functions of both sexes. Only later in evolution did the two sexes become clearly differentiated. In any event, women possess a vestigial penis called the clitoris, while men possess stunted female breasts. The clitoris is the most sexually excitable part of the female anatomy.

There are two glands near the opening of the vagina which do not show on our diagram. Called respectively Skene's gland and Bartholin's gland, it was long thought that their purpose —like that of Cowper's gland in the male—was to provide the necessary lubricants for comfortable intercourse. We now know that while Bartholin's gland in particular does produce an oily secretion during sexual excitement, most of the lubricant a woman needs for comfortable intercourse comes from a phenomenon somewhat similar to sweating which takes place in the walls of her vagina when she is sexually aroused.

The ovaries are the storehouses for a woman's eggs, or ova, all of which are present in her body at birth. There are probably between 300,000 and 400,000 of them in each baby girl; unlike the sperm, they are not manufactured after the individ-

ual has achieved sexual maturity. Until the age of puberty—
which generally takes place in a girl between the ages of twelve
and fifteen—nothing happens to these eggs; they are just there.
Commencing at puberty, however, one egg ripens each month
—alternating between the two ovaries. This process is known
as ovulation. The ripened egg moves into the Fallopian tubes
which extend from the ovaries to the uterus or womb. If sperm
from a male happens to be in a woman's vagina at the time a
ripened egg is in the Fallopian tubes, it is attracted to the egg,
penetrates it, and conception (another term for onset of pregnancy) has begun. As soon as a spermatozoon (singular of
spermatozoa) has thus penetrated an egg, no other spermatozoon is able to do so.

It was once believed that identical twins are caused by two
spermatozoa penetrating an egg simultaneously. We now
know this is impossible. Identical twins, like single babies, are
produced by one sperm and one egg; because of an unusual
arrangement of chromosomes, however, the initial cell divides
into two organisms instead of remaining one. Fraternal (non-
identical) twins appear in the very rare instances when both
ovaries yield eggs in the same month and both are fertilized,
each by a separate sperm.

If no sperm is present to fertilize the egg, it passes on down
the vagina and is expelled from the body. No one has ever
actually seen the egg as it leaves the body. It is less than
one-hundredth of an inch in diameter; about three million of
them could be accommodated in a thimble.

Unlike the male urethra, there is no one passage in a woman
which carries both her urine and her sex secretions. It is only
near the mouth of the vagina that the outlet from the bladder
reaches the same general outer opening from her body.

In commenting earlier on the fact that some boys worry
during adolescence about the size of their penises, we noted
that girls may experience similar concern over their breasts
(called in slang, *tits* or *boobs*). This is especially true in our
culture, where such publications as *Playboy* so often extol the
alleged advantages of very large breasts. The fact is, however,
that the size of a girl's breasts are in no way related either to
her own sexuality or to the probability of her being attractive
to a boy. Some males prefer large breasts, others small ones;
just as some find blue eyes appealing, others brown. By the

way, girls sometimes worry because their breasts do not seem to be exactly the same size. This is of no greater consequence than the fact that our arms, legs, hands, eyes, and ears also vary in their dimensions. None of us is precisely symmetrical. In any event, the most important thing for a girl to remember is that a boy will be attracted to and will love you—all of you—not just any one specific part of you.

Life begins

When an egg has been fertilized, it then normally moves into the womb, which is to be its home for the ensuing nine months. It slowly develops into a human infant, obtaining all its nourishment from the body of the mother. At one time it was believed that the fertilized egg—or for that matter, even the spermatozoon before it reaches the egg—looked exactly like a miniature person, which only had to grow in size during the period of pregnancy. We now know this is not so. The cell which results from a sperm fertilizing an egg contains microscopic chromosomes and genes; it is these which carry the various characteristics and traits which the infant inherits from

DEVELOPMENT OF THE HUMAN EGG

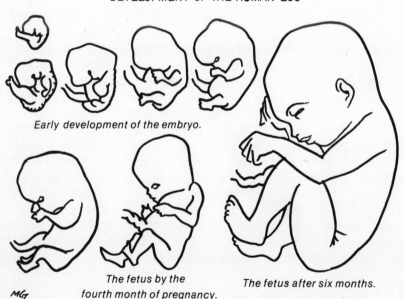

Early development of the embryo.

The fetus by the fourth month of pregnancy.

The fetus after six months.

MG

132   *Love, sex, and marriage: a Jewish view*

both parents. As it slowly grows from one cell to a full human being, the fetus, as it is called, retraces some of the steps which life generally followed in its development through evolution. At one early stage, it resembles a fish. Later it assumes the appearance of an amphibian, then an ape, and finally, a human being. It is interesting to note that a human egg cell, at the moment it is fertilized, weighs one-twenty-millionth of an ounce; after developing into an average adult, its weight has multiplied fifty billion times. Yet in that initial microscopic cell are contained all the physical, emotional and spiritual potentialities of the adult!

The womb is the best possible host for the developing life it harbors. It is so anxious to perform its duties well that each month it prepares for a possible guest. As ovulation is about to take place, the walls of the womb thicken with extra blood supply, ready to feed the fertilized egg if it arrives. If no such guest makes an appearance that month, the nourishment provided in advance becomes unnecessary, sloughs off the walls of the womb and passes out through the vagina. This process is called menstruation; it is often referred to as a girl's "period." A woman menstruates each month unless she is pregnant. A small quantity of blood—usually half a cup or less—along with some of the mucus from the uterus wall, flows out of her body.

Here is another of the marvelous provisions of nature to which we have already referred. You know that blood always tends to clot as it flows from the human body. Were this not so, we would risk bleeding to death from every nosebleed or scratch. If, on the other hand, menstrual blood were to clot, it would block the vaginal passage, make the bearing of children impossible, ultimately causing infection and death. The only normal circumstance we know of in which blood flowing from an opening in the human body does not clot is in the process of menstruation!

Menstruation can last anywhere from a couple of days to about a week. While it is occurring, a girl can pretty much go about her normal routine of activity except that she wears a protective napkin or tampon.

Some girls find the days preceding and during menstruation to be difficult. Physically, they may experience cramps. Emotionally, they may be unusually tense or easily aroused to anger or tears. A considerate fiancé or husband will try to be especially tender and considerate where this is the case. Many girls prefer to avoid such strenuous exercise as swimming while they are menstruating. If a girl who usually enjoys activity of this kind seems on occasion unwilling to participate, a wise boy gets the point without asking embarrassing questions. Come to think of it, there is no reason for such questions to be embarrassing at all. Boys and girls should be as comfortable discussing menstruation as they are talking about any other physiological function.

Girls vary in their reactions to menstruation. Some find it only a minor inconvenience; some dread it with great apprehension; most are to be found sonewhere between these extremes. There are psychological as well as physical factors accounting for these differences. If a girl unconsciously resents her femininity, or if her mother always anticipated her own period as a catastrophe, she herself is likely to suffer more than is necessary. In that event, it would be wise for her to consult a gynecologist, a physician who specializes in problems involving a woman's sexuality.

It was once universally believed that there was something unlucky or unclean about a menstruating woman. It was therefore considered dangerous to have any contact with her. This may be, in part, the origin of separating the sexes in an Orthodox synagogue. After all, one could never tell which women might be menstruating at a given religious service. Even so enlightened and intelligent a rabbi as Nachmanides wrote, in the thirteenth century:

> It appears to me that in days of yore menstruating women were totally sundered from society. They were not allowed to come near anyone, or to speak to anyone, for the ancients knew that their very breath is harmful. It seems that they were kept separate in a tent which was out of bounds to everyone else. Here is a saying in the talmudic tractate נִדָּה *Niddah* (the Hebrew term meaning a menstruating woman): "One may not touch a נִדָּה." R. Yohanan says: "It is forbidden to walk behind her, or to tread on the ground where she has trodden. It is likewise forbidden to make use of her labor."

Nachmanides carried these restrictions to the point of prohibiting a physician from even feeling his wife's pulse during her period.[1] And Rashi, the great Bible commentator, wouldn't hand his house key directly to his wife while she was menstruating.[2]

Today we recognize all this to be sheer superstition. Ancient peoples are not to be condemned; they were operating with the limited knowledge of their time. There is no excuse, however, for a modern person to believe such nonsense. A menstruating woman, provided she follows simple rules of hygiene to keep herself clean, is living through a perfectly natural phase of her life. She should be treated (and should treat herself) as normally as possible, and is no more to be shunned or avoided than a person with a nosebleed.

Just as some boys begin to produce sperm earlier or later than the average, so there are girls whose menstruation commences sooner or later than in most cases. Usually a woman continues to menstruate monthly until she reaches the age of about forty-five to fifty-five. The stage at which menstruation gradually ceases is called menopause or change of life. Thereafter, it is impossible for a woman to become pregnant. She can continue, however, to enjoy an active sex life with her husband.

The greatest wonder of all

Nothing on earth is more beautiful or important than the fact that a man and woman who truly, deeply love each other can, through the expression and consummation of that love, create a new human being. Nature has provided for the survival of all its species of life through reproduction. But nowhere is this process as meaningful as in human life.

It is, of course, through sexual intercourse—also called coitus —that humans become parents. The enlarged and stiffened penis is inserted into the vagina which is also made large enough, through stimulation, to receive it. It is then moved back and forth, with increasing excitement, until the male comes to a climax known as an orgasm. When this happens there is an ejaculation of semen in spurts. The contact between penis and vagina causes an orgasm in the woman too, with much the same pleasurable physical sensation, but with no ejaculation. It is difficult to describe an orgasm to a person who has never experienced one. Perhaps the closest analogy would be the release and titillation one feels in a robust sneeze, though the comparison is surely less than perfect.

We have already mentioned that a woman's clitoris is the most sexually sensitive part of her anatomy. It is by stroking the clitoris—either manually or with a man's penis during intercourse—that she reaches her orgasm. Some women are more effectively brought to climax when the clitoris is massaged indirectly, through neighboring tissue, than by direct contact. Freud and his early followers taught that there are two kinds of female orgasm: clitoral, which means to say, centered in her clitoris; and vaginal, where the climax or peak is experienced deeper in her vagina. This distinction is no longer considered valid by most experts. It is now recognized that all female orgasms—whether in intercourse or otherwise—result from stimulation of the clitoris. At the moment of climax, however, the sensation is so overpowering that it is felt throughout the vagina, indeed, in the entire pelvic area.

Each spermatozoon is so small that ten thousand or more, placed side by side, would cover less than an inch. Each also has a lashing tail which propels it up into the vagina in the direction of the Fallopian tubes. If there is a ripened egg waiting there and just one spermatozoon penetrates it, pregnancy has begun. If not, the sperm gradually dry up or drain out of the vagina.

You may have seen articles or reports on the possibility of so-called *test-tube babies*. These refer to experiments in which an egg is taken from a female during ovulation, is fertilized by a male sperm outside her body and, after two or three days, is reimplanted in her womb to develop normally. The theoretical advantage of such a procedure is that it might enable a woman who otherwise could not conceive nevertheless to have a child. The first successful human birth of this kind occurred in England during the summer of 1978.

There has also been talk among researchers about fertilizing a human ovum as described above, but, instead of returning it to the womb, developing it to the point of normal birth in a laboratory vessel called a petri dish. This too, at the moment, is only a theoretical possibility.

What effect would the cultivation of fetuses outside a woman's body have on her emotional relationship to her children? Might it in any way affect the child? How do you feel about this possibility?

Primitive peoples of course practiced sexual intercourse and the women became pregnant, but they failed to establish a connection between the two. They invented a number of fanciful explanations to account for pregnancies. A tribe in eastern Australia still believes that girl babies are fashioned by the moon, boy babies by the wood lizard. In Queensland it is commonly supposed that the thunder god makes babies from swamp mud and puts them into a woman's womb. Elsewhere it is believed that a woman becomes pregnant through sitting over a fire on which a certain kind of fish has been roasted, or because she has successfully hunted for a particular species of frog.

In animal life below the human level conception takes place in one of several ways. In some, especially certain fish, the female lays eggs outside her body, the male comes along shortly afterward and, without even seeing the female, deposits over the eggs a substance from his own body which fertilizes them. In other animals, the male injects a fluid from his body into that of the female while the egg is still forming within her body and before the shell has appeared. The fertilizing element thus becomes a part of the egg itself, so that after it is laid, only the attention of the female is needed in order for the egg to hatch. In a number of species the male is almost incidental; once he injects the necessary fluid for fertilization into the female, either she devours him (literally!) or he goes off to die by himself.

Intercourse among human beings differs in a number of very important ways from the same phenomenon in other animals. Among these differences are the following:

1. With very few exceptions—dolphins and whales, for example—only among humans do the male and female generally face and see each other during the act of intercourse.

2. Only among humans does intercourse serve purposes other than propagation of the race. It is doubtful whether females other than women are even capable of experiencing an orgasm. Intercourse in the rest of the animal kingdom occurs

only when the female is ready to be impregnated and only for the purpose of pregnancy. Intercourse in human life occurs when a husband and wife who love each other want thus to express their love. And in addition to the fact that it sometimes results in pregnancy, at all times in a good marriage it increases the very love which it expresses.

3. Only among humans does intercourse have a spiritual as well as a physical aspect. Only with us does it lead to the formation of families and the creation of a kind of love which endures even beyond the time of life when intercourse between husband and wife may cease.

4. Thus far we have mentioned only those ways in which sex is a more wonderful and exalted experience among humans than in any other branch of life. There is one way, however, in which it can also be more degrading. We are the only species in which the male can sometimes overpower the female, forcing her to have intercourse against her will. Forced coitus is called rape. What it means, plainly and simply, is that sex in human life can be either immeasurably glorious or unforgivably depraved. The choice is ours.

No baby, please

Only human beings are capable, if they wish, of preventing intercourse from resulting in pregnancy. This is referred to as birth control or contraception. It can be accomplished in several ways. The most common are:

a. for the male to wear a thin sheath called a condom (also a "rubber" or a "safety") on his penis to prevent any sperm from entering the vagina;

b. for the female to insert a diaphragm which covers the opening between the vagina and the uterus, thus preventing sperm from fertilizing a ripened egg;

c. to insert a medicinal jelly into the vagina which can kill sperm without injuring her;

d. to use a contraceptive foam which, if injected into the vagina before intercourse, can kill sperm;

e. to have a physician insert a small metal or plastic ring in the womb (called an intrauterine device, or IUD) which, for some reason we do not yet fully understand, seems to make conception impossible; or

f. for the female to take a pill which prevents ovulation, thus making it impossible for an egg to be fertilized. The pill, however, is taken not just in anticipation of each act of intercourse, but for twenty days of each month under the direction of a physician; otherwise it is not dependable. The contraceptive pill produces unpleasant side effects in some women. There is reason to suspect, moreover, that it may increase the incidence of phlebitis (a blood clot) or cancer, though most researchers are convinced that this danger is outweighed by the fact that the pill is the most certain single method of birth control we know. A woman who is on the pill should be checked by her physician regularly to make sure no undesirable or dangerous side effects appear.

Experiments are currently under way on several additional birth control methods. As this is being written, however, none of them is ready for general use. One is a "morning after" injection or pill, which would be given to a woman some hours after intercourse. Strictly speaking, this is more like abortion than birth control. It would not prevent conception, but would force the fertilized egg to be discharged through her vagina instead of becoming embedded in her uterus and developing there. Work is also in process on a pill which, taken only once a month, would protect a woman against pregnancy for that time span. And on a capsule which, inserted by needle, would prevent pregnancy until or unless it were removed.

Pending perfection of such a permanent method as the last, some men and women who are positive they will never want more children, resort to a surgical procedure called sterilization. If a woman's Fallopian tubes are cut or tied, she can continue to have intercourse but will never become pregnant. The same objective is achieved in a man by an operation known as a vasectomy, in which the vasa deferentia are cut, preventing any passage of semen into his urethra. The danger of sterilization is that, should the individual change his or her mind about having children, such surgery is difficult, if not impossible to reverse.

In addition to the birth control methods described above—all reasonably effective if properly used, the pill being most dependable—other methods are extremely unreliable. Boys, for example, have been known to use crude, homemade condoms, fashioned from rubber balloons or Saran Wrap. Such substitutes provide virtually no protection. Even a professionally manufactured condom can fail if it contains so much as a microscopic hole or if it slips off the penis during intercourse.

A diaphragm, to provide protection, must be fitted for size by a physician, who also gives instruction on how to insert it and how long after intercourse to keep it in. It is also best to combine a diaphragm with a contraceptive jelly or foam. While the IUD generally works, it can slip out, unknown to the woman who still relies on it for protection.

Some women rely on douching after intercourse—washing out the vagina with a device similar to an enema bag in order to remove any sperm which may have been deposited there. Because a douche has a limited range, and especially because sperm are energetic enough to reach beyond that range toward the uterus before a douche can be used, this is among the least reliable methods of birth control.

Another of the least reliable methods is the so-called rhythm system. This system is based on the fact that there are certain days in the menstrual cycle when there is no ripened egg present, hence no possibility of becoming pregnant. While this is true, there is enough variation in ovulation and menstruation in any one woman to make the calculation of this safe period so complicated that it cannot be used with any great assurance.

An extremely unreliable method which some couples foolishly use is called withdrawal. This means commencing coitus but not completing it; as soon as the male feels his orgasm beginning, he quickly withdraws his penis from the vagina to prevent sperm from entering the woman's body. In addition to the fact that this is an unhealthfully frustrating practice for both sexes, it is undependable as a method of birth control because sometimes semen begins to flow from the penis even before the actual orgasm. The attraction of sperm for a ripened egg, moreover, is so great that even when deposited outside a woman's body, near the lips of her vagina, they can swim toward the Fallopian tubes and cause conception. There have been women who became pregnant in this manner without actually experiencing intercourse.

Withdrawal is mentioned in the Bible. It was the practice among Jews in ancient times that, if a married man died without having a male child, his brother was obliged to marry the widow and to impregnate her so that she might give birth to a son who would bear her dead husband's name. A man named

Onan found himself in precisely this situation. Apparently he married his widowed sister-in-law but was not willing to make her pregnant. We read:

> But Onan, knowing that the seed would not count as his, let it go waste (or: spoil on the ground) whenever he joined with his brother's wife. . . .[3]

Ever since, withdrawal during intercourse has been known as onanism.

With all our research and new knowledge on birth control, it would seem entirely reasonable to expect a drastic decrease in the number of unwanted pregnancies. Yet such a decrease has not taken place, especially among unmarried young couples. Indeed, one prominent gynecologist has written: "The truth is that doctors today are seeing more women who are unwillingly pregnant than ever before."[4]

A nationwide study of nearly 5,000 teenage girls, made in the early 1970s by two sociologists at Johns Hopkins University, revealed that one-third of all brides eighteen years old or younger were pregnant when they married. Nearly 30 percent of all unmarried American teenage girls who had intercourse became pregnant.[5]

A 1973 study made by two Princeton University sociologists showed that "despite advances in birth control techniques . . . more than a third of the women . . . practicing birth control over a five-year period became pregnant anyway." A breakdown into specific methods showed the following rates of failure: the pill—5 percent; IUDs—5 percent; condoms—10 percent; diaphragms—17 percent; foam—20 percent; douches —over 40 percent.[6] Although no attempt was made to distinguish married from unmarried couples, for obvious reasons the rate of failure among young couples who are not married is bound to be significantly higher than among those who are married.

Unfortunately, no statistics on birth control failures more recent than 1973 are at hand. There is every reason to believe, however, that they would be quite similar to those cited above.

More than a million teenagers become pregnant each year, two-thirds of them against their will. In the decade 1967–1977, at a time when the birth rate among older women declined sharply, the rate for girls between fifteen and seventeen years old nearly doubled. This, surprisingly enough, despite the fact that reliable contraceptive devices were more conveniently available than ever.[7] The risks are frightening: babies born to girls in this age category are two to three times more likely to die in their first year—as are babies born to mothers in their twenties; the probability of their being born retarded or afflicted with cerebral palsy is many times greater; the rate of maternal death in childbirth is 60 percent higher than for mothers in their twenties.[8]

Sometimes the reason for birth control failure is careless or improper use of a method which could have been effective. Sometimes a couple who used no contraceptive device, because they had no intention of having intercourse, were swept off their feet by passion. There are also couples who think or feel that to plan against pregnancy in advance reveals a prior intention to have intercourse which is somehow more "immoral" than to intend self-control but to be overcome by passion.

In addition to all this, there are complicated, unconscious psychological reasons accounting for some "unwanted" pregnancies. They may, in fact, be very much wanted. A girl may be desperately eager to prove her femininity—or a boy his masculinity—by having a baby. Or one of them may be trying to force the other into marriage. Or determined to punish a parent by exposing him or her to embarrassment as well as heavy financial obligation. Not infrequently an unmarried girl who has endured the trauma of pregnancy and been given all the information she needs about birth control will nevertheless become pregnant again. Obviously, she is trying by her behavior to say something very important about herself, to herself —and to others.

Despite all the liberalization of attitude in recent years, the agony attendant upon an unwanted premarital pregnancy should not be taken lightly. Any rabbi or physician can testify from his own professional experience to the agony experienced by two unmarried young people who discover that, despite their most careful calculations, they have conceived a new life. What should be the most sacred and exalted moment in human experience becomes cheap and besmudged. Incalculable anguish is suffered by the couple, as well as by their parents. If they marry, friends lift suspicious eyebrows when their first child appears in less than nine months. Sometimes a shadow of guilt and remorse hovers permanently over a marriage which might otherwise have been a wonderful relationship. Not even this is the whole story. The anguish suffered by a girl who eventually learns that she is not pregnant—but who is horrified by a tardy menstrual period, knowing that she has had intercourse and *could be* pregnant—is not to be discounted lightly. The one and only sure way for an unmarried girl to prevent pregnancy is to avoid intercourse or any other experience which could place male sperm in or near her vagina.

Pathetic echoes of the enduring tragedy and heartache which afflict the parents of an unmarried pregnant girl are evident in the following excerpts from a letter published in *The Saturday Review* of August 15, 1964. In response to an article on "Campus Mores," published in an earlier issue of the magazine, a distraught father wrote:

> To all those college students, high school students, teenagers and others who want to indulge in sexual intercourse without marriage I would propound this question and demand an answer: "Are you personally prepared to assume full responsibility for pregnancies, illegitimate births, or physical or psychological damage that may result to you or your sexual partner because of these acts and to relieve your parents and others of the burden of such results?" . . . As the father of a daughter who made a "mistake" in college, gave the child for adoption, underwent psychiatric treatment for two years, and then had to go back to school to try to make some kind of new life, and who necessarily threw much of the burden on her family, I would say that sexual "freedom" is first of all a matter of responsibility and the ability and willingness to assume it. To those who have not the willingness and ability to assume responsibility, the freedom should be denied. In general, I would say that sexual intercourse is for responsible men and women and not for irresponsible boys and girls. . . .
>
> This letter is a testimony of a deep and harsh experience that has not ended after eight years and may never be

ended, for there is little hope that my beautiful daughter will ever be anything like what she might have been.

Another danger

Our survey of important information on sex would be incomplete if we did not include a few paragraphs about venereal diseases. These are principally two: syphillis and gonorrhea. They are transmitted from one person to another almost always through intercourse and are among the most dreaded of all diseases. In both sexes they can result in blindness, in deformed children, in paralysis and mental deterioration. In order to secure a marriage license it is now necessary in most states first to have one's blood tested to make sure neither party suffers from a venereal disease. But there is no way in the world of insuring that a partner in premarital coitus is free from infection.

Here again, there are some who minimize the danger, saying that we now have drugs which can control and even cure these diseases. Though we do in fact have such medication, successful cures depend on early diagnosis and treatment. Most parties to a premarital sex adventure are understandably not anxious to disclose this fact, even to a physician. As a result, in many cases the disease is not recognized until early treatment is impossible.

Unfortunately, the statistics here are as devastating as they were in the case of unwanted pregnancies. An article in *The New York Times* of May 6, 1962, written by Dr. Howard Rusk, bears the alarming heading, "Syphilis Cases Rise." It reads in part:

> The battle against venereal disease is far from won even with such available allies as penicillin and other new therapeutic tools.
>
> The 18,781 reported cases of infectious syphilis in the United States in the fiscal year 1961 was not only double the 1960 rate but triple the 1959 rate and was the greatest number reported since 1950. . . .
>
> Even more shocking than the marked increase in infectious syphilis is the fact that the greatest increase has been

among young persons. The disease increased 59 percent in the fifteen to nineteen year age group and 73 percent in the twenty to twenty-four year age group between 1959 and 1960.

Later in the same article Dr. Rusk attributed this frightening situation to, among other things, "lowering of moral standards" and "inadequate parental control of teenagers."

The trend reported by Dr. Rusk in 1962 has continued. You may at some time hear the convenient and apparently comforting rationalization that venereal diseases are a major threat only in the lower socioeconomic classes or among certain racial groups. Government studies show this to be untrue. Experts of the United States Public Health Service assure us that the horrifying increase disclosed in 1964 "is not confined to any race, sex, socioeconomic group or geographic area," that it has occurred quite generally throughout the nation.

Not even the most alarming statistics, however, tell more than a small part of the tragic truth. Because so many victims of venereal disease do not consult a physician, and because frequently doctors—to spare embarrassment to families they know well—fail to report such cases to public health authorities, the facts are undoubtedly uglier and more widespread than medical records indicate.

This is especially true among those in their late teens. According to the United States Communicable Disease Center in Atlanta, between 1960 and 1974 the rate of venereal disease among men and women under the age of twenty increased by 200 percent. How can we explain this? In part, it is due to greater sexual permissiveness. To a considerable degree, the birth control pill is also responsible. A condom, while less reliable than the pill for contraception, does provide some protection against venereal disease. The pill provides none. The only intelligent procedure for any person who has the slightest reason to suspect that he or she may have contracted a venereal disease is to consult a reliable physician at once.

You may at some time hear the convenient and apparently comforting rationalization that veneral diseases are a major threat only in the lower socioeconomic classes or among certain racial groups. Government studies show this to be untrue. Experts of the United States Public Health Service assure us that the horrifying increase disclosed in 1964 "is not confined to any race, sex, socioeconomic group, or geographic area," that it has occurred quite generally throughout the nation.

What is a man? What is a woman?

You may already have discovered that adolescence can be simultaneously a painfully agonizing and ecstatically happy time of life. More than any other stage of human development, it is marked by an intense search for identity. During these years you know that you are no longer a child, yet you sometimes wonder whether you are really an adult. On the same day—within a single hour!—you may do some things which are patently childish, others which are amazingly adult. A large part of this quest for identity is your urgent need to become not only an adult generally but a man or woman specifically.

What or who is a man? Many males mistakenly suppose that the answer is one of sexual prowess. The larger a man's penis, the stronger his physical desires for members of the opposite sex, the more frequently he enjoys intercourse and the greater the number of his partners in coitus—the more manly he is. Right?

Wrong! Quite the contrary: The more compulsively a human male needs to "make" every attractive girl he sees, the less probable it is that he is really a man. In all likelihood he is trying to compensate for a gnawing sense of uncertainty and insecurity, to prove to others but especially to himself that he is what in fact he very much doubts himself to be. Such a person may succeed in demonstrating that he is a sexual athlete; this, however, is by no means the same thing as being a man.

Two Catholic writers on marriage and the family (Barbeau, Clayton, and Myra, *Your Manhood or Your Womanhood in Marriage —An Interfaith Guide for All Couples,* Association Press, 1970, p. 19) have illustrated this truth as follows:

> Recently a young man, married only a few years, commented: "I used to have five guns: three rifles and two pistols. I sold them all recently. I haven't been interested in them since I got married. I needed them to prove I was

manly, I guess, the great hunter, the ready man with the weapon, whatever. Anyway, she's made that sort of thing unnecessary. She's convinced me I'm a man. Not just in bed, either, because I was lousy at that, too, before she got me to see that it wasn't anything I did, it was who I was that counted."

You most probably remember the story of Joseph and Potiphar's wife. Joseph, having been sold by his jealous brothers into slavery and brought by his masters into Egypt, has become chief steward in the household of an Egyptian official named Potiphar. We read in Genesis 39:7–20:

After a time, his master's wife cast her eyes upon Joseph and said, "Lie with me." But he refused. He said to his master's wife, "Look, with me here, my master gives no thought to anything in his house, and all that he owns he has placed in my hands. He wields no more authority in this house than I, and he has withheld nothing from me except yourself since you are his wife. How then could I do this most wicked thing and sin before God?" And, much as she coaxed Joseph day after day, he did not yield to her request to lie beside her, to be with her.

One such day, he came into the house to do his work. None of the household being there inside, she caught hold of him by his coat and said; "Lie with me!" But he left his coat in her hand and got away and fled outside. When she saw that he had left his coat in her hand and fled outside, she called out to her servants and said to them, "Look, he had to bring us a Hebrew to dally with us! This one came to lie with me; but I screamed loud. And, when he heard me screaming at the top of my voice, he left his coat with me and got away and fled outside." She kept his coat beside her until his master came home. Then she told him the same story, saying, "The Hebrew slave, whom you brought into our house, came to me to dally with me; but, when I screamed at the top of my voice, he left his coat with me and fled outside."

When his master heard the story that his wife told him, namely, "Thus and so your slave did to me," he was furious. So Joseph's master had him put in prison where the king's prisoners were confined.

Why did Joseph refuse to have intercourse with his master's wife? Was it because he was afraid of sex? Would he have been more a man had he yielded and gone to bed with her? Is it manly to reject a woman's sexual advances? Was Potiphar's wife more a woman because of her strong feeling for Joseph and her desire to have intercourse with him?

This last question brings us to the other side of our inquiry: What is a woman? Much of what has already been suggested applies here, too. It is a grotesque mistake to suppose that the more men a female can attract and seduce the more womanly she is. Certainly sex has something to do with being a man or a woman. *Something*—but not *everything*. It is the total person who qualifies as man or woman not just genitals.

It's easier to say what manliness or womanliness is not rather than what it is. Perhaps the best way to approach a positive answer would be by referring back to the criteria of maturity traced in Chapter 5. A person who has done reasonably well in meeting these standards and who sees and uses his or her sexuality, not as the be-all and end-all in itself, but as one important part of a whole personality—that person is well on the way toward being a man or woman.

Such a person understands two additional important truths about sex: (1) It is one of the most important drives in human experience; as such, it cannot successfully be denied or repressed, nor can it be turned on and off at will. And (2) the sex part of us is intimately related to every other part, especially to our emotions. The way we feel about life in general and the opposite sex in particular has much to do with our specific sex behavior. The opposite is equally true. How we act sexually affects our emotions and our attitudes toward life and other people. In short, sex is not a segment or compartment of our being. It is a strong impulse, part of our very essence, which is inseparably related to everything we are or do.

Path of wisdom

There is almost no sexual problem that cannot be solved if faced honestly and with competent help. There are many which can become bothersome if allowed to fester without adequate help. For this reason we would encourage you to discuss whatever problems of this kind you may have with an older person. It does little good to talk about them only to others your own age. Those who talk loudest and boldest are seldom the ones who really know the most.

The wise thing for each young couple to do as their marriage date approaches is to schedule one or more premarital conferences—one with their rabbi, another with a physician, preferably a gynecologist, a doctor who specializes in the female reproductive and sexual system. The rabbi will discuss the spiritual aspects of marriage. The physician will examine both bride and groom, discuss with them any problems of sexual adjustment they think they may encounter, give them the birth control information they need, and try to answer their questions.

Unfortunately, not every rabbi or gynecologist is competent to provide this kind of help; some of them may be as ignorant or "hung up" on sex as the couple themselves. Where this is the case, better counseling may be available through a local office of Planned Parenthood or a sex information service.

For instance

A. The education committee of the temple was meeting to discuss a course in marriage preparation which the rabbi proposed to give to juniors and seniors of the high school department. This book was to be the text; each member of the committee had been provided with a copy in advance, and they all had read it.

While most members of the committee were enthusiastically in favor of the course and thanked the rabbi for his suggestion that it be given, some had serious misgivings. One said, for example: "I'm not a prude, but I must admit that certain pages of this book embarrassed me; I wouldn't want my seventeen-year-old daughter to read them. It's all right to give our high school youngsters sex information in general, but I don't approve of going into such minute detail. The diagrams especially bothered me. Can't we leave anything to the imagination?"

"I agree," another member said eagerly. "What bothers me even more is the information given in Chapter 8 about birth control. Don't you think it's time enough for young people to learn about such things when they are ready for marriage? I don't mind telling you I'm even worried a little that this kind of information may encourage some of our boys and girls to go farther sexually than they otherwise would."

This last comment evoked vigorous disagreement from one woman on the committee. "Oh no," she exclaimed, "how can you even think such a thing? Our boys and girls come from decent, ethical homes, where they have been taught the difference between right and wrong. I can't believe that any of them would violate the sex ethics they have been taught by their parents. As a matter of fact, my objection to this course is that sex education belongs in the home, not in the religious school. We shouldn't usurp the rights of parents."

"I don't agree with any of these objections," said the newest member of the committee. "I like the idea of the course and I approve the book. My only suggestion would be that certain chapters or parts of them should be taught separately to boys and girls. I think, for example, that if the diagrams and discussions on the male and female sex organs were covered in separate groups—with the rabbi teaching the boys and a woman physician or nurse instructing the girls—there would be less embarrassment. Otherwise, I'm all for it!"

What would your reactions be if you were on this committee? Would you have voted for or against the course? Why? How would you have responded to each of the arguments summarized above? Are there other objections which could have been voiced at this meeting? How could they be answered? Has any part of this book thus far embarrassed you?

B. After Professor Magoun had finished a lecture to a group of Jewish high school students which included much of the information of this chapter, he invited written questions, which he then proceeded to answer. These, of course, were anonymous. One student wrote the following: "I find that your method of analyzing and describing the sexual process in front of a large group goes against my moral sense. It seems immoral and disgusting to speak of these matters in such a way. Perhaps between two or three people it would be more natural, but this does not seem correct."

How do you feel about this reaction? Do you agree or disagree? Do you think this student would have felt better if he or she had first read this book, then come together in a large group to discuss it? What would you be inclined to guess about the questioner's knowledge of sex? About his (or her) sexual conduct and future sex adjustment?

C. Todd and Jane had been engaged for ten months, had set the date of their wedding, and had already seen the rabbi for a premarital conference. At his suggestion, they had also gone to see a gynecologist who had talked to both of them and examined Jane. Up to that time everything had gone very well; after that day, however, the roof caved in.

While the gynecologist was discussing birth control with them, he said it would be possible for him to fit Jane for a diaphragm and give it to her to take with them on their honeymoon. Todd flushed perceptibly, though neither Jane nor the doctor noticed it. On the way home he was silent and sullen. Jane's efforts to find out what was wrong proved fruitless. Later that night when they were alone, Todd finally told her what had been bothering him. He knew, he said, that a girl whose hymen is unbroken cannot be fitted for a diaphragm. Several of his friends who were already married had told him that their brides had been advised by their physicians to return after the honeymoon to obtain a diaphragm, but that in the meantime some other method of birth control would have to be used temporarily.

To Todd this could mean only one thing: Jane was not a virgin. If her hymen was broken or stretched and her vagina was large enough for a diaphragm to be fitted, he was convinced that she must already have experienced intercourse with someone else. Whenever they had talked together about sex, both had said they had never had intercourse, nor did they want to with each other until after the wedding. Todd still loved Jane very much, but he did not see how he could marry her or how they could be happy after she had deceived him in one of the most important areas of life.

How would you have felt had you been in Todd's place? What would you have said or done in Jane's place? Who was at fault? Could this situation have been avoided? Would any argument now convince Todd? Would you advise them to go ahead with their wedding plans or to call the whole thing off?

D. Gail, who is thirteen years old, has not yet started to menstruate. She has been told all about it by her mother and older sister but is extremely apprehensive about the fact that some time in the fairly near future she will no doubt have her own first experience. As long as she can remember, her mother and sister have called their periods "the curse." For days before each flow starts and until it is just about finished, they have complained about being depressed and feeling a variety of aches and pains. Gail's mother usually spends three or four days in bed each month at that time.

Gail has heard many arguments between her parents and remembers occasions on which her mother complained to her father bitterly about "the curse," saying that no man could ever appreciate what a woman has to endure just because she is a woman.

As a consequence of all this, Gail isn't happy about being a girl and having to face the prospect of menstruating for many years. She looks with envy at her brother Bob, knowing that he will never have this worry.

How wholesome or realistic is Gail's attitude? Who is to blame for it? Are her mother and sister justified in resenting the inconvenience and discomfort of menstruation? Is there anything that could be done to help Gail? Why do some women find their periods so much more difficult than others?

E. Meanwhile, unknown to Gail, Bob has his own problems. It was just about a year ago that he had his first "wet dream." He awakened in the middle of the night—only half aware at first of the fact that he had just been interrupted in the midst of an exciting dream about sex. As soon as he became almost fully awakened, he realized that some kind of liquid had emerged from his penis. At first he thought perhaps his bladder control had failed, but this didn't seem probable at his age and anyway it soon became apparent that the liquid was not urine. That was the only time Bob has awakened during such a dream, but on several occasions since then he has found stains in the morning on his pajamas and sheets. This embarrasses him; he wonders whether his mother and the maid have noticed them.

The first time this happened, Bob began to worry that there was something wrong with him, that the liquid which came from his penis during the night was the semen he had heard about; but the fact that it was leaking out must mean that he would never be able to live a normal sex life or have children. This had become almost an obsession, usurping his mind even at times when he tried to study or read. The one boyfriend with whom he had tried to talk about it told him this just meant that he needed sexual intercourse and should try to find a girl who would be willing to try it with him. Then his semen wouldn't have to escape as it had during the night. But Bob was afraid to follow this advice; he continued to have occasional nocturnal emissions and continued to worry. At times he wished he were a girl so that, like Gail, he wouldn't have to face such a problem.

Could Bob's worries have been prevented? Was his friend's advice sound? If you were Bob, what would you do? If you gave him this chapter to read, would that resolve the situation? What can you tell about their parents and home life from the feelings of Bob and Gail?

9

"True, you are bright-eyed and bushy-tailed, but that just doesn't happen to turn me on."

The
same,
yet different

It is perfectly obvious that individual men and women, boys and girls, differ widely. An ancient *midrash* tells us that, whereas a human being, in creating many coins from a single mold, produces objects which are identical and indistinguishable, God, in fashioning all humankind according to the same pattern, made each one unique. Not even so-called identical twins are exactly alike; they differ from each other both physically and emotionally.

Nowhere are these individual differences more apparent or important than in the area of sex. We have already had occasion to observe that young people vary a great deal in the size of their sexual organs as well as in the age at which such sexual functions as menstruation, breast development, and wet dreams begin. Most young people are very much concerned with what is *normal* in sex development and behavior and whether or not they qualify for normality. We shall return to this later.

In addition to the uniquenesses which distinguish each individual from all others, there are also broad categories of differences in the sex attitudes and conduct of large groups. It will be the business of this chapter to inquire into some of these variations.

Foremost among them are the significant differences between males and females generally, quite aside, obviously, from anatomical characteristics. Contrary to mental growth and general maturation, adolescent males begin to function sexually at an earlier age than females, probably reaching their peak of physical sex capacity in their late teens. Girls do not achieve this peak until five or even ten years later. It goes without saying that this has important implications both for dating and for the early years of many marriages. Most boys are more speedily and directly aroused to sexual excitement than are girls. The sight of a shapely woman, casual physical contact with her, a photograph of a nude or seminude, even the very thought of sex, can produce an erection almost at once. This can be embarrassing if it occurs when a boy is standing before his class to recite. Girls are not exposed to such awkward moments, not only because they are sexually aroused much more slowly, but also because—unlike an erection—the flow of vaginal secretions which signals their sexual arousal is obviously not visible.

Don't misunderstand this distinction. Girls are not less sexual than boys; when aroused, they can want, need and enjoy sex just as much as males. The point here is that they reach this stage more slowly and indirectly. Very few girls are excited, for example, by the kind of photograph which can so immediately affect a boy. They are more likely to start with a more generalized feeling of emotional warmth and romance, moving slowly from that to a more specific desire for sex.

Reliable research indicates that almost all boys have had an orgasm by the age of fifteen; less than half of the girls have had one by that time. This difference in timing applies to women throughout their lives. Contrary to men, who ordinarily require very little preparation before intercourse, most women need to be introduced to coitus through what is commonly called foreplay, that is, affection, kissing, fondling and petting. Men who overlook this difference, who proceed to intercourse at their own natural pace without considering the condition or needs of their mates, do not share a mutually satisfactory sexual experience.

It must be quickly added, however, that there are differences even within differences. A minority of women are aroused and excited sexually as rapidly and directly as men. Some girls walk faster than the average, eat faster, read faster, work faster. Similarly, some respond faster to sexual stimuli. There is no such thing as a rigid standard of normality which brands as neurotic anyone who differs from it.

Most men are exhausted and satisfied after a single orgasm, requiring at least a half hour—sometimes considerably longer —before they are able to repeat. Some women are capable of enjoying multiple orgasms in quick succession. This does not mean that they are oversexed. The term *nymphomaniac* refers to a woman who is sexually insatiable, who cannot be satisfied no matter how many sexual experiences she has. This is a very rare condition; the fact that a woman can enjoy several orgasms in succession does not mean she is a nymphomaniac or in any other way abnormal. Neither does it cast any suspicion of inadequacy upon a woman who is content with a single orgasm. Both can be normal.

The gap in arousal time between boys and girls accounts for more than a few clumsy situations on dates. It is extremely important for males and females to understand each other's anatomy and physiology if they are to avoid embarrassment. This applies especially to girls who may unwittingly do or say something which comes through to their dates as something quite different from what was intended. Dr. Wardell B. Pomeroy, former president of the Society for Scientific Study of Sex, understands and expresses this situation very well:

> Because it is difficult for a girl to understand how much more sexually oriented boys are than she is, she may often, without having any understanding of what she is doing, say or do provocative things that will be constantly frustrating to a boy, particularly if petting does not follow. Sometimes it is only a matter of vocabulary, of double meanings not intended. For example, a girl may say at the end of a date, "My parents are in bed. Come on in and we'll have a good time." By that she may mean nothing more than listening to some music and having something to eat without parents being around. Most likely, however, a boy will translate her casual remark as "the coast is clear, and we can pet." Then he finds that what he thinks is an open invitation is something else, and the girl is shocked by his advances and resists them. As a result, he is left irritated and frustrated because he has picked up the wrong cues. . . .
>
> It would help girls if they could keep in mind constantly how much more sexually oriented boys are and that remarks they make will usually be interpreted in that way.[1]

While boys are more likely to be the aggressor, it is not always or necessarily so. A Harvard psychiatrist has told me that with increasing frequency he finds women to be the initiators of sexual encounters on the campus. This is likely to be truer on the college than on the high school level, but it can happen at any age. Incidentally, Dr. Pomeroy writes, not only about the girl who misleads her date innocently, but also about those who may do so intentionally, trying to see how far they can encourage a boy to go before deliberately, sadistically stopping him. Quite probably a girl who does this hates men and needs to demonstrate how much power she can wield over them. Whatever her motive, it goes without saying that this kind of behavior is dangerous and terribly unfair. A first essential for healthy relationships between boys and girls—indeed, for all persons generally—is that each must understand, accept and respect the other.

No cause for guilt

Nearly always when we speak of *wanting sex* or *having sex* we refer to intercourse. This is an unfortunate mistake. Touching, kissing, putting your arm around a person—all these are forms of sexual behavior. Coitus isn't the only manner of experiencing an orgasm either. Boys know that; very nearly all of them have already masturbated as have a somewhat smaller yet significant number of girls. For those who may not yet have practiced it, masturbation—sometimes referred to also as *jerking off* or *whacking off* or *getting off*—consists of manipulating the penis or clitoris, by hand or with some other object, to the point of causing an orgasm. There is good reason to believe that by adulthood virtually 100 percent of males and about 60 percent of females have at one time or another masturbated.

Probably more guilt has been incurred in this way than any other. Until recently, masturbation had been prohibited by both medical and religious leadership. Among the alleged consequences, against which generations of boys in particular have been sternly warned, are: blotched skin, tuberculosis, dyspepsia, heart disease, epilepsy, blindness, paralysis, insanity, and sexual impotence. Quite a list! The fact that not even this false catalogue of catastrophes succeeded in eliminating the practice of masturbation attests to the strength of the sex drive.

Thomas Aquinas called masturbation "nocturnal pollution." In Judaism it was referred to as "adultery by the hand." Sometimes the term *onanism* is mistakenly believed to refer to masturbation; we have already seen that in fact the sin of Onan was *coitus interruptus,* withdrawal before completion of intercourse. Our ancient rabbis applied the same principle to both: It is wrong to "waste" semen, the source of new life.

This is one of the many matters on which liberal Jews must respect our tradition without necessarily following it. Most of the ethical insights of Judaism are at least as valid today as when they were first conceived by our ancestors. In some areas, however, because we have knowledge which was unavailable to them, it becomes necessary for us to revise or even discard their judgments. We have already come upon one such point of departure in discussing isolation of menstruating women. The same thing is true with reference to the treatment of certain diseases. Were we to limit ourselves now to the medical knowledge and procedures of those who wrote the Torah, we would obviously be handicapping ourselves in our endeavor to maintain and improve health.

So it is with masturbation. Limited to the knowledge of those who so sternly warned against it in the past, we would doubtlessly feel exactly as they did. But we are not so limited. Medical and psychiatric experts are unanimously agreed that masturbation is *not* harmful; it does *not* cause any of the disasters once attributed to it. The only harm resulting from masturbation is the profound but unwarranted sense of guilt it has induced in the past.

Once this unjustifiable guilt is removed, far from being harmful, masturbation may even be advisable. Through it, young people may learn to achieve orgasm and find a way to relieve their sexual tensions without inviting into their lives some of the dangers and risks involved in premarital intercourse. Girls, who sometimes experience difficulty in reaching an orgasm, can discover through masturbation just what pressures and motions on the clitoris are best calculated to bring them to a sexual climax. Boys, who find it much easier and more natural to reach orgasm, can learn through masturbation how to delay it, a technique which may be invaluable later when it becomes necessary to slow down their own progress in coitus so that their wives may match their degree of arousal. Dr. Eleanor Hamilton, an experienced marriage counselor, has summarized the advantage of masturbation:

> This can be a healthy and normal way to enjoy sexual feeling when you are not ready or able to share loving sexuality with a person of the opposite sex. . . . Young persons who have developed their sexual feeling and their ability to come to orgasm through masturbatory techniques have a better chance to enjoy fully satisfying sexuality in marriage. . . . A person who has learned how to come to orgasm through masturbation is much more

likely to be a good sex partner in marriage than one who has not.[2]

A psychologist who has specialized in marriage counseling concurs:

Women who have previously masturbated to orgasm have been found to be far more likely to reach orgasm during coitus the first year of marriage than are women who have never masturbated to orgasm before marriage.[3]

These statements may be shocking to some adult readers, among them perhaps your parents. It is important to emphasize, therefore, that there is nothing casual or whimsical about them. They summarize some of the best research of recent years in the area of human sexuality and marriage. Not only can masturbation be a desirable practice in the years between puberty and marriage, there are some circumstances in which even a married individual may find it to be advisable. True, it can never equal or even approximate the suffusion of love between two persons which accompanies sexual intercourse at its best. Neither, however, does it involve the very real dangers inherent in alternative behavior choices.

Usually a person who is masturbating fantasizes or daydreams about a sexual incident involving himself. He may view an erotic picture, read a sexy passage in a book or just rely on imagination. There is no more reason to feel guilty about such fantasies than about masturbation itself. Unlike New Testament Christianity, Judaism does not equate thought with act, fantasy with deed. So long as sexual fantasies do not permanently and entirely replace reality, they can serve a useful purpose in our sexual development. It is scarcely necessary to add that masturbation, like other forms of orgasm, should be a private form of behavior.

Sometimes masturbation is accompanied by viewing pornographic pictures, photographs of nudes or seminudes or even of couples engaged in sexual contact. These may appear together with verbal descriptions of sexual encounters. Many magazines contain such material; they are available on most newsstands.

Is it sinful to use pornography in this way? Not really—
though a word of caution is in order. This kind of literature and
photography nearly always cheapens sex. We shall have occasion shortly to think about the relationship of sex and love in
human experience, about the truly wonderful way in which
only human beings can combine the most pleasurable physical
excitement with the highest degree of spiritual joy in their
sexual lives. Most pornography deals with sex only on the
crudest, purely physical level. It makes the human body, a
wonderfully beautiful thing, into an object of display, often
exaggerating its physical dimensions and describing intercourse as a purely animalistic kind of experience. It portrays
sex as something one person does *to* another for his or her own
gratification, not as an experience shared by two persons to
express and enhance their love.

Most boys—and probably an increasing number of girls—at
least occasionally make use of pornographic material. There is
no reason to feel guilty about that. It is well to remember,
however, that there is little room for tenderness or mutual
commitment or love in pornography. Unless we include a great
deal of tenderness and mutual commitment and love in our
sexual lives, we fail to become fully human.

A word should be added here about sexual curiosity and
experimentation in early childhood. Often parents are horrified to discover that their children—perhaps while playing
"doctor" or "house"—are examining each other's genitals or
even playing with them. A very large proportion of little children do this kind of thing at one time or another. It is a natural
consequence of childrens' curiosity about themselves and others. Any guilt you may now still feel about such behavior years
ago is unrealistic.

To pet or not to pet

Petting is another possible way to reach orgasm without intercourse. You will recall our earlier definition of petting as the
fondling by either sex of those parts of the other's body which
are most sexually excitable.

This serves an important purpose in nature's scheme of
things. It is the prelude and preparation for coitus, nature's

preface to full sexual relations. Remembering our earlier comment that girls and women generally are slower in being aroused, petting helps a woman catch up to her mate so that she too is ready for intercourse and orgasm. Thus her vagina becomes enlarged and lubricated to allow for comfortable insertion of the penis.

What choices do young people have with regard to petting?

1. They can firmly determine to resist all temptation, never to indulge in it at all. Because their sex drive is normally so persistent at that age, and especially if they date one person steadily and exclusively over a long period of time, this is a highly unrealistic and improbable alternative. It would serve no useful purpose to look the other way or to pretend to the contrary.

2. They can "play it by ear," setting no policy in advance, just acting as the spirit and urge move them. Again, because sex can be an explosive reality, this is not wise procedure. The more actively our glands function, the more difficult it is to apply rational controls to our behavior. The middle of a raging blizzard is no time to check on whether the storm windows have been installed. Couples, therefore, should agree on a mutually acceptable policy in advance, determining how far they intend to go, then resolutely abiding by their decision.

3. A third possibility is to agree on petting but to terminate it before either partner has an orgasm. Aside from the fact that this decision may require even more self-control than not to pet at all, the frustration of proceeding almost to the point of orgasm, then stopping, can be nearly intolerable. A boy who has done this may actually feel physical pain in his testicles; occasionally a girl may also experience a pain in her groin as a consequence. In such situations it may be well for a person to masturbate soon afterward in order to relieve the tension.

4. A couple confronting this dilemma may agree to pet to the point where both of them achieve orgasm. This has the advantage of relieving tension and providing intense physical pleasure, without the disadvantages and guilt which may be caused by proceeding to intercourse. Is there a difference of substance between intercourse and petting to orgasm? Is there such a thing as a "technical virgin," a girl whose boyfriend or date has given her an orgasm but without penetration?

People will differ in their responses to these questions. My own disposition is to say yes, there is a significant difference; such a girl remains entitled to consider and call herself a virgin. A counselor with many years of experience on the college campus agrees:

> Ideally, neither premarital intercourse nor petting to orgasm is a satisfactory solution to the sexual needs of men and women. But this is no reason for denying that one may be better than the other as a resolution of the dilemma in which the contemporary student finds himself.[4]

It is not at all uncommon, when young couples have intercourse, for the woman to fall short of an orgasm. The resultant nervous strain can be severe. It is not necessary for both partners to have an orgasm every time they have intercourse. If, however, one or the other persistently fails to reach a climax, there will be serious frustration and strain. Many experts on sex are convinced that petting to the point of mutual orgasm is healthier and affords better preparation for marriage than intercourse which does not provide an orgasm for both partners.

A further word or two is necessary for those who may elect this fourth option. For one thing, they should remember our previous comment that even without coitus it is possible for sperm deposited near the vagina to move up to the Fallopian tubes and to fertilize an ovum. In this manner, pregnancy can result from petting to orgasm—even without intercourse—if the male ejaculates too close to the opening of the vagina.

Finally, promiscuity in petting can be almost as harmful as promiscuity in full intercourse. We have already remarked on the very strong association in human behavior between sexual conduct and love. That association, essential for the fullest enjoyment of marriage at its best, is jeopardized by petting to climax as a casual experience or just for the sake of the physical enjoyment which can be obtained also from masturbation. Two of the experts whom we have already quoted have written wisely on this point too. Dr. Hamilton:

> . . . Mutual petting to orgasm by partners who love, respect and care for each other's well-being, and who have

learned how to direct their impulses so that they experience orgasm but do not expose themselves to the creation of a child, may be one step on the road to sexual maturity —one form of sexual expression for the young person who, in general, may not yet be ready for the full responsibility or implications of intercourse but who is ready to share his love sexually with a partner. . . .

Petting, if it is to be truly rewarding, must be a natural outgrowth of love. If it is not, if it is only indulged in "for kicks," it tends to have little significance other than momentary pleasurable sensation. However, when petting is a genuine reaching out of one human being to another whom he loves, all manifestations of that love take on a significant and long-remembered character.[5]

Still with reference to petting, Hettlinger adds:

Divorced from deep and meaningful personal respect and love, it is likely to seem, in the cold light of another day, demeaning and debasing for both parties. The line between these practices and full genital union is real; but it is a very fine one. The man who, out of consideration for his fiancée or because he wishes to reserve the final act for marriage, finds release and mutual comfort in petting may indeed have found the best available solution.[6]

You must have noticed that, in posing the several alternatives on petting, nothing was said about permitting it to culminate in full intercourse. We have no intention of ignoring this option; it will be included later in a full discussion of premarital intercourse. Perhaps this is the proper place, however, for a brief word about the effect of alcohol and drugs on sexual behavior. It is commonly supposed that the two are stimulants which increase both the probability and the enjoyment of sex. But there is a paradox involved here. While it is true that both alcohol and drugs, by lowering our resistance and controls, can lead to conduct we would not ordinarily accept, it is also true that they sometimes actually decrease our capacity to perform sexually. They are likely also to induce carelessness in the use of contraceptives.

Abortion

In our earlier discussion of birth control (see Chapter 8), we purposely said nothing about abortion. The two are really quite different; although both prevent the development and birth of a child, contraception accomplishes this by foreclosing the fertilization of an ovum, abortion by removing a fetus from the womb after it has begun to develop. This is usually done by a relatively simple surgical procedure through the vagina, during which the walls of the uterus are scraped, thus removing the fetus. Abortion can also be accomplished by use of suction or injection of a saline solution. The best and safest time is between the eighth and tenth weeks of pregnancy; after that, it becomes increasingly risky. Beyond a certain point the operation can no longer be done through the vagina but requires an abdominal incision.

Until only a few years ago, abortion was declared illegal by every state in this nation. As a result, some girls, driven to desperation by the discovery that they were pregnant, either tried to induce abortion themselves or sought illegal abortions. In the hope of accomplishing the former, they would use something like a bleach or a coat hanger or violent exercise. All such methods, in addition to being highly ineffective, are horribly dangerous. The procedures followed by illegal abortionists aren't much better, often resulting in severe infections, profuse bleeding, inability ever to have a child, or even death.

In 1973 the Supreme Court of the United States decreed that during the first third of her pregnancy, no law can deny a woman the right to have a medically supervised abortion if she and her physician agree on its advisability. Since then, some states have made legal abortion possible too, although there are still major differences among the states. Performed in a hospital by a competent physician at the proper stage of pregnancy, abortion is a safe procedure with almost no risk.

The Catholic Church and some other religious denominations are vigorously opposed to abortion, perhaps even more than to birth control. This is because they believe that from the moment of conception the fetus is a human being with a soul. To abort it, therefore, is, in their eyes, murder. The rejection of abortion by some people is highly emotional. Shortly after stating on television my view that under certain circumstances abortion should be allowed, I received a hysterical letter from a man who, among other things, wrote: "It is most disturbing that child murder has the support of a person whose authority should be lent to the cause of decency. Your espousal of abortion puts you in company with those who ran the concentration camps of Nazi Germany. . . . The fact that you are a rabbi evinces the decay of Judaism as a moral force."

> How do you react to these words? Do you agree that abortion is to be equated with child murder? With the executions of the German concentration camps? Under what circumstances would you justify abortion? Is it the best alternative?

Judaism does not agree with the Catholic position on abortion. For one thing, our rabbis never considered the fetus to be a נֶפֶשׁ *nefesh*, a human being with a soul. Until it had been actually born, legally and morally it was thought of as a part of the potential mother's body, as one of her limbs, for example. According to talmudic law, if a רוֹדֵף *rodef*, a pursuer, threatens my life and the only way I can possibly save myself is to kill him first, I am justified in doing so. In any situation where a continuation of pregnancy would jeopardize the life of a mother, the same principle was applied; the fetus is considered to be a רוֹדֵף ; its life is secondary to that of the mother and is to be sacrificed, if necessary, in order to save hers. In the מִשְׁנֵה תּוֹרָה *Mishneh Torah,* Maimonides's great legal code, he summarized the matter as follows: ". . . The sages ruled that, when a woman has difficulty giving birth, one may dismember the child in her womb—either with drugs or by surgery—because he is like a pursuer seeking to kill her."

Suppose there is no immediate physical threat to the mother's life? Here the rabbis are not of a single mind; some are liberal, others strict in judging the matter. Even the strictest, however, agree that, if continued pregnancy would cause extreme mental anguish to the mother, so serious as to carry a threat of either suicide or hysteria on her part, abortion is allowed. In 1913 an Orthodox responsum (rabbinic reply to a request for a legal judgment) dealt with the specific case of a pregnant woman whose mental health was at stake. It decreed:

"Mental health risk has been definitely equated to physical health risk. This woman who is in danger of losing her mental health unless the pregnancy is interrupted would accordingly qualify."

Similarly, if a pregnant woman is anguished over the possibility that delivering another child might harm one already born or that the fetus she carries may prove to be a defective child, some Orthodox rabbinic authorities would uphold her right to abort.

There are some Orthodox rabbis, however, whose views on abortion are scarcely distinguishable from the Catholic position. They are inclined to oppose it under all but the most extreme circumstances. It seems to me that they thus depart radically from the liberalism of genuinely traditional Judaism. In a curiously paradoxical way, it is sometimes possible for a non–Orthodox Jew to reflect the spirit of Jewish tradition more accurately on a specific matter than do some Orthodox Jews. That spirit clearly allows abortion where the physical or mental health of a mother would otherwise be threatened.

This should not be misinterpreted to mean that Judaism looks lightly upon abortion or would approve of abortion merely for reasons of convenience. We shall see later that our tradition approves birth control; this, not abortion, is the recognized way for a couple to enjoy intercourse without producing a child. Yet, under special circumstances such as those described above, abortion was considered acceptable.

Some women—probably not as many now as in the past—suffer serious emotional stress after having an abortion. At the very least, a woman who is contemplating such a step should have the benefit of skilled and sensitive professional counseling both before and after her abortion. The performance of an abortion can pose difficult emotional problems for some physicians, too, especially if their religious or medical background has predisposed them to oppose this act. If you are interested in an extremely tender, poignant description of one doctor's reaction to the first abortion he performed, read pages 20 to 24 of *Sex without Tears* by Dr. Boyd Cooper (Charles Publishing, 1972).

Homosexuality

Another variant form of sexual behavior is homosexuality, which may involve either two men or two women who derive their sexual satisfaction together. They may achieve orgasm either through mutual masturbation or, in the instance of males, through insertion of the penis of one into the anus of the other or through oral-genital contact to be discussed shortly. Women homosexuals are called lesbians. The word *gay,* preferred by the homosexual community, is used for both male and female homosexuals. Colloquial terms for women homosexuals are *butch* or *dyke;* men are sometimes called *fairies, fags* or *queers.* This is another area where the wildest and weirdest kind of emotional, even hysterical reactions are often heard. Surely the better part of both wisdom and humaneness is to approach the subject as rationally as we can.

We do not really know what causes homosexuality. According to one theory, it results from chemical imbalances. Another explanation is that it comes from unhappy, unhealthy relations between the child and the parent of the same sex. Still others have suggested that all of us grow through a period of latent homosexuality, that some are arrested at that point, never developing to heterosexuality. Some psychiatrists believe that homosexuality is an illness, though a majority of them have by now come to consider it instead, a variant form of behavior, not necessarily a symptom of illness in itself. There are individuals who are bisexual, able to enjoy sexual relations with members of either sex. There are also some who, though generally heterosexual, may be driven to homosexual behavior under such restrictive circumstances as being in the army or in prison where contact is possible only with members of their own sex.

Though there is still so much about this phenomenon that we do not know, it occurs quite commonly in the animal world in cows, monkeys and chimpanzees among others. Often homosexuality in humans is accompanied by a high degree of artistic sensitivity. Among the famous men who are known to have been homosexuals are Leonardo da Vinci, Michelangelo, Tchaikovsky and Walt Whitman. It is a mistake to assume that all homosexuals are identifiable by their mannerisms. Very masculine-looking male professional athletes as well as quite feminine-appearing women and girls have been known to be counted among them.

There are as many different kinds of homosexuals as of heterosexuals; both can be either healthy or neurotic. In some instances two homosexuals live together in a stable, loving relationship which resembles a heterosexual marriage.

Young boys and girls frequently harbor fears that they may be potential homosexuals. In most cases these fears are groundless. The fact that an individual may even have had one or two such experiences or may have been seduced by a member of the same sex does not by any means indicate that he or she will be permanently or exclusively homosexual. Nor is there any truth at all to the notion that masturbation either signals or causes homosexuality. If, however, a young person has persistent and gnawing fears that he or she may be leaning in that direction, the wisest course is to consult someone who is both knowledgeable and trustworthy. Here, as in all areas of sexual development, our greatest enemy is ignorance.

For many reasons, not the least of which are the obvious implications for the future of the family, Judaism has traditionally opposed and rejected homosexuality. This undoubtedly accounts for the biblical warning: "A woman must not put on man's apparel, nor shall a man wear woman's clothing; for whoever does these things is abhorrent to the Lord your God."[7] The subject is mentioned more explicitly in the story of Sodom, a city whose men demanded of Lot that he surrender his male guests for their sexual enjoyment.[8] What is only hinted or suggested earlier becomes directly prohibited by law in the Book of Leviticus: "If a man lies with a male as one lies with a woman, the two of them have done an abhorrent thing; they shall be put to death—their bloodguilt is upon them."[9]

Is this biblical decree still valid? Would the reference in Deuteronomy preclude the wearing of identical jeans by boys and girls? Do you see any advantages in such unisex apparel? Any disadvantages?

There is no doubt that here again the attitude of liberal Judaism differs considerably from that of ancient Jewish tradition. No Jewish leader even today would recommend homosexuality or would put it on a par with heterosexual relations. Yet there is strong feeling that, so long as a homosexual relationship is between consenting adults, so long as no one is being forced or coerced, so long as the sexual behavior of two such individuals is on a private basis, it is not society's business to interfere.

This squares with a widespread change in the attitude of American society as a whole. Due in no small measure to the Gay Liberation movement, homosexuals have been encouraged to discard their former feelings of secrecy and shame, to declare themselves for what they are and to insist on obtaining their rights. However we may differ in our attitudes on the subject, there is little room for disagreement among enlightened individuals that homosexuals are at the very least entitled to equality in every respect. Dr. James McCary spoke for most liberals of all faiths when he wrote:

It should be remembered that homosexuals . . . can be as religious, moralistic, loyal to country or cause, inhibited, bigoted or censorious of other types of sexual variance as anyone else can. Also, they manifest no greater number of serious personality problems than one would expect to find in the normal population. . . . Fortunately, Western societies are finally making an effort to evaluate homosexuality with compassion rather than with condemnation.[10]

In 1974 the Union of American Hebrew Congregations was faced with a difficult dilemma when a congregation consisting predominantly though not exclusively of homosexuals applied for admission. After prolonged debate on a very high level, the UAHC Board of Trustees accepted the application.

What do you suppose were some of the arguments on both sides during this discussion? How would you have voted? Why? Do you think the admission of such a congregation will increase the incidence of homosexuality among Reform Jews? Do you think our definition of love (see Chapter 2) could apply to two homosexuals? Why?

If you wish to know more about homosexuality, I recommend a book written for young people, Morton Hunt's *Gay—What*

You Should Know about Homosexuality (Farrar, Straus & Giroux, N.Y., 1977).

And finally

Our catalogue of variations and differences in sexual behavior would be incomplete if we failed to mention at least briefly a few additional phenomena. Though all of them are rare, it is important for you to know what they are.

Exhibitionism means the desire or need of an individual to display his or her genitals in public. The exhibitionist is usually an inadequate, insecure person who hopes to shock others. The most effective way of dealing with them, therefore, is to ignore them. Seldom do they become aggressive or act out their sexual desires.

Voyeurism is the technical term applied to those whom we more commonly call "peeping toms," men or women (more often the former) who derive special sexual pleasure out of watching others in the nude or while they are having intercourse.

Transvestism refers to those who like to wear the clothing of the opposite sex. This applies primarily to undergarments of a distinctively sexual nature, not to the blue jeans already mentioned. In some cultures women have traditionally worn pants while robes or gowns were included in the wardrobe of men. Such garments need not be related to transvestism. Though we are not yet sure what causes this kind of behavior, we do know that it is not necessarily an indication of homosexuality.

Transsexualism is something different. Also called *sex–role inversion,* it designates individuals who have the anatomical equipment characteristic of one sex but prefer to be members of the opposite sex. From time to time such individuals actually resort to plastic surgery in order to accomplish their desires.

Bestiality is the practice of having intercourse with animals. For obvious reasons, this is likely to be found more often among farm than city persons.

Sodomy gets its name from the story of Sodom, referred to a few paragraphs back. Strictly speaking, it means male homosexual intercourse. The term is frequently used also, however, for bestiality and for anal intercourse.

You may have heard the term *sixty-nine,* used to describe two people who simultaneously establish oral-genital sex contact with each other. When it is the female mouth in contact with the male penis, the term usually employed is *fellatio; cunnilingus* means the opposite, contact of the male mouth with the female vulva. Many couples include oral-genital experience in the foreplay which precedes intercourse.

What's normal?

This is by no means an easy question to answer. Most thoughtless people would immediately assume that whatever they themselves do sexually is normal; everything else is abnormal. But that's too easy an answer. While it would be going too far to say that every form of sexual conduct described in this chapter is normal, the fact remains that our concept of normality must be considerably broader than it has been in the past. Perhaps it would be reasonable to say that any form of sexual behavior between two consenting adults—forced upon neither, repugnant to neither—is acceptable for that particular couple.

Some such definition as this would surely apply in marriage. Each couple must decide what its normal sexual behavior is to be. So long as neither of them and no one else is hurt—now or in the future—most of us would go along in considering their actions to be normal for them.

This is a decision you will have to make for the rest of your life. Our hope, in this chapter as well as in the discussions yet to come, is that we can help you make this choice.

For instance

A. Elaine, thirty-three years old and married eleven years, doesn't have a very good sex life with her husband who is her senior by fourteen years. His desire for sex doesn't come close to matching hers. When they do have intercourse, sometimes she fails to achieve an orgasm; at other times, she does reach a climax but feels the need for more. By this time, however, her husband, having had his orgasm, is likely to be sound asleep.

Knowing that men reach the highest point of their sexual potential in their late teens, Elaine has been making overtures to Don, a nineteen-year-old college student living across the street. So far, this has amounted only to flirtation, but she is hoping to establish a sexual relationship with Don, expecting that they may be sexually more compatible than she and her husband are.

> Evaluate Elaine's feelings and hopes. What consequences can you foresee if she continues on her plan? Can you suggest better alternatives?

B. Lois is one of the most popular girls in her high school. Extremely attractive, she has more requests for dates than she can possibly accept. One reason for this, she believes, is that she tries to let every boy who dates her have a good time. They all seem eager to pet, and she allows them to do so. Even when she may not enjoy the experience herself, she derives much satisfaction from knowing that, as a woman, she can attract and please men.

Other girls in her school, knowing something of her reputation, are quick to criticize her immorality and to accuse her of being promiscuous. This, however, is not true. Lois is a virgin and intends to remain one. She prides herself on knowing how far to go and when to stop. The moment she senses that her date is on the verge of going too far, immediately she puts a stop to their petting. She feels that she is always in control. So long as this is so, Lois considers herself a moral person.

> What do you think? Is she moral? Are the girls who criticize her moral? Is it necessary for a girl to permit or encourage petting in order to be popular? For a boy to initiate sexual activity on dates in order to prove himself a man? Does a girl feel unwanted or rejected if her date doesn't "make a pass at her"?

C. Reading this chapter hasn't changed Jon's feelings about masturbation at all. While he is somewhat reassured to learn that this practice doesn't cause all the harm he has been told it does, he nonetheless feels contaminated and contemptible because he masturbates regularly. Numerous times, in moments of great disgust, he has solemnly sworn to stop. After a few days, however, he is driven by an unconquerable urge to masturbate again. The semen he ejects disgusts him. He looks upon himself as being weak and unmanly, yet there seems to be nothing he can do about it.

If the facts of this chapter haven't altered Jon's attitude, what might? How can you explain his feelings? The inconsistency between his feelings and his conduct? What accounts for his extreme revulsion? How might it have been prevented?

D. Suzie finds it more and more difficult to handle her feelings about sex. She occasionally pets, though never to the point of climax. Each time she feels cheapened and frustrated—guilty over the fact that she has petted at all, tense and anxious because of unfulfilled sexual desire. She knows that some girls resolve this kind of problem by masturbating but finds the very thought repulsive. Though she can understand a boy's need to masturbate, she thinks girls should be able to control themselves better than that. It seems to her to be "unladylike" for a girl to "play with herself" to the point of orgasm.

Is Suzie correct in feeling that boys and girls differ when it comes to masturbation? With her attitude what it is, why doesn't she just stop petting? What would you recommend? Why?

E. The thing that bothers Len most about his masturbating is his fear that it may lead to homosexuality. It seems logical to him that a boy who derives sexual satisfaction from his own body is likely to develop into the habit of finding such fulfillment with other males rather than females.

Lately one of Len's friends has told him that their coach persuaded him to have a homosexual experience with him and that he found it exciting and enjoyable. He has invited Len to come along next time.

Are Len's worries realistic? Should he stop masturbating? Accept his friend's invitation? Reassure himself by having intercourse with a girl? What do you recommend? Why?

10

CATHY by Cathy Guisewite

FIRST IRVING SAID HE HATED THE WAY I MUSH UP MY ICE CREAM BEFORE I EAT IT... AND THEN I SAID THAT ANYONE WHO LIKES PINEAPPLE SUNDAES IS STUPID.

THEN IRVING SCREAMED AT ME FOR NOT FIGURING THE TIP OUT IN ONE SECOND, AND I SHOUTED AT HIM FOR WADDING UP HIS NAPKIN ON HIS PLATE.

©1978 Universal Press Syndicate

WAIT A MINUTE, CATHY. THIS DOESN'T SOUND LIKE A VERY SERIOUS FIGHT TO ME.

ARE YOU KIDDING?

THE BIGGER THE FIGHT, THE LITTLER THE THINGS WE YELL AT EACH OTHER ABOUT.

Do all religions agree on sex?

The only honest answer to the question which heads this chapter is *no*. There are many aspects of sex, to be sure, on which all the religions with which we are familiar in the United States are in substantial agreement. There are others, however, on which there is considerable disagreement. In discussing both the similarities and the differences, we shall be concerned only with those religions which are usually found among our neighbors and friends, which means to say: Judaism, Catholicism and the various Protestant faiths.

It would be foolish to pretend that there is one Jewish attitude toward sex or one Christian point of view. While Catholics come closer to unanimity than any other group, even among them there are some differences of opinion on sex. Still—as we examine the historical record—it is possible to discern major divergences between what may be called the main Jewish and the main Christian points of view.

Christianity on sex

Generally speaking, Christianity through much of its history has been negative and suspicious in its approach to sex. Unlike nearly all the biblical and talmudic leaders of Judaism, so far as we know, Jesus was never married. In order to divorce him from any possible taint of connection with sex, Christian tradition even resorted to the belief that Jesus was born to a virgin. Paul, who was the real founder of Christianity, looked upon sexual desire and especially coitus as evil. He expressed the wish that all men might be capable, as he was, of remaining celibate (male virgins). Because he realized that most were not, as a concession to human weakness he said: "It is better to marry than to burn."[1]

At the conclusion of a long New Testament passage comparing marriage to celibacy, Paul says: "So that he who marries his betrothed does well; and he who refrains from marriage will do better."[2]

His attitude carried over into most of the early history of Christianity. Summarizing his view and that of the New Testament generally, one Christian authority has written: "In this idea of marriage as an accommodation to human weakness and a hindrance to the fullest service of God there is but little appreciation of its dignity and high calling; nor do the writers of the New Testament show much sense of the joys and privileges of family life. . . ."[3] The same writer, in commenting on the preponderant Christian attitude in the centuries following the completion of the New Testament, has said: "While none denied that marriage, relatively speaking, was a good thing, it was nevertheless tolerated rather than commended." Also: "Of the joys, privileges and opportunities of home and family life we find little appreciation, while hardly more than lip service is paid to the blessing of children."[4]

On rare occasions a voice of protest or disagreement was raised within the church; but generally, a negative view of sex and a rather reluctant acceptance of intercourse within marriage as a concession to human weakness and the only means of propagating the race prevailed. These were the characteristic outlooks of Christianity throughout most of its history. One evidence of this is that in some Christian denominations— most notably but not exclusively Roman Catholicism—religious leadership is limited to men and women who do not indulge in what we would consider to be a normal sex life. Thus do these faiths indicate their conviction that the highest form of human life is that of the celibate and the virgin.

In the extreme Christian view, sex desire and its fulfillment even within marriage were considered scarcely more ethical. St. Jerome, for example, wrote: "He who loves his own wife too ardently is an adulterer." St. Augustine said: "Intercourse even with one's legitimate wife is unlawful and wicked where the conception of offspring is prevented." In a similar vein, the church fathers condemned the use of cosmetics and other adornments by all women, on the ground that these might increase their sexual attractiveness in the eyes of men. According to Tertullian, even the natural, unadorned beauty of women "ought to be obliterated by concealment and neglect, since it is dangerous to those who look upon it."[5]

In mentioning earlier the daydreams which frequently accompany masturbation, we drew a distinction between fantasy and reality. New Testament Christianity accepts no such differentiation in sexual matters. Thought is equated with deed. Thus Jesus: ". . . every one who looks at a woman lustfully has already committed adultery with her in his heart."[6]

Despite significant changes in the sexual attitudes of modern Christianity, more of which in a moment, the traditional point of view has by no means been completey abandoned. The eminent nineteenth-century Danish philosopher and theologian, Soren Kierkegaard, who is still admired and quoted by many Christian authorities, almost seems to be echoing the views of earlier Christians when he writes:

It is an abominable lie to say that marriage is pleasing to God. From the Christian point of view it is a crime, and what is odious about it is that by this very crime the innocent individual is introduced into that community of criminals which is human life.[7]

Saint Augustine even attempted to read his own views of sex back into the minds and lives of the Hebrew Patriarchs, Abraham, Isaac and Jacob. He said they would have preferred to fulfill God's commandment to "be fruitful and multiply" without indulging in coitus, but this was manifestly impossible. He assumed, therefore, that they experienced intercourse with their wives only reluctantly, and as a duty.

There is no evidence in the world to indicate that Augustine was correct about the feelings he attributed to the Patriarchs. The Christian views on sex cited above would have been impossible within Judaism. They have been gradually abandoned in modern times by many Christian groups too. It is now increasingly accepted by the leaders of a large number of Christian denominations that an active sex life between husbands and wives is a good thing, even apart from their desire to have children. Insofar as they have come to this point of view, however, it is important to recognize that they have moved away from the historic position of Christianity on sex and toward that of Judaism.

Judaism on sex

What has the Jewish view been? For the most part, that sexual intercourse between husbands and wives is a good thing—desirable and wholesome—intended by God, not only as a means of creating succeeding generations, but also to fortify and reinforce the love of married couples. True, there is an occasional expression within authentic Judaism which sounds suspiciously like Christianity, but this is the exception rather than the rule. The following statement by Maimonides is a particularly curious and rare one: "We ought to limit sexual intercourse altogether, hold it in contempt, and desire it only rarely. . . . The act is too base to be performed except when needed."[8]

Much closer to Jewish tradition is the rebuttal to this statement uttered in the next century by another authoritative spokesman for Judaism, Nachmanides: "It is not true, as our rabbi and master asserted in his *Guide for the Perplexed,* praising Aristotle for teaching that the sexual urge is a source of shame to us. God forbid that the truth should be in accordance with the teachings of the Greek! . . . The act of sexual union is holy and pure. . . . The Lord created all things in accordance with His wisdom, and whatever He created cannot possibly be shameful or ugly. . . . When a man is in union with his wife in a spirit of holiness and purity, the Divine Presence is with them."9

How can we determine who was closer to the view of authentic Judaism on sex—Maimonides or Nachmanides? Does it make any difference?

One of the shorter books of the Bible is devoted in its entirety to the physical side of love. True, in Jewish tradition, *The Song of Songs* was looked upon as an allegory depicting the love of God and the Jewish people for each other. But there can be no doubt that it was originally written as a series of passionate love songs. It contains the very beautiful words you may have heard in an Israeli song or seen engraved on wedding rings: דּוֹדִי לִי וַאֲנִי לוֹ *dodi li va'ani lo* (my beloved is mine and I am his). In this book are also to be found descriptions of a woman in pursuit of her loved one (3:1–4), of her physical beauty as seen by him (4:1–5) and of his beauty as it impresses her (5:8–16).

Both Bible and Talmud describe and discuss matters of sex with uninhibited honesty. King David is portrayed as having indulged in intercourse with the wife of another man and being punished for it. In the Talmud there is an interesting discussion as to the best time for a man and his wife to have intercourse. Our tradition even includes a suggested prayer of considerable meaning and beauty, to be recited by a man before coitus with his wife.

One such prayer, recommended in the *Zohar,* concludes with: "I take my stand in the realm of holiness; I garb myself in the holiness of the Divine King." This is particularly significant because the *Zohar* was the primary source of medieval Jewish mysticism, and in all other faiths the mystics were especially averse to sex even between married couples. A longer, more meaningful prayer, to be recited before intercourse between husband and wife, appears in an eighteenth-century collection of Jewish prayers:

O Lord, my God and God of my fathers, ground of all the universes . . . may it be Your will that You emanate from Your spirit of power unto me and give me might and strength in my organs and my body that I might regularly fulfill the commandment pertaining to my sexual cycle; that there be not found in my organs, body or passion any weakness or slackness; that there be no forcing, unseemly thought, confusion of mind or weakening of power to prevent me from fulfilling my desire with my wife. Rather, now and forever, let my passion be ready for me without fail or slackness of organ, at any time that I should desire. Amen.

There follows then a paragraph asking for a healthy son.[10]

Rabbinic literature recognizes the fact that the sex urge varies from person to person, that consequently one man may require intercourse more frequently than another. According to the *Shulchan Aruch*, "each man is obliged to perform his marital duty according to his strength and according to his occupation. Gentlemen of leisure should perform their marital obligation every night. Laborers who are employed in the city where they reside should perform their duty twice weekly, but if they are employed in another city, once a week. Donkey drivers [should have marital relations] once a week; camel drivers, once in thirty days; sailors, once in six months. As for scholars, it is obligatory for them to have intercourse once a week, and it is customary for this to be on Friday nights."[11]

How can we account for this passage? On what basis did Jewish authorities decide how often men in different occupations should have intercourse with their wives? Is there any validity to their reasoning?

Unlike many ancient and medieval cultures, in which only men were deemed to have sexual desires, Judaism recognized the sexual needs of women and insisted that they be satisfied. Thus a husband was forbidden to leave on a long journey without first having intercourse with his wife, and was enjoined to have intercourse with her again as soon as possible after his return. The bridegroom was bidden to be respectful of his wife's natural timidity in their first performance of coitus: "The Torah teaches gentle manners: the bridegroom should not enter the marriage chamber until the bride gives him leave."[12] Contrary to the strictures of Christianity against the use of cosmetics by women, Meir of Rothenburg, the outstanding rabbi of the thirteenth century, said: "Let a curse descend upon a woman who has a husband and does not strive to be attractive."[13]

Intercourse between husband and wife, according to Judaism, must always be a beautiful experience. Every form of sexplay between them which helped to make it so was approved. The same Maimonides whose curious, almost un-Jewish statement on sex has already been quoted, said elsewhere: "The sexual union should be consummated only out of desire and as the result of the joy of the husband and wife. . . . He must not approach her when he thinks of another woman and certainly not when he is under the influence of alcohol or while they are quarreling and hatred divides them. He must not approach her against her will or force her to submit to him out of fear."[14] In the final portion of this statement Maimonides was simply reiterating a view which the Talmud had expressed many centuries earlier: "He who coerces his wife will produce unworthy children."[15]

Another rabbi of talmudic times urged that each act of coitus between husband and wife be as exciting and fresh as was the first on their wedding night.[16] Finally, Judaism taught long ago that active sex interest and sex life between married mates is to continue beyond the wife's ability to bear children. Even if a man and woman young enough to have children know that it will never be possible for them to have children together, it is still legitimate for them to marry and enjoy intercourse.

Sex is for women too

The Bible catalogues three primary obligations of husbands to wives: food, clothing and sexual rights. The Talmud then singles out sexual rights as the most important of these by stipulating that a woman may, by prenuptial agreement, surrender her right to food and clothing—but never to sexual gratification! The famous schools of Shammai and Hillel disagreed on how long a man could deny sexual intercourse to his wife before she would be entitled to ask for a divorce. According to the former, two weeks; according to the latter, only one.

Perhaps the most amazing aspect of these statements is that they were issued—all of them—by men addressing themselves to other men. At a time when, among other peoples, women were valued only as receptacles for male gratification and impregnation, Judaism revealed a most astonishing sensitivity to the fact that women possessed active sexual needs.

Men were even obliged by our tradition to anticipate the sexual moods of their wives, to initiate intercourse when it was reasonable to suppose a feminine desire for it. They were instructed, moreover, to increase a woman's sexual pleasure by commencing with exciting foreplay. The following remarkable instruction is from a thirteenth-century marriage manual, *Iggeret Hakodesh,* usually attributed to Nachmanides, though the authorship is not entirely certain:

> . . . Engage her first in conversation that puts her heart and mind at ease and gladdens her. . . . Speak words which arouse her to passion, union, love, desire and eros—and words which elicit attitudes of reverence for God, piety and modesty. Tell her of pious and good women who gave birth to fine and pure children. . . . Speak with her words, some of love, some of erotic passion, some of piety and reverence. . . . Hurry not to arouse passion until her mood is ready; begin in love; let her orgasm take place first. . . ."

Quite obviously, in addition to the most admirable kind of sensitivity, the rabbis were aware of some of those physiological differences between men and women which we have previously reviewed.

They were curious, as we are, as to what caused a fetus to be conceived as male or female. Granting the sexism of their preference for boys, it is deeply significant that they said: When the woman experiences her orgasm first, a son results; if the husband comes first, it will be a daughter. In short, if a man wanted a son, he had better attend to the sexual needs of his wife!

The teachings of some religions in regard to sex make it very difficult for young people in those denominations to cope with their own feelings of sexual desire. Adolescence, after all, is a time of increasing sexual interest. It marks the emergence of a person from childhood into adulthood—the time when all the organs and glands of the body are ripening for full use in marriage. At such a time it would be unnatural for any of us not to feel a strong physical attraction for the opposite sex. To tell a young person that it is wrong to feel what nature itself impels one to feel is to create an almost intolerable problem.

Judaism helps us face this difficult but wonderful period of life in a wholesome way. It tells us we should not feel guilty over our strong feelings of sexual desire; if God did not want us to experience such sensations, he would have created us differently. Judaism teaches that life is good and sex is good—if we accept it and learn how to control and use it for our advantage and richest growth.

Clearly, then, there has been major disagreement between Judaism and Christianity regarding sex. The fact that today the difference is less than it once was is a tribute to the ancient insight of our tradition. It would be dishonest to pretend that every Jew in the world knows or follows the traditional attitude of our faith toward sex. Those who do, however, can live a healthier, more wholesome life, with greater probability of happiness in their marriages.

Debate on birth control

One consequence of these differences on sex in general has been a wide disagreement on birth control. The natural result of the old Christian belief that sex is a necessary evil and coitus is permissible only as a means to conceive children was a strong opposition to any method of contraception which would enable married couples to enjoy intercourse for its own sake, without intending to produce a child. Originally, both Catholics and Protestants were opposed to birth control. Among Protestants there has been a steady inclination toward change, so that many of the leading Protestant denominations, as they have moved closer to our Jewish view of sex in general, have also relaxed their antagonism to birth control.

The change in the Roman Catholic Church has been slower and less substantial. At first the church taught that under no circumstances did a married couple have the right to cohabit (another term for coitus) without intending pregnancy as a consequence. More recently, however, Catholic authorities have moved to the point where they approve the rhythm method. This they accept as being a *natural* method of family planning. All other methods they consider *artificial* and to be condemned. There have been suggestions, some even from within the Catholic Church, that perhaps the contraceptive pill may in time be approved as *natural*. There has been no change thus far, however, in official Catholic opposition to the pill and all other techniques of birth control which are deemed to be *artificial*.

In the modern Jewish view this distinction between two kinds of contraception is not valid. Even the Talmud recognized certain circumstances under which the practice of birth control was recommended. The methods then known were nowhere near as sophisticated or certain as ours, but the principle was identical. Judaism believed then—and does now—that the noblest fulfillment of a marriage is the birth and rearing of children. It believes equally, however, that God created us with sexual desires and needs because He considered these to be good; and that partners in marriage should live as full a sex life as they desire, utilizing whatever methods they wish for birth control in order that they can continue to express their love in intercourse without producing more children than they want or can properly love.

There are Jews—even rabbis—who oppose contraception. This opposition may be due to a misunderstanding of the tradition; or to uneasiness over sex despite the tradition; or to a legitimate fear that if we Jews approach zero population growth, especially after six million of us were exterminated during the Holocaust, we may risk our disappearance as an identifiable people. The modern Jew confronts a most painful dilemma between a knowledge that the human population of this earth must be curbed if disaster is to be averted, and an insistence that it is important—for us and for humankind in general—that we Jews survive.

Are sex and love the same?

If Judaism was wise in anticipating many of the insights of modern psychology in terms of sex generally, it was no less perceptive with regard to the relationship between sex and love. We have already referred to the truth that a good sexual adjustment is more the consequence of love than its cause. Some people have from time to time considered sex to be just a psychological tension—similar to an itch which is to be scratched in the most convenient way, or to hunger which is to be satisfied by whatever edible food happens to be available. Such an attitude, in addition to being inaccurate, is unworthy of human beings as spiritual creatures.

For instance

A. Mark's parents are members of a fundamentalist Protestant sect which accepts every word of the Bible as being literally true. They believe that smoking, drinking and card playing are all serious sins. They are equally convinced that sex is evil and they disapprove of all physical expressions of affection between men and women.

Mark had grown up without questioning his parents' ideas. They had never really bothered him until he fell in love with Sally, whose thoughts about sex were very different from his. Sally's family is Protestant too but they belong to a liberal church. Their attitude toward sex is similar to that of Judaism as you have come to know it in this chapter.

Sally and Mark had discussed their differences regarding sex a number of times, especially since they became formally engaged last spring. Though they are no closer to agreement now than in the beginning, Sally isn't particularly worried. She is confident that, as she puts it, "nature will settle the argument," and that Mark will want to express his love for her sexually after they are married.

> If you were a marriage counselor and this couple came to you, what advice would you give them? What do you think is their chance for a happy marriage? What makes people feel about sex the way Mark and his parents do? Is Sally correct in her confidence that things will take care of themselves after their wedding?

B. Mrs. Langfort—despite the fact that she has been married over twenty years and has given birth to two children—is convinced that sex is evil. She insists we can see this at the very beginning of the Bible, in the story of Adam and Eve. "At first they were naked in the Garden of Eden and didn't even realize that it made any difference—isn't that so?" she asks rather demandingly. "Then, after they had eaten of the tree of the knowledge of good and evil, and for the first time became aware of their nakedness, they were expelled from Eden, isn't that so? Well, what more proof do you need that God knew sex was evil when He first created it?"

Mrs. Langfort has taught her views of sex to her children and practically forced them on her husband. Because of her feelings she will not permit her sixteen-year-old daughter to be alone with a boy. She is afraid the girl may not be able to resist the temptation that may confront her. She permits her to date only if at least one other couple goes too, and she will not allow her to bring a date into the house at the end of the evening.

> Are the facts of the Adam and Eve story correct as Mrs. Langfort recounts them? Is her interpretation of the facts accurate? How, if at all, would you answer her on this point? Is it possible for a Jewish woman to feel this way? What kind of marriage would you suppose Mr. and Mrs. Langfort have had? What kind of marriage would you predict for their daughter? How would you feel if you were their daughter? What would you do?

C. Phil and Madeline have been married five years. Their sex life has been good; they both enjoy intercourse and both experience orgasms practically every time. Yet they spend an increasing amount of time arguing and fighting. Sometimes it seems the only time they agree on anything is when they are in bed. In the past couple of years Madeline has been using sex as a weapon, warning Phil that if he doesn't do as she asks, give her what she wants, she will deny him the sex he wants next time. He on his part becomes furious when she threatens him this way. "Don't act as if you were doing me the biggest favor in the world!" he practically shouts at her. "Sex is something to which I'm entitled, not a gift you can give or withhold as you please. Anyway, you're not the only woman in the world; if you don't want to satisfy my needs, I can find someone who will!"

> Does it sound realistic for a couple that quarrels so much to find mutual pleasure in their sex life? How good would you say their marriage is? In what ways is it good? In what ways not? Does a woman have the right to use sex for punishment and reward as Madeline has done? Do you blame Phil for reacting as he does? Why?

D. Kathy's parents had been opposed from the beginning to her match with Stan. Devout Catholics, they would by far have preferred their daughter to marry within her own church. After almost a year of opposition, however, they relented—especially since Kathy had successfully urged Stan to have a church wedding and to promise that their children would be educated as Catholics.

It seemed that the only remaining issue was the question of birth control. Kathy made it clear that, in accordance with the teachings of her church, she would accept no method of contraception except the rhythm method. She agreed with Stan that they could not afford to have children for several years at least, but said she would feel guilty discarding her religious principles in so important a matter. Stan said he supposed one method of birth control was about as good as another. If this was what Kathy wanted, it was all right with him. So they agreed that they would have sex relations after their marriage only at such times as Kathy was "safe" from becoming pregnant.

With all important possible disputes apparently ironed out in advance, do you think Kathy and Stan could anticipate a good marriage? What issues can you see that might cause them trouble? Is Stan apt to be happy for the indefinite future with their solution to the problem of contraception? Why? Is the problem permanently solved for Kathy? Why?

11

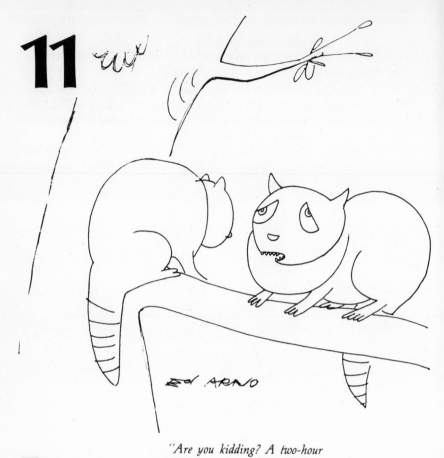

"Are you kidding? A two-hour mating season and you have a headache?"

To wait . . . or not to wait

As has been suggested, the most important decision of your life will most probably be your choice of a mate for marriage. This, however, is not an immediate decision; it will be several years before you need to make it. Yet there are many options confronting you now and in the near future which will seriously affect your eventual selection of a husband or wife and the quality of your marriage.

Among these interim but extremely important decisions is whether or not to experience premarital intercourse. The only person on God's earth who has a right to decide that question is *you*. Others can suggest or advise; only you are in the final position to judge. On this matter, I have a point of view which I shall state as clearly as I can, not because I would attempt to dictate nor because I expect that every reader will agree with me, but rather out of the unhappy, sometimes almost despairing conviction that too many people never even make this choice consciously. They just drift along, allowing the mood of the moment to make it for them.

Nothing is more important than for young people to shape a firm policy in advance and then to govern their daily decisions accordingly rather than to act entirely on impulse or whim so that a whole series of non-decisions becomes a policy after all. A sailor who is just out for an afternoon of fun can permit the wind to take him where it will. Come to think of it, though, even he must from time to time calculate where he is, how long it will take him to return to port and possible changes in the weather. The sailor who has a destination—a place he must reach by a stipulated hour—must do more than this.

A good marriage is one of the most important destinations you will ever have. Though it may still seem remote to you, it is essential that you begin to decide now what kind of marriage you would like to have, the quality of sex life you want in it and the steps to be taken during the intervening years if you are to succeed. Whatever your decision regarding premarital sexual intercourse—and, again, it must and can be only yours —it should be made after the most careful consideration of all relevant facts, of all the options available to you, and the probable consequences of each. The purpose of this and the next two chapters is not to tell you what to do but to trace the options and where they are likely to lead.

Voice of the past

What does Judaism teach about premarital intercourse? It will probably surprise, perhaps even shock, you to learn that nowhere in either the Bible or the Talmud is there an explicit prohibition of intercourse before marriage. The closest the Torah comes to such an injunction is in the following passage:

> If a man seduces a virgin who has not been betrothed [engaged] and has intercourse with her, he must make her his wife by payment of the bride price. If her father refuses to give her to him, he must still pay the bride price for virgins.[1]

Elsewhere, another passage repeats substantially the same law, adding that, because he had violated her virginity before betrothing or marrying her, he had forfeited the right ever to divorce her.[2]

Does this mean that, except for the special circumstances described above, ancient Judaism condoned premarital intercourse? Not so fast! The absence of a direct law on this matter can be understood only in the larger context of social conditions prevailing among Jews at that time. We must remember that marriage took place at a much earlier age then and, indeed, was often arranged by parents when the prospective bride and groom were little children. Most couples were wedded in their late teens after a full year of betrothal. The status of the betrothed couple, moreover, went far beyond that of engaged couples today. It actually involved a condition of quasi–marriage, so much so that, if a couple decided during their betrothal not to marry, they were required to obtain a kind of divorce from the rabbis. With betrothal in the mid-teens and marriage a year later, what need was there for laws prohibiting premarital intercourse? If a betrothed girl had intercourse with any man other than her future husband, this was in the legal category of adultery, to be punished as it would be if the couple were already married.

How about intercourse between the two while they were betrothed? There is no doubt that in the development of talmudic law this was deemed to be immoral and indecent. Yet it did sometimes occur; and, when it did, the only punishment was that the couple had to marry at once instead of waiting for the normal end of their betrothal period. Which means that the rabbis, while they condemned such intercourse, treated it quite differently from casual coitus between couples who were not betrothed to one another.

Like all other aspects of sexual ethics, this became more of a problem in medieval times. One wonders whether Rabbi Isaiah Horowitz, in the early seventeenth century, was venting his ire more against the offending couple or against his colleagues who looked the other way when he wrote:

> Be very careful that before nuptials the groom shall not sit near the bride, as is the custom in this wicked generation, when not only this is the case, but he even hugs and kisses her. Woe unto the eyes that see this and the ears that hear of this. How surprising that the sages of our day allow this great sin to go on without calling a halt to it.[3]

A century later Rabbi Jonathan Eybeschuetz declared:

> I shall from now on endeavor with all my might to set up restrictions and I shall not permit the engagement contract to be written until both parties obligate themselves by solemn pledge that they shall not touch each other until their wedding.[4]

Because of eroding communal standards in medieval times, and because couples were no longer betrothed and married at so young an age, it became necessary for the first time that Jewish law prohibit premarital intercourse explicitly as it had implicitly through the centuries. Maimonides included such a provision in his מִשְׁנֶה תּוֹרָה *Mishneh Torah,* the great twelfth-century legal code. We leave for later the question of whether this posture of traditional Judaism remains valid for us today.

A revolution?

Your decision regarding premarital intercourse will be made against the background of the sexual revolution about which so much has been written and spoken in recent years. Has there in fact been such a revolution? Have society's standards of sexual attitudes and behavior in fact changed so radically?

These are not easy questions to answer. Even the very careful scientific studies on hand are open to some doubt. For one thing, such investigations depend upon the responses of subjects who either volunteer or are willing to respond to questions about their sex lives. Even assuming their total honesty, we must wonder whether they constitute a fair sampling, so that the results are typical of society at large. Not everyone is willing to discuss personal intimacies with strangers, even with reliable scholars. Many experts in the field have warned us that those who are willing are likely to consist disproportionately of individuals who are open to more sexual experience than the average. The results, while accurate for them as a select group, may be off the mark as far as the total population is concerned. Still, these are the only data we have, and—with all due reservations about their overall validity—we must learn what we can from them.

We must remember also that there can be differences between sexual attitudes and sexual behavior. Not all those who express liberal views on premarital intercourse have themselves experienced it. Indeed, one study actually suggests an inverse relationship. College students in the intermountain region of the United States were compared to their peers in Denmark.

> One conclusion . . . was that the Danes had the most liberal attitudes but the least premarital activity. The intermountain students disapproved most explicitly of premarital relations but engaged in such relations more frequently. . . .[5]

With precautions such as these clearly in mind, how extensive has the sexual revolution of our time actually been? What can we learn from the following estimate?

> . . . The race of girls is getting bold and run after the fellows into their rooms and chambers and wherever they can and offer their free love.

Before you become too involved in affirming or denying this accusation, relax. It was made by Martin Luther in 1544 and was directed against students at the University of Wittenberg. Obviously, ours is not the first generation in which authorities have condemned the real or alleged conduct of the young. In the case of the United States today, which is it—real or alleged?

Investigations made in 1967 at Stanford University and the University of California at Berkeley revealed that in the middle of their junior college year 40 percent of males and between 28 percent (Berkeley) and 38 percent (Stanford) of females had experienced intercourse.[6] All competent observers are agreed that the change among women has been more dramatic than among men. The probability is that males of college age don't differ too substantially from their counterparts a generation ago. What is significant is that fewer among them are experiencing intercourse with prostitutes or casual pickups, more with their fellow students. Studies of sexual behavior among women and girls are therefore the most significant and revealing.

A 1972 report to the Presidential Commission on Population Growth and the American Future, made by two Johns Hopkins University professors, showed that 44.1 percent of American girls aged nineteen had experienced intercourse. This is an average for the whole country; in the lower socioeconomic classes it was higher than this; in the middle and upper classes, it was lower. At least as significant as the statistics themselves is the fact that 60 percent of the girls who were no longer virgins said their coitus had been with only a single male partner while half of the total indicated they expected to marry that partner.[7] Other studies come pretty close to the same estimates on the incidence of intercourse among young women in the United States today. They show that more girls masturbate than before, that there is more sex but less promiscuity among them, that coitus is increasingly associated with affection and with a relationship which is intended, at least by the girls, to be permanent.[8]

In 1977 some 24,000 high school juniors and seniors who are leaders and achievers were surveyed. Seventy percent said they had never had sexual intercourse; 56 percent stated a preference that their future husband or wife be a virgin.[9] An earlier similar survey covering roughly the same number of young people showed that where 34 percent of Protestant students reported they had experienced intercourse and 25 percent of

Catholics, only 17 percent of the Jewish students were in this category.[10]

Two footnotes about premarital intercourse among men should be appended at this point. One has to do with a young man's image of his own masculinity, the other with peer pressure. Both are encompassed in the following observation:

> Young men, whose heightened sex drives are equaled only by their feelings of adolescent insecurity, are particularly susceptible to the idea that their masculinity is measured by the number of women they have seduced. To retain his masculine image in the eyes of his peers, a young man may boast about sexual exploits which have occurred mainly in his imagination. His listeners, however, accept these exaggerations as truth, and each dejectedly concludes that *he* is the only young man in the world who does not have erotic escapades with voluptuous females.[11]

Our second and final comment in this connection about men is related to our earlier observations about the double standard. Studies made some few years ago in England showed that, while 51 percent of the male respondents indicated they would like to have intercourse before marrying, 64 percent of the same group expressed a preference that their brides be virgins!

An investigation among college men in this country showed that 50 percent of them approved premarital intercourse for a woman, yet 75 percent said they would prefer to marry a virgin.[12]

Question: What right does a man who has himself experienced premarital intercourse have to criticize or condemn his future wife if she does the same? *Answer:* Absolutely none! Only a man who has remained chaste himself has any right to judge his bride on this score. There is no justification for a double standard. We shall have more to say about this later.

Although there is reason to believe that fewer men now demand virginity in their wives-to-be than was once the case, more frequently than you might suppose, boys who voice very liberal attitudes on the subject in theory, feel a strong preference for a bride who has not had intercourse with anyone else.

Insofar as we can be reasonably confident, then, this is the extent of our contemporary sexual revolution. There is much more open, honest discussion of sex. Attitudes toward premarital coitus are certainly more accepting. And there has undoubtedly been some increase in full sex relations before marriage, particularly among girls. We should not overlook, however, the fact that intercourse among the young today is probably more closely associated with strong affection, even love, than in the past.

My guess is that some of the statistics just given, by what they show of increased rates of premarital intercourse, may have shocked older readers but may have surprised you or your friends almost as much by falling so short of what you had supposed the situation to be. In any event, this information is offered as accurate background for what follows, not because we suppose for one foolish moment that questions as important as these can be determined by popular vote. It is important for you to know the situation as it actually exists, but you will have to make up your own mind in the determination of values and standards for yourself.

And so

Enough of background. It is time to approach the core question: to wait or not to wait. One of the major deficiencies of the famous Kinsey sex reports is that they classify every orgasm, no matter how or with whom achieved, as an "outlet." This kind of quantitative oversimplification is most misleading. It overlooks the fact there are several ways of achieving an orgasm and that even intercourse can carry different qualitative overtones to different people at different times and under different conditions. Rabbi Eugene Borowitz has done us an excellent service in outlining the various levels on which two heterosexual individuals can have intercourse.[13] With only minor modifications, I intend to follow his pattern here. For reasons which will become apparent as we proceed, these levels will be numbered in reverse.

Level five is that of conquest or force. Little need be said about it. We already know that the technical term for this kind of conduct is rape, a phenomenon which may be found only among human beings. If a male dog were to force himself sexually upon a female against her will, at a time when she is not ovulating and is therefore not receptive to his advances, not only would she resist him ferociously, if necessary she would even attack his sex organs. Although rape is nearly always thought of as a practice of male against female, in theory I suppose it could be the opposite way around. In any event, no time need be wasted here in condemning it. Women have organized in recent years to advise each other on how to avoid or resist being raped, offering compassionate guidance and help to those who have been thus victimized. To the rapist, sex is plainly and only an instrument of power, a way of imposing himself and his will on someone weaker, a vain attempt to simulate a self–confidence which doesn't exist.

It is especially with reference to rape that the term "making love" as a synonym for intercourse is so transparently inaccurate. At its best, of course, intercourse is a manifestation of love. But it can also indicate hate, fear, insecurity or a variety of other emotions which are far from love. Dr. Karl Menninger, perhaps the dean of American psychiatrists, stated this truth with dramatic effectiveness:

> The orgasm of a terrified soldier in battle, that of a loving husband in the arms of his wife, that of a desperate homosexual trying to improve his masculinity and that of a violent and sadistic brute raping a child are not the same phenomena. The muscles and nerves and secretions may be the same but the orgasms are not the same, and the sexuality is not the same.[14]

Level four is that of the "healthy orgasm." It emerges from a perception of our sexuality as a strong physiological need (admittedly true) which it is healthy to express, unwholesome to repress. The underlying assumption or code is simple: when hungry, we eat; when thirsty, we drink; when afflicted with an itch, we scratch; when desirous of sex, we seek intercourse. One writer, in commenting on this level of sexual activity, has said that "sex, presumably, will become purely fun, like surfing—or hygiene, like Swedish calisthenics."[15]

The most popular expression of the "healthy orgasm" philosophy of sex is in *Playboy* and similar periodicals, in books with such titles as *The Love Machine* and in such promotional slogans as "Two Views of the Sex Game." Sex is interpreted as little more than mechanical adjustment or sport. The ultimate aim is to become a sexual athlete or gymnast, to discover exotic positions and procedures for intercourse that one has never thought of before. Two male respondents to a campus study of sexuality have illustrated this level about as well as anyone:

> Yeah, I've tried the 187 positions described in the manual. Maybe I'm exaggerating when I say 187 because some of the positions are practically impossible—after training for gymnastics, I might make all of them. How do I feel about these experiences? No feeling really. It's sort of a physical readiness program. It's more fun than jogging. I'm ready to settle for less activity.

> I can't say I've specialized in positions, but I could brag about the number of partners I've had. How do I feel about these experiences? Well, I believe sex has to be something more than physical. . . . I hope to find something more when I get married.[16]

This is one of the levels of sexuality available to you; like each of the others, yet to be considered, it offers you both advantages and disadvantages.

Before proceeding, let's go back for a moment to the thought that it may be harmful to one's health to frustrate so intense a natural urge as sex. If that meant total and absolute repression—no release of sexual tension even through masturbation or petting—it would most probably be true.

Yet we should remember that premarital intercourse at an early age may also involve serious physical or emotional risk to one's health. Dr. Elizabeth Whelan writes:

> There is now increasing evidence that some of the emotional side effects of a premature permissive sexual relationship may have long-range effects on the development of personality, damaging a person's emotional stability.[17]

Others have voiced similar warnings. George F. Gilder, formerly a member of the Harvard faculty, wrote:

> When sex becomes a temporary release, to be prompted as well by one woman as by another, or by sex magazines; when sex becomes a kind of massage . . . one's whole emotional existence is depleted.[18]

Dr. Whelan cites specific studies to support her view, then continues:

> Statistics have shown that girls who begin to have intercourse early in their life (roughly, before the age of sixteen) are twice as likely to develop cancer of the cervix than are those girls who delay intercourse until some time in their twenties. The reason youthful sex increases the chance of developing this form of cancer is unknown. It has been suggested that sexual organs which are not fully mature are more susceptible to whatever the agent is which causes cervical cancer.[19]

This should be an important consideration in arriving at your decision regarding intercourse as "healthy" orgasm.

This brings us to *level three which Rabbi Borowitz labels "mutual consent."* Where level five definitely and level four probably exemplify the desire of an individual to fulfill his or her own sexual needs, the partner being only a means to that end, here on level three we come to consideration for both participants. Two people feel a desire for sex at the same time. Finding each other to be physically attractive, they agree to satisfy their mutual need. The situation is really not much different from that of a man and woman who agree to scratch each other's itchy backs. Neither is imposing anything upon the other or taking advantage of the other. Instead of one individual's seeking a healthy orgasm, two agree to do so mutually and simultaneously. It is clear—isn't it?—that thus far each level has been a bit more restrictive than the preceding one; which means to say, each category of intercourse imposes additional criteria which must be met before two individuals proceed to the experience of intercourse.

The same thing is true as we proceed to *level two, that of love.* Here, for the first time, intercourse becomes part of a relationship between two whole personalities, not just two genital systems. As one competent observer has commented: "Penises and vaginas can't love each other; only people can do that." Intercourse as an expression of love reverses what some people believe to be the sequential relationship between the two. Very often the assumption is that first two individuals are sexually attracted, then they enjoy successful intercourse which increases the attraction, finally this leads to love. Without denying that perhaps this does occasionally take place, many experts in the field of marriage feel that the opposite is truer. That is, first two people, who of course are initially attracted to each other, deepen their relationship as persons to the point of love, after which they express this love, among other ways, by sharing intercourse. Dr. Erich Fromm, the renowned psychoanalyst whom we have quoted before, has expressed this concept as well as anyone:

> Because sexual desire is in the minds of most people coupled with the idea of love, they are easily misled to conclude that they love each other when they want each other physically. . . . If the desire for physical union is not stimulated by love, if erotic love is not also brotherly love, it never leads to union in more than an orgiastic, transitory sense. Sexual attraction creates, for the moment, the illusion of union, yet without love this "union" leaves strangers as far apart as they were before—sometimes it makes them ashamed of each other, or even makes them hate each other, because when the illusion has gone they feel their estrangement even more markedly than before.[20]

Rejecting "the notion that mutual sexual satisfaction was supposed to be the basis for satisfactory love relations and especially for a happy marriage," Dr. Fromm adds:

> The underlying idea was that love is the child of sexual pleasure and that, if two people learn how to satisfy each other sexually, they will love each other. It fitted the

general illusion of the time to assume that using the right techniques is the solution, not only to the technical problems of industrial production, but of all human problems as well. One ignored the fact that the contrary of the underlying assumption is true. Love is not the result of adequate sexual satisfaction, but sexual happiness—even the knowledge of the so-called sexual technique—is the result of love.[21]

Those who advocate that intercourse be restricted to love say that various types of human behavior are appropriate to different degrees of relationship. One politely nods toward a casual acquaintance, shakes hands with a person to whom he or she has just been introduced, affectionately hugs an old friend, passionately kisses a mate. To shower a casual or new acquaintance with hugs and kisses would be highly questionable if not comic behavior. The question, then, is: At what degree in the relationship between two persons is sexual intercourse appropriate? The answer, for those who take their stand here: On the level of love, not before.

Rabbi Borowitz expresses this view eloquently:

> I think highly of friendship, but sexual intercourse seems to me a rather extravagant way in which to express it. One should think so much of self, and what his most intimate giving of self means, that he should not do so without the most worthwhile reason. Or, to put it more positively, I value intercourse too highly as an interhuman experience for me to find it an appropriate act with a person who is only a friend.[22]

Finally, there are those who would be even more restrictive by *reserving intercourse for marriage.* They would point to the fact that it is easy, under the persistent urging of sexual desire, to confuse love with infatuation. A psychiatrist has described a young girl, one of his patients, as saying: "I believe one should have intercourse only when in love, so I am constantly in love." Without being quite so ridiculous or bold as that, many individuals act on a similar premise. Adherents of level one remind us of the time test we used in our second chapter to distinguish love from infatuation. To this, they would add that there is a difference between "love for now" and "love forever." When two persons not only feel the strongest kind of interpersonal relationship but are ready on that basis to commit themselves to each other, to assume what they hope will be permanent responsibility for each other, then intercourse between them becomes appropriate and proper. Rabbi Borowitz summarizes this level in the following words:

> Lovers do not make love simply to achieve or produce rich sensation but because they love each other. They do not love for the sake of achieving orgasm, but achieving orgasm is fully appropriate between them because they love. Indeed because they know and trust each other fully, they may hope to find in their lovemaking a personal fulfillment and joy that no other setting for sexual intercourse could provide.[23]

Here, then, are the levels on which a man and a woman may experience intercourse, the alternatives among which you must ultimately make your personal choice. I have tried to keep my own opinions out of this chapter, to be as objective as possible in stating the alternatives. Yet it would be unfair both to you and to me if I were to let the matter rest there. In Chapter 13, therefore, I shall speak for myself. Chapter 12 expresses a point of view which accepts premarital intercourse.

Because chapters 11, 12 and 13 really belong together, the "for instance" cases for all of them will be deferred to the end of the discussion as a whole.

12

"I'm on my way to dispatch two dragons, dethrone a soulless tyrant, and rescue the Grail—I'll try to catch you on the way back."

Not to wait

Written by Judith Fales, M.A., former instructor in Sociology, Kean College, Union, New Jersey

If you and I are going to talk about the positive aspects of premarital sex, we ought to begin with a few cautions.

Firstly, we know that responsible people do not generally

advocate young couples' having premarital intercourse. They believe that, if this is going to happen, it is best for everyone involved that such sexual relationships take place between people who are as emotionally mature as possible, people who really care about each other, who are concerned about each other's feelings and desires.

Secondly, we all are aware that no advice is right or good for everyone in all times and places. The "old" morality created guilt and fear for our older brothers and sisters or our parents who chose to ignore it and decided to have sexual intercourse before getting married. Similarly, the "new" morality creates its own kind of guilt for those of us who honestly want to keep our virginity until we are married. This fact, incidentally, shows us that guilt is culturally caused and so can be culturally erased. Which means to say that a particular society, by declaring a given kind of conduct to be wrong, can make its citizens who nonetheless practice that which has been forbidden feel guilty. In another society, which accepts the same behavior, those who practice it feel no guilt. The author of this book provides us with a fine example when he tells us that masturbation was at one time thought to be wrong, evil and even sinful. All of us who masturbated then felt some degree of guilt. Most people today accept masturbation as a healthy part of sexual development. Hence today's young people feel little or no guilt when masturbating.

We need to be aware, however, that this new morality also carries with it a new type of burden for us. There is the possibility that we might lose our freedom, our sense of self-responsibility, this time, not because our parents are imposing their wills on us, but because our peers, our friends and classmates are pressuring us to conform. "We all do it, so you must, too, or you will not be popular, you will not belong!" We must reach our own decision without undue pressure from *anybody* else.

As a final word of preliminary warning, none of us would give the same suggestions or advice to an unmarried sixteen-year-old that we would give to an unmarried twenty- or thirty-year-old. What we would say to these different age groups would depend on their emotional maturity and, as we all know, emotional maturity is difficult to come by and even harder to define.

With these cautions in mind, let's look at the reasons why one might choose *not* to wait.

When we examine history, we see that premarital sex was of little concern in most societies. After all, when people were engaged as young children and married by their early teens, marriage took place at the same time as strong sexual awakening and interest. Sometimes, in fact, people actually got married before they had any strong interest in sex.

Today's world looks very different. Our modern, wealthy Western world has prolonged the process of growing up. First comes adolescence, the teenage years, when most of us are not expected to work, unlike people of this age in the past. In all probability you will continue going to school, remaining financially dependent on your parents. Then we have postadolescence; these years of going to school and maturing are extended into our early twenties. Finally, comes what we might call post–postadolescence. It is becoming more and more common for people well into their twenties, even into their early thirties, to put off taking on the two responsibilities that society has used to define adulthood, namely, working full time and starting one's own family.

You can probably reason out for yourself why growing up now takes such a long time. Life is more complicated now than in the past. Our scientific, highly technological world needs lots of highly skilled workers. To become a scientist, engineer, physician, or even a teacher requires greater preparation than it did even when your parents were adolescents. People have to go to school for more and more years, getting more and more degrees, in order to do the jobs that have to be done in our world. Going to college and then on to graduate school has started to replace or postpone marriage since few of us can afford to do both.

Yesterday and today

As long as people married young, their sexual needs could be satisfied at about the time they were most felt and in a way that society found acceptable—within marriage. Today, however, marriage occurs much later than this period, and there are some of you who may even consider not getting married at all. It seems unrealistic to expect young and not-so-young people to wait more and more years to have the enriching experience of sexual intercourse. What made sense in yesterday's world doesn't make sense to many of us today.

People have intercourse for reproduction and/or for pleasure. Before our scientists invented modern contraceptives, especially the pill, we could not separate these two. If we experienced coitus for pleasure, we risked getting pregnant or impregnating our partner. This was a matter of proper public concern since society was responsible for feeding and educating its children. Now, however, we can avoid pregnancy. Many people believe that society no longer has the right to concern itself with an individual's sexual behavior now that birth rates can be controlled.

We have already seen that society is also responsible for many of the negative aftereffects of having premarital intercourse, in other words, for guilt and remorse. These negative feelings are most likely to happen to us if our society has restrictive rules about premarital sex.[1] Such restrictiveness takes sexual responsibility out of your own hands, thus robbing you of your independence and producing guilt in those of you who prefer to make your own decisions about what you do or do not do sexually. We also have to realize that our same society which says, "Don't!" to premarital intercourse has pushed sex and sexuality at us in movies, in books, and in advertising. (Evidently, cars will not sell unless the ads for them show beautiful, sexy women sitting in them!) Society has bombarded us with a double message . . . "Be sexual or you will be lonely, unhappy, unwanted, but don't carry that sexuality through to its logically and emotionally consistent conclusion, the act of intercourse."

Our society has also helped create a separation between sex and love. We are told to develop the ability to love in a mature way but not act out that love in sexual intercourse until after a marriage ceremony takes place. And then, so we are led to believe, inexperience in sex will be cancelled out by loving tenderness on the wedding night and all will be well! We may well ask how we can consider the sexual part of love as inappropriate, wrong or immoral before marriage yet find it fully acceptable and satisfying after marriage.

Young men have been especially affected by this separation

between love and sex. Because American society has shut its eyes to, perhaps even winked in approval of, boys' "sowing their wild oats" and, at the same time, has said "nice girls don't," these young men have experimented with sex in "back alley" ways, frequently with such partners as prostitutes or casual pickups. These partners bore little if any resemblance to the women they would eventually marry. The result was that little respect for their partners developed; there was little concern for their partner's sexual or emotional satisfaction and also little commitment and responsibility.

A lot of our research shows that an increasing number of today's young couples are not usually interested in quick, promiscuous relationships but are rather concerned with creating intimate and caring relationships based on concern for each other and a sense of responsibility. It is possible for an unmarried couple to show more mutual concern and care than a married couple. This responsibility appears to include an obligation to prevent pregnancy by the use of contraceptives. Not all married couples take their vows seriously, and not every unmarried couple is immature, trying to escape from the commitments that are supposed to be part of marriage.

One of the most commonly mentioned reasons for accepting premarital intercourse is that sex is both a physical and an emotional need, a natural part of life for each of us. This argument does not suggest that we become animalistic, going out and indulging in all kinds of sexual experimentation with lots of people just to satisfy our needs. It does suggest that sexual desire, when combined with affection between the people involved, is healthy and should be satisfied.

Not only does the denial of satisfaction in sex make us physically uncomfortable but, according to Freud and his followers, unsatisfied or repressed needs can cause emotional problems at some future time in our lives. Some parents who were raised in the Victorian era suppressed all sexual behavior in their children, even in young adults. As a result, in later years many of these children experienced unsatisfactory sexual adjustment, even frigidity, after they were married.

Before and after

One of the arguments used by people who are against premarital intercourse is that nonvirginity at the time of marriage is related to subsequent marital unhappiness. No such relationship was found in the only major study considering this question in the 1960s.[2] There is probably no way for us to measure the exact nature of this relationship, but it might be fair to speculate that, if as many as three out of four American marriages have some kind of sexual problem (among others, Masters and Johnson say that this is the case), premarital sex might contribute to increased marital happiness. It could do this both by giving us experience in an area which everybody agrees is a significant part of marriage and by allowing us to decide whether or not our sexual partner is compatible with us before a marriage actually takes place.

We have also been told that those who experience premarital intercourse are more likely than others to commit adultery, that is, to indulge in extramarital intercourse after marriage. The Kinsey research of 1948 suggests this. It may well be, however, that this correlation between premarital and extramarital sexual behavior is the result of some of the factors existing at that particular time. Society's insistence, for example, that "sex is only really right in marriage" may have led some couples who had experienced premarital intercourse to feel so guilty that they married even though they were not mature enough or compatible enough to do so. We certainly know that people got married in the past because they felt sexual pressures and not because they had truly decided that marriage was for them. (We should mention that Kinsey himself cites evidence that those who achieved premarital sexual success, defined as the ability to have an orgasm, were likely also to enjoy marital sexual success.) There is little, if any, more recent evidence to prove that premarital intercourse increases the probability of extramarital intercourse. We do know that recent research concerning young people's *attitudes,* which, of course, may very well differ from their actual *behavior,* indicates increasing permissiveness toward premarital intercourse but no corresponding increase in permissiveness about extramarital sex.

Being sexually intimate with another person can give us

growing knowledge about ourselves and our partner. This knowledge includes not just a check for sexual compatibility but also more information about such important matters as concern for another, kindness and thoughtfulness and any tendency to exploit another. It is incompatibility in all these areas which has helped produce our tremendously high divorce rates. Sexual and emotional intimacy before marriage may help us be more careful in our choice of mates, thus reducing the number of divorces. Instead of sexual or quasisexual traits ("Man, is he/she sexy!") being stressed exclusively in evaluating future mates, we can give more emphasis to such traits as honesty and openness.

I urge, at this point, however, that you keep one important point in mind. It isn't likely that intimacy, sexual or otherwise, between *immature* couples will help you choose your mate more wisely. This is as true for married couples as it is for unmarried ones. In fact, it is distressing to see how many people who write on this subject contrast "mature" married couples with "immature" unmarried couples, as though the state of matrimony automatically makes everybody who enters it responsible and mature.

We must also remember that living together before marriage does not, according to recent research, mean greater chances of your marriage being successful. The divorce rate for couples who have lived together, sometimes for years, and then married, is as high as for those who did not live together.

This may be because they were still immature, or it may mean that there remains some degree of commitment and/or responsibility which is withheld in the absence of a legal ceremony. Whichever the explanation, the result is that compatibility while living together unmarried is an unreliable test for living together successfully as a married couple.

Another point we might make here is that, although people getting married in the past did so "until death do us part," it appears that an increasing number today feel that this may be unrealistic, given how long we live. Their feeling, rather, might be expressed by "until death do us part, unless we find ourselves unhappy and then we can get a divorce."

Yes, premarital relationships end. But so do marriages—and with far more upset for the individuals involved. If the pressures from unfulfilled sexual needs can be eliminated, we can at least hope that marriages taking place now at an earlier age because of these pressures will *not* occur and that finding out more about nonsexual areas of compatibility will become more common for us. The pressures which lead to unhappy marriages will be present to some extent even if petting to mutual orgasm is practiced because the ultimate sexual experience is that of intercourse.

Because Dr. Anthony Storr, a British psychiatrist, so eloquently expresses the importance of the sexual aspect of relationships, the author cites him here and will cite him again in Chapter 13. "Sex is so important, so pervasive and so intimately connected with every aspect of personality that it cannot be separated from the person as a whole without impoverishing even superficial relationships." How much more important, then, is sex in the development of loving and enriching relationships, the kind that we all hope to have some day, as well as in self-development!

Women have changed

Finally, we ought to consider another thing that has been happening in our society which has influenced attitudes and behavior relating to premarital sex. The women's revolution, which will be discussed in a later chapter, has had a tremendous impact on our knowledge of female sexuality and premarital sex. All past studies of such behavior have shown that young males engaged in premarital intercourse far more frequently than had females. Women have historically been considered to be asexual or nonsexual creatures. It was man's desire to have intercourse and woman's duty to oblige. Many people believed that women had no sexual desires until their husbands introduced them to the joys of sex in general and intercourse in particular.

Women have rebelled against this double standard. They have begun to insist that "if it's normal and acceptable for men, it's normal and acceptable for us." This position is being reflected in more recent studies which show that the rates of premarital intercourse have increased far more noticeably for women than for men. While our society was preaching "Don't!" for all, it was practicing "Don't!" mostly for women.

And American women are no longer buying this brand of sexual discrimination.

These, then, are the positive aspects of premarital sex. The choice between waiting and not waiting is yours to make. You can make that choice wisely only by accurately evaluating your own personality and maturity.

13

LOVE BIRDS
$5.98 PR

To wait

My own view—after weighing the evidence on both sides as carefully as I can, after more than four decades of marriage, after a long career of counseling many couples—is that the wisest and happiest course is to restrict sexual intercourse, certainly to the level of love, quite possibly to that of marriage.

Let me preface this honest statement of my view by approaching a question you may have asked when Rabbi Borowitz's classification of the levels on which intercourse may be experienced was first presented in Chapter 11. Isn't it possible to have intercourse on one level before marriage, then on a different and superior level afterward? This isn't an easy question to answer, in part because we must rely on common sense and our general knowledge of human behavior and feelings rather than on any kind of documentary evidence or clear-cut scientific data which might qualify as absolute proof.

The answer, moreover, may not be the same in every case. If we are talking about switching from level two before marriage to level one later, yes, it certainly is possible. If what we have in mind is one or two premarital experiences on level two or three, *perhaps* a postmarital shift to level one is possible. The greater the number of partners, the less likely is a dramatic shift.

We must remember what has already been said about the extremely close connection between sex and every other aspect of our emotional life, indeed, of our total personality. Intercourse is not an isolated episode, divorced from the human being who precedes and follows it. Our first experiences with coitus, moreover, are likely to make an indelible impression, to be associated with an emotional aura which will attend later experiences also. It is extremely difficult, perhaps even impossible, to have intercourse with a variety of partners over an extended period of time on a level lower than the second, then to shift gears, as it were, and live the rest of one's sex life after marriage on the first.

Sex can be a relationship of genitals to genitals or of whole persons to one another. Each time individuals enjoy it on the former level, they teach something to their bodies, their emotions, and their minds; they establish and then reinforce a pattern which it may never be possible to erase. Admittedly, this may be less true of individuals who decide to have intercourse during their engagement, that is to say, on level two. More on that later. But it will nearly always be the case with high school and many college students who are by no means ready yet to relate the whole of themselves to the whole of another person in a permanent partnership.

A psychiatrist and a writer who collaborated on a book combining the insights of psychiatry and religion wrote this:

Sexual intercourse is but one item in a total human relationship and it provides emotional fulfillment only as it is an expression of mature love between a man and a woman in marriage. Advice that overlooks this is likely to have dangerous results.[1]

The late Dr. Max Levin, clinical professor of neurology at the New York Medical College, felt very much the same way:

Sex is more than a mechanism for procreation, and it is more than an avenue for sensual gratification. It is a function that promotes the growth of character. It is in the realm of sex that people reveal most clearly their real character and the degree of their emotional maturity. The behavior of man and wife in the sex act is the most sensitive index of their capacity to give, of their refusal to receive satisfaction unless they also give it.[2]

To some extent, our sexual values—like all the standards and judgments by which we try to live—are socially determined, that is to say, influenced by the society and culture in which we live. Judith Fales makes this point in Chapter 12, but I believe she overstates it. Eskimos think it ethically desirable to terminate the lives of their aged before debility can set in; we try to keep our elders alive as long as possible. Some societies will not allow a girl to be married until she has demonstrated her prowess as a sex partner or, perhaps, even become pregnant; at least verbally, many people in our society still put a good deal of value on virginity. There are cultures in which a host has shirked his duties if he has not offered a male guest one of his wives for the night; most of us continue to condemn adultery.

It would be a serious mistake, however, to assume that cultural determination is the *entire* picture. Nature, including human nature, operates by law. Certain patterns of behavior go along with other patterns and produce inevitable consequences. This is easy to demonstrate physically. If I hold your head under water for ten minutes, not allowing you to use an oxygen tank or scuba apparatus, you will drown regardless of the society in which you live. If you foolishly touch a high-tension electric transmission wire, you will perish whether you are an Eskimo or an American. It is more difficult to demonstrate this truth ethically than physically, but it prevails nonetheless. The sexual values which encourage premarital pregnancy and a wife-for-the-night as a token of hospitality are found in societies which are recognized in other respects to be inferior to ours. The more sensitive people are generally, the more highly their spirituality has evolved; the farther removed they are from sheer animal behavior in other respects, the more inevitably will their acceptance of sex as a purely physical aspect of life make it impossible for them to enjoy it as anything more than that.

An analogy may be helpful here. The eye is an extremely sensitive organ, able to detect minute shadings of color. Were individuals to ignore this fact, however, to expose their eyes persistently and without protection to the brightest sunshine, perhaps even to stare directly at an eclipse of the sun, they would destroy the exquisite sensitivity of their eyes. Our ears are perceptive enough to identify and enjoy very slight differentiations of musical tone. A man who spent his entire working day in the vicinity of jet planes, however, without in some way protecting his ears, would find it impossible to enjoy a symphony that night. If his ears were thus abused over a long span of time, they might permanently lose their sensitivity. I am convinced that, in much the same manner, a man or woman who chooses to experience intercourse on less than the highest sensitivity level of which he or she is innately capable will, after a time, damage or even destroy that capacity.

If it were a simple or easy thing to transpose one's sexual behavior from one level to another, it would be logical to assume—would it not?—that those individuals who have experienced premarital coitus would, by and large, refrain from extramarital coitus, from adultery. Careful and reliable research, however, indicates that this is not the case. It shows that with both sexes there is a higher incidence of adultery among those who went all the way before marriage than among those who abstained. We do, in fact, carry our premarital sexual attitudes and behavior patterns with us into marriage. Speaking of the men he had studied, Dr. Ira L. Reiss explains:

These men separated sexual behavior and affection in their premarital coitus. It is therefore not difficult for them to engage in extramarital coitus purely for pleasure. . . . This sort of training may well be conducive to double standard extramarital intercourse in later years.[3]

His analysis, if valid, would apply no less to women.

Before we leave the matter of shifting from one level to another, a word should be inserted about two additional subjects of great importance: morality and guilt. I use *morality* and *ethics* synonymously despite the technical differences which distinguish them. And I do not mean by these terms artificial norms which we are obliged to accept just because a great person pronounced them in the past. My view of ethical values emerges from what has already been said about the natural consequences of certain actions. Whatever course of action will, in the long run, inherently bring the greatest amount of fulfillment and happiness to the largest number of persons concerned—this is what I call *ethical* or *moral.* I believe that the higher the level of sexual intercourse between any two individuals the more moral is their behavior. I am convinced that the higher this level the greater will be the *ultimate* happiness to the two of them, their respective mates if they do not marry each other, their children and society as a whole.

Two psychiatrists who have written one of our best college level books on sex are authors of paragraphs which acknowledge the reality of morals and their close association with guilt:

According to an old saying, a stiff penis has no conscience. The world, however, is not populated by penises and vaginas but by men and women, and they do have consciences. In fact, the moral questions related to sex, as well as to any other area of life, may well be the most critical ones. They certainly are the most difficult. . . .[4]

Sexuality involves powerful emotions—not only love *(eros)* but also feelings of guilt. The former tends to predominate before and during the sexual encounter, it seems. When a question of morality is involved, however, feelings of guilt tend to appear the following day or even months or years later. Guilt feelings may be regarded as the "voice of conscience," but actually their origins are extremely complex and may be totally irrational. Again, we shall leave debates over whether or not conscience is a God-given faculty to the theologians, but we cannot deny the reality of guilt feelings. Situation ethics emphasizes the processes that occur before an act. That the individuals believe *at the time* that what they are about to do is right is the important variable. But what of the potentially painful aftermath of guilt feelings, irrational as they may be?[5]

Without the slightest doubt, the guilt attached to sex by most of our parents and many of us has been excessive, emerging in large part from the traditional Christian concept that sex is dirty and reprehensible. In counteracting that extreme, however, we must be careful not to adopt its opposite which is no less unrealistic and harmful. Guilt is real; far from being only a product of our culture, it inheres in human nature. It may be easy for some of us to rationalize almost any kind of conduct we desire by assuring ourselves that we ought not and will not feel guilty over it. Yet, in an insidious and treacherous way, even the most self-confident of us may be victimized by corrosive guilt long after our conduct has been concluded and presumably forgotten.

Back to our five levels

Let me turn now, in my statement of personal views, to specific comments on the five levels of intercourse spelled out in Chapter 11. We are dealing in this discussion with natural rules and norms of human behavior which are true wherever men and women live. The attitudes of society may change from decade to decade; the relationship between feelings and actions and the consequences which follow certain kinds of behavior do not change. For that reason, some of the supporting quotations given in this chapter, though they may have been written a few years ago, are still relevant and valid.

I would hope that none of my readers would justify coitus on the lowest level, that of conquest or force. Yet occasionally something of the brutality characteristic of this dimension may be found in the sexual conduct of those who are on a different level. You have heard, for example, of sadomasochistic sexuality. Sadism refers to the neurotic need of some persons to brutalize or torture others; masochism is the opposite—satisfaction gained from suffering as a martyr. There are men and women who especially enjoy intercourse when it involves physical pain for themselves or their partners. There is obviously a close relationship between this and coitus on its lowest level.

Intimations of this level may be found also in some of our language about sex. Brief mention was made of this earlier in our discussion. If you think for a moment of the two four–letter verbs most frequently used in vulgar speech for intercourse, you will realize that both of them refer to unpleasant things which one person does *to* another, not to happiness which is enjoyed *with* another. They are never used in a favorable or loving context, only in aggression and anger. When used in a nonsexual context, they always describe cheating another person, taking advantage, wreaking vengeance. This is deeply symptomatic of an unwholesome, unloving attitude toward intercourse—which belongs on level five.

Dr. Lewis Thomas emphasizes this in tracing the origin and development of what he calls "the most famous and worst of the four-letter Anglo-Saxon unprintable words." It comes from an Indo-European word meaning "evil and hostile, the sure makings of a curse." From that, it developed through several tongues with connotations such as foe, fated to die, feud. "The unspeakable malevolence of the message is now buried deep inside the word, and out on the surface it presents itself as merely an obscenity."[6] So much for level five.

How do I react to level four, that of healthy orgasm? Of course I recognize the urgency of our sexual drive stressed by the advocates of this dimension. There is no denying the fact that it would be unhealthy, even if possible, to thwart our sexual urges completely. But this is not the only alternative to intercourse at a very early age; we have already observed that —aside from wet dreams, an automatic response for males— both masturbation and, assuming a relationship of very deep affection, petting to orgasm provide other ways of relieving the physiological pressure which attends sexual attraction.

The major defect of sex seen only as healthy orgasm is its

failure to reckon with the unbreakable ties between sex and our total personalities, to which reference has been made several times. Richard Hettlinger underscores all our earlier comments on this:

> *Playboy* treats (sex) as a desirable accessory which can be changed according to the whim of the moment. Yet, if we have learned anything from Freud and his successors, it is surely that we are not people with or without sex, as we choose, but sexual beings—and that to deny or degrade our sexuality is to degrade our very selves. "Sex," writes a contemporary British psychiatrist [Dr. Anthony Storr] "is so important, so pervasive and so intimately connected with every aspect of personality that it cannot be separated from the person as a whole without impoverishing even superficial relationships."[7]

The only apparent distinction between this and level three is that *mutual consent* invites *healthy orgasm* for two rather than one. This is surely an improvement though my basic criticisms of the *Playboy* philosophy would also apply here. A development which gone too little noticed to date is that with increased acceptance of premarital and extramarital intercourse, there has also come a dangerous decrease in the amount of *feeling* and *deep pleasure* which attends these adventures. Dr. Rollo May is but one of many psychoanalysts to note that more and more of his patients are complaining not about prohibitions and inhibitions against sex, as was once the case, but about the absence of feeling and passion in their sexual lives.[8] A fifteen-year-old girl named Alice, suffering as a drug addict, wrote in her diary: "It's strange how much sex I've had and yet I don't feel as though I've had any."[9]

Neither Alice's sad comment nor Dr. May's observation would have surprised Freud. Knowing how fallacious the popular assumption is that the less we surround intercourse with restrictions the more enjoyable it will become, he wrote: "In times in which there were no difficulties standing in the way of sexual satisfaction, . . . love became worthless and life empty. . . ."[10]

Perhaps the most valid criticism of contemporary American

life made by the counterculture is aimed at its technological impersonality. When our sex lives also become nothing more than the satisfaction of physical desires through learning the proper skills, but without deep and lasting emotional concomitants, we exaggerate the worst qualities of our civilization. Only sexual intercourse associated with the very roots of our emotions can alleviate the mechanical barrenness of our lives.

Permissive sexual behavior affects more than just our personal lives. Near the beginning of this chapter I mentioned that extreme sexual permissiveness is usually found in societies generally less civilized than ours. Several scholars have noted an important correlation here: Human progress and creativity seem to accompany a measure of restriction on sexual activity. In the words of one such scholar, "There would have been no modern Europe if the sexual behavior of early European man had been as spontaneously unrestricted as that of the natives of Samoa whose sexual freedom so enthralls Margaret Mead."[11] In short, neither extreme—that which represses or that which permits—is good for our personal welfare or the advancement of civilization. I firmly believe that only when intercourse assumes its proper place in the entire psychic economy of human beings does it serve the purpose meant for it by nature and God.

This brings us again to level two, intercourse associated with love. No one has expressed this level of sexual ethics more perceptively than Phyllis and Eberhard Kronhausen:

> *If we deeply love one another,* and we find in sex a way of showing its deepest levels; if we find that, during and after and because of it, we are both straining to grow in stature in the other's eyes; if we find that, because it is loving, the release of the sex energy also releases, rather than uses up, our deepest creative energies; if each time there is a sexual interlude, we find that we love and respect and admire each other more afterwards, then, and only then, but so sensitively and wonderfully then, *it is right.*[12]

The great Jewish philosopher, Martin Buber, has introduced us to the distinction in human relations between I–It and I–Thou.

I–It means treating another person as if he or she were only a thing. If I move a chair aside because it stands in my way, there is an I–It relationship between the chair and myself. It makes no difference to the chair where it is placed or how many times it is moved. But, if I rudely bump into you because you happen to be in my way, it does make a difference to you. You are a human being, with feelings, fears, hopes and needs very much like mine. I have no right to use you for my own purposes. I must relate myself to you on an I–Thou basis. If not, I act as if only I were created in God's image, not you.

This is true in all our relationships with other people. It is especially true in our sex relationships. When one person exploits another only for the gratification of personal sexual desires or ego, that person has forgotten one of the most precious principles of Judaism.

This is to a great degree true even in the case of mutual consent intercourse, where the individuals concerned are really using each other as *its* for physical pleasure of both.

I find instructive in this regard a description of animal intercourse by Julian Huxley, the great British biologist:

> . . . Many birds will attempt to mate with a stuffed dead female as readily as with a live one—provided that it is set up in a certain pose; and the sperm for artificial insemination in cattle and horses can be obtained because the mating urge of bulls and stallions is aroused by suitable dummies as well as by live cows or mares.[13]

In my judgment, when intercourse between a man and a woman is on a level devoid of love, it resembles this kind of animality more than the fullest potential of sex on a truly human level. I fully agree with Rabbi Borowitz when he writes: "There is a radical difference between loving someone because he is sexy and having sex with someone because of your love."[14]

There are some persons—more often men than women—whose early sex education or "miseducation" makes it difficult for them to associate intercourse with love. Dr. Harold Greenwald describes them as follows:

Unfortunately . . . there are many people who are quite capable of having great sexual pleasure only when there is no love present because they have been educated that sex is something you do with bad people, not with those you love like your mother or sister. So these people need the pleasure of illicit sex, such as prostitution, because that is what is exciting to them. It is difficult for them to combine love and sex.[15]

Such individuals are unfortunate. They should be understood, accepted and helped but not emulated. There are also some persons whose childhood experience makes it difficult or impossible for them to enjoy great music, literature or art. Our efforts in such cases should be directed toward correcting the earlier mistakes which threaten to deprive them of great joy and avoiding similar errors with those who are still children. Our hope must be to increase the number of people who are capable of enjoying intercourse on its highest human level as the ultimate expression of love between a woman and a man.

One of the lowest and least human levels of intercourse is that of the prostitute and her customers. Of course, a prostitute is a woman willing to have coitus with any man who will pay her fee. Sometimes these women are "managed" by a *pimp,* a man who solicits their customers, rents rooms for them, collects the money due them and pays each a set salary.

Among many ancient peoples, prostitution was not only permitted, but it was considered sacred. Young girls were enrolled for the purpose of having intercourse with the priests, and this was thought to be a form of worship. However, even in ancient Judaism, all forms of prostitution were condemned.

Modern studies reveal, as you may already have suspected, that there is almost never an emotional relationship between prostitute and customer. There is considerable reason to doubt whether most prostitutes even experience orgasms. They make themselves available, not for love, not even really for their own pleasure, but merely for the money they can thereby obtain.

For obvious reasons, prostitutes are a principal source of venereal infection. Even in those countries where prostitution is legal and regulated, a prostitute can pick up a venereal disease from her first customer, after she had been medically examined, and transmit it before she is next inspected.

It is probable—though not provable—that at least in the middle and upper social classes fewer men patronize prostitutes now than a generation ago. Most males who indulge in premarital or extramarital intercourse are likely to prefer it with a partner for whom they can feel affection if not love.

Here we must revert to the vexing problem first encountered when we attempted to distinguish love from infatuation. With young people of high school or early college age, the great danger in acceptance of the love criterion for intercourse is the likelihood of their confusing infatuation with love. Then the question arises as to the number of partners with whom one can experience intercourse on what he or she honestly believes at the moment to be the level of love, only to discover later that it wasn't love at all. With how many before the sensitive, delicate connection between coitus and love becomes permanently blunted? With how many? I don't profess to know the answer. But I do know that there is such a "point of no return," and I would urge every young person to keep this in mind.

On the verge

How about intercourse between two individuals who are actually engaged to be married? We have already seen that our rabbinic ancestors were ambivalent about coitus during the betrothal period; while they considered it to be indecent, the only punishment was to hasten the actual marriage. Bearing in mind that our so-called engagement is far more tentative and less definitive than the old Jewish betrothal, we still must recognize the great difference between sex which is more or less casual and that which takes place between individuals who are already committed to marry. Even during the engagement, sex may still be separated from the total relationship of whole human beings to one another, the meshing of personalities, the trusting, loving, responsible caring—all of which accompany a good marriage.

In addition, engagements are not infrequently broken. More than once during the years I have had a wedding ceremony, at which I was supposed to officiate, canceled only a few days in advance, after all arrangements had been completed and invitations had been sent.

In some cases premarital intercourse may even be the precipitating cause of breaking an engagement. We can only speculate about this, but we know for a fact that the guilt which can unexpectedly follow such intercourse is capable of playing incredible tricks on one's feelings about his or her partner. There is an example of this in our Bible. In the book of II Samuel we are told that King David's son Amnon felt so passionate a desire for his half sister Tamar that he conspired to be alone with her and begged her to have coitus with him. When she refused, he forced her with his greater strength. No sooner had they finished than we read: "Then Amnon hated her with exceeding great hatred; for the hatred with which he hated her was greater than the love with which he had loved her." The writer of this tale possessed profound psychological insight: he knew that often one projects personal guilt after such an experience onto one's partner. The consequence is that love—or what had appeared to be love—turns to hate.

That this is more than just biblical fancy or pure theory is attested by the research of Burgess and Wallin into the success of engagements. They concluded that "the engagement success scores of persons who had intercourse tend to be lower than the scores of those who were continent."[16] Though the studies leading to this conclusion were done many years ago, I am unaware of any evidence to the contrary that has been produced since then. It is hard to argue too vehemently against intercourse by a mature engaged couple prior to their wedding ceremony. There are undoubtedly circumstances which necessitate a long postponement of that ceremony and in which they might find it both desirable and necessary not to wait. Even then, careful consideration should be given to the reasons for patience outlined above.

Obviously, there is a vast difference between such a couple and two young people of high school or early college age, for whom this book is primarily intended. Here we must revert to something which has been suggested previously: those who are most inclined to go all the way at an early age are *not* the most secure and mature. One scholar summarizes his studies of this truth by writing:

First, teenagers who trust themselves and their ability to contribute to others and who have learned to rely on others socially and emotionally are least likely to be involved in irresponsible sexual activity. . . .

Second, teenagers who have learned to be comfortable in their appropriate sex roles (boys who like being boys and wish to be men, and girls who like being girls and wish to be women) are least likely to be involved in activities leading to indiscriminate sexuality. . . .

Third, both boys and girls have a need to discuss serious problems with adults who they feel can be helpful, that is to say, trusted.[17]

The overall relationship between a young person and his or her parents is another factor of great importance in determining responsible or irresponsible sexual activity. Very often intercourse at an early age, as well as premarital pregnancy, can be a desperate lunge for happiness and love which an individual feels was not received from parents. Dr. James McCary, whose wise words have been quoted several times, puts it this way:

A close, accepting, and loving family relationship is far more effective in controlling the sexual behavior of teenagers than are threats of dire punishment. Studies have indicated that girls who get along well with their fathers and mothers and boys who get along well with their mothers are far less likely to become sexually involved than those who do not.[18]

A true test?

Because they recognize the danger of divorcing sex from all other aspects of a healthy marital relationship, some couples have turned to cohabitation, living together prior to marriage. We tend to think this kind of experiment is of very recent vintage. Not so! A Yiddish newspaper in New York used to conduct a column in which advice was given to questioning readers on all sorts of personal and social problems. Though the following letter appeared in 1965, it obviously refers to an incident in cohabitation that goes back to the early years of this century:

My husband and I were young immigrants when we got acquainted. I was not quite nineteen and my husband was a few months under twenty–one. We were members of an idealistic group who dreamed of building a heaven on earth for everyone. We believed in "free love."

My husband and I were alone here because our parents had remained in Europe. We fell deeply in love, and after a two weeks' friendship we decided to live together. We were not the only ones at that time to do so. It was the fashion, then, for "free love" among many liberal, idealistic young men and women. . . .

The fact that we never married legally, however, has been on our minds for many years—more than ever of late. This is because we are approaching our old age and our world is different. I tell my husband often, lately, that we should do something about it because we even feel guilty before our children. My husband thinks as I do about this, but he doesn't want to stir up the whole thing.

My brother lives in a city thousands of miles away, and, since I haven't seen him in many years, I told my husband that we should go to visit him for a few weeks and there we could settle everything. I mean, get a marriage license and go to a rabbi to be married properly. We waited fifty years, and that's long enough. My husband is undecided and puts it off. I would, therefore, like to hear your point of view and your suggestion.[19]

If you were the editor, how would you respond? Why do you suppose this couple felt as they did after fifty years of living together? Is their guilt realistic? Can we learn anything valuable about cohabitation from their experience?

Though not at all a brand–new phenomenon, it would seem that more couples are cohabiting now than in the past. If they are mature, if they come to feel they have passed the test and then marry, it is hard to condemn them out of hand. Yet I must confess to strong reservations. What if, after living together for several months or even years, they break up? What effect does this have on each of them now and on their future marriages to other partners? Suppose they have a child while living together? A question posed with reference to premarital intercourse intrudes again insistently: with how many persons can one cohabit, even in good faith, before the whole prospect of marriage becomes meaningless?

I have counseled couples who have lived together for varying periods of time and been amazed to discover how very little they had learned about each other or their probable compatibility. In one instance I felt compelled to say to them: "You two haven't really been living together for the past year; you've just been playing house." What I fear most is that, without the element of commitment and responsibility which goes with mature marriage, the alleged test isn't really a test at all. When two individuals are on a trial basis, their premise being that, if the wind blows too vigorously or the water gets too rough, all they need do is ask out, this is an altogether different relationship from one in which the two partners are pledged to work out their problems, however vexing, and to use their failures as well as their victories to cement a closer, more significant relationship. This does not mean to say or even imply that a couple who find their marriage to be impossible should be condemned to continue it. Not at all. But I am uneasy over the degree to which cohabitation is anything more in most instances than a facsimile of marriage; and a facsimile is neither a model nor a true test.

A woman in my congregation, after listening to a sermon dealing with this topic, reminded her husband of troubled moments early in their marriage and said: "My God, what happiness and growth and joy we would have missed if we had just walked out then instead of remaining together to work at it!" This kind of reaction makes me wonder whether some of the couples living together do not risk cheating themselves in the long run.

Though I have tried, even in offering my own opinions, to avoid dogmatism and accept alternatives, there is one ethical issue on which I must speak with uncompromising obstinacy. Any couple choosing to share intercourse on a level less than that of marriage—or, for that matter, even a married couple

when a child is not wanted—has an inescapable moral obligation to use the best contraception available and to refrain, if
necessary, from coitus until a reliable method is at their dis-
posal. If only the complication or corruption of their own interpersonal relationship were at stake, that would be one thing.
The vigor of my conviction, however, is occasioned by the
inestimable damage that can be done to an innocent child who
did not ask to be born and who was unwanted.

True, there have been some recent advocates of parenthood
for unmarried singles. With due respect for the courage and
love a few such individuals may be able to give to a child, I very
much doubt whether any unborn child would opt to be born
into this kind of status. The very first essential in any ethic of
sexual behavior—for those who reject my views no less than
for those who agree—is not to gamble with the stakes so ominous to an innocent victim. Intelligent and skilled use of birth
control is a prerequisite for every couple not ready or qualified
to conceive a child.

Lest we forget

I have—helpfully, I hope—interrupted myself in this chapter
to the point of almost forgetting the topmost level designated
by Rabbi Borowitz for intercourse, that of marriage. Although
many of my personal comments on this may easily be inferred
from what has already been said, a few additional, specific
reactions need also to be stated.

Judaism has excelled in recognizing the subtle but intensely
important relationship between sex and love in a good marriage. It is clearly more than a verbal coincidence that the word
used by our Bible for intercourse is יָדַע *yada,* meaning *knew.*
Thus we read in Genesis: "And the man knew Eve his wife; and
she conceived and bore Cain. . . ." Our faith teaches that
intercourse at its best was intended by God and nature to be
considerably more than just physical gratification and pleasure, as important as they are. It involves two people *knowing*
each other—respecting and caring for each other deeply in
both physical and spiritual dimensions—loving each other
enough to desire a permanent sharing of their lives, leading to
the creation of new life.

Does premarital intercourse improve the prospects for a good marriage? Judith Fales, the author of Chapter 12, is not the only one to suggest that it does. I have my doubts. For one thing, I do not agree with her that full sexual relations before marriage make it more probable that a couple will concentrate on other nonsexual aspects of compatibility. It is a rare couple who meet with instantaneously mutual success sexually. A man and woman who are committed to a permanent partnership on many levels can gradually work toward improving their sexual lives. Where both permanence and commitment are lacking, two pitfalls can be present. Immediate sexual success can convince them they are right for each other when in fact they are not. Or initial disappointment in sex can encourage them to break off when they might in the course of time have achieved an excellent sex life through patience and love.

Those who believe that successful sexual experience with a variety of partners can increase the prospect for a happy marriage should be reminded that such success is not transferable. Sexual adjustment is so intimate a thing that success with one partner gives no assurance of similar success with another.

It is true that intercourse can be associated with love or be devoid of love either in marriage or outside marriage. All other things being equal, however, marriage provides the setting best calculated to maximize the close connection between sex and love.

This may be even truer for women than for men. Some research indicates that a woman is able to achieve orgasm only if she fully trusts her partner and believes their relationship to be permanent.[20] For both sexes, the first experience of intercourse is likely to make a lasting, even indelible impression which can carry over to subsequent coitus. And that first experience—especially if it is not accompanied by strong feelings of love and trust—can be a disillusionment and disappointment.

A number of studies would seem to support my view. Premarital coitus is by no means the only factor involved. It would be ridiculous to claim that every marriage in which both bride and groom waited for each other will be happier than every marriage in which either or both had intercourse previously with others. Yet many experts have concluded, on the basis of sober research, that—all other things being equal—the odds favor couples who have been celibate. The statements of several of these experts follow.

Dr. Elizabeth Whelan, authority on the sexual needs and experiences of young people, writing about extensive youthful experimentation with intercourse:

> This type of initiation to sex hardly provides the kind of background which leads to healthy sexual adjustment in marriage. Indeed, it may well interfere with the enjoyment of sex in later years.[21]

Dr. Francis Harding, Ohio State University College of Medicine, is convinced:

> [The young person who has experienced premarital intercourse] cannot expect his eventual marriage to be the best and most enduring of all possible relationships, if previously his relationships . . . have been exclusively physical and transient.[22]

Dr. Harold Christensen, professor of sociology at Purdue University:

> There have been a dozen or so serious studies that have attempted to determine if premarital sexual experience in any way affects the outcome of the marriage. Though the results in some of these have been inconclusive, the preponderant finding has been that marriage is more successful where premarital chastity has been maintained.[23]

Dr. Lynn Scoresby, associate professor of Child Development and Family Relations, Brigham Young University:

> My observation as a counselor, having spent time in various parts of the U.S. with married couples who have and have not experienced premarital sexual relations, suggests that, in an extremely high percentage of cases, premarital sexual experience does not positively affect marriage but

may instead bring into a relationship some negative by-products. . . .

Though [couples] may be more sexually experienced and proficient, they often discover their mental and emotional ability to extend themselves to [one] partner is significantly reduced, thus hurting their chances for a full, profound and complete marriage.[24]

Dr. Clarence Leuba, professor of psychology at Antioch College:

Investigations of happiness in marriage indicate that those who were virgins at the time of marriage or who had had intercourse only with the person they eventually married were happier on the average than those who did not fall into either of these two categories.[25]

The case should not be overstated. There are other scholars who disagree with those quoted here. My own disposition is to see positive advantages in reserving intercourse for one's eventual marriage partner.

We ought not leave our consideration of intercourse on the topmost level without a word about adultery, which means to say, extramarital coitus. Jewish tradition is clearly opposed although, to be honest, its strictures are aimed more explicitly and punitively at women than at men. The Seventh Commandment is as definite as it is terse. The writer of Proverbs, referring to "the evil woman" and "a harlot," warns his readers not to lust after them:

Can a man take fire in his bosom,
And his clothes not be burned?
Or can one walk upon hot coals,
And his feet not be scorched?
So he that goes in to his neighbor's wife;
Whoever touches her shall not go unpunished.

The prophet Hosea, who felt deeply on this subject because his own wife had been faithless to him, applies the prohibition against adultery as much to men as to women when he thunders in God's name:

I will not punish your daughters when they
    commit harlotry,
Nor your daughters-in-law when they commit
    adultery;
For you yourselves consort with lewd women,
And you sacrifice with harlots.

The Talmud too underscores the importance of sexual faithfulness between husband and wife. It declares: "In marriage a
person reserves his partner for himself as a sacred object."[26]
    There is reason to suspect, perhaps to believe, that more
adultery occurs today than in the past. Some writers have even
claimed that enjoying intercourse with a partner not one's
husband or wife can enhance a marriage. I think this depends
entirely on what kind of persons are involved and what they
want their marriage to be. If their relationship is exclusively
physical, one in which they relate to each other's enjoyment
and satisfaction only in bed, then I suppose it doesn't really
make much difference when or with whom they experiment
sexually. But, if their partnership even remotely approaches
what marriage should be, if their intercourse emerges from and
leads to a total relationship between two loving persons, it
seems to me quite ludicrous to believe that sexual adventures
with other partners can do anything but severely damage their
life together. Even in a good marriage, either or both partners
may feel sexual attraction toward another or fantasize about
acting out their feelings. But they will value what they have
together too highly to risk destroying it.
    Just as the adolescent who is boldest in experimenting with
intercourse is likely to be the least secure and mature of his
peers, so the married person who is impelled toward adultery
betrays not an abundance but a woeful lack of mature sexuality. As a psychiatrist puts it, "All too often extramarital affairs
fulfill poorly realized neurotic needs or are thinly veiled attempts to humiliate or otherwise hurt the marital partner."[27]
    No one has described the inevitable effect of such behavior
better than a Catholic and a Jewish teacher respectively. The
first, Dr. George N. Shuster, writes: ". . . The psychological
impact of infidelity—on the man and the woman involved, on
the injured partners and particularly on the children of the
married couples—is far greater than we had previously
thought. Anyone who thinks that adultery, gone into however

lightly and however gracefully, cannot completely shatter the life of the injured partner is terribly mistaken."[28] The second, Rabbi Borowitz, agrees: "Adultery is not just a transgression of an old law and a personal promise but a change in the relationship one has with his spouse. Sexual fidelity bespeaks ultimate personal faithfulness, exclusive regard, unique concern. Adultery therefore is never trivial and though we may forgive, if we love, we cannot cease caring."[29]

In conclusion

The final returns are not yet in. Many young people, in justifiably rebelling against some of the hypocrisies and artificialities they see in the sexual mores of their parents' generation, are convinced that the new permissiveness—both before and after marriage—will improve the quality of their own lives in wedlock. I wonder. Life often has a way of mocking our most profound convictions and expectations. It would not surprise me if the verdict of the future were to be that the extreme embraced by some of today's youths produces as many maladjustments and mistakes as the opposite extreme against which they so vigorously rebel. Drs. Lunde and Katchadourian are among the experts of repute who share and confirm my doubt: "One would imagine that such intimacy would serve to screen out the more incompatible matches, but current divorce rates and the persistence of sexual problems in troubled marriages suggest that it does not."[30]

To wait or not to wait? The decision is yours. Not to make a decision is a decision in itself. If you are wise, you will ponder the material in chapters 11, 12 and 13—indeed in the entire book—as responsibly as you can. You will examine your own feelings honestly, observe the marriages of your parents and older friends, speculate on the kind of marriage and sex life you want eventually to have, consider the probable consequences of each alternative and adopt for yourself now a policy for the future. That policy will ever be open to new appraisal in the light of new knowledge and experience. The decision is yours, and you are the one who will have to live with it—you and your future mate . . . and your children.

For instance

A. Special to *The New York Times*
   Coral Gables, Fla., July 13
A policeman who was suspended this week for living with a woman to whom he is not married intends to fight in court the action by the chief of police.

Jeffrey W. Vance and four other police department employees were ordered by Police Chief William Kimbrough to end their cohabitant arrangements. Three policemen and a female police clerk obeyed the order, but Officer Vance refused and was suspended for 30 days without pay.

(*The New York Times*, 16 July 1974)

> Who is right in this dispute? What effect might Officer Vance's defiance have on young people in the community? Should a public official live on a standard of ethics different from that of others? Should a rabbi? Why?

B. Dan has been carrying on a heated discussion with his rabbi on the subject of the marriage ceremony. It began when the rabbi lectured to a group of college students on the Jewish wedding ritual. Dan was silent during the discussion period but later wrote his rabbi a letter of objection and has since met with the rabbi several times to exchange views further.

What bothers Dan is the idea that a few words spoken by a clergyman can make legitimate what would otherwise be improper. "What counts," he has insisted over and over again, "is not what ceremony two people expose themselves to, but whether or not they love each other. If they do, it is perfectly proper and right for them to live together. If they don't, no ceremony or ritual can make their life together good." He has also expressed the idea that wedding rituals have been invented by religious leaders throughout history, mainly in order to control people's lives. As far as he is concerned, when the time comes for him to settle down with the girl of his choice, a civil ceremony—or, for that matter, none at all—will suffice.

> How much of what Dan has said is correct? How much of it is mistaken? Why? Does the wedding ritual add

anything to the relationship between two people? Is there any difference between a religious and a civil ceremony?

C. Frank and Rose have never made a good sex adjustment in the six years of their marriage. From the beginning Rose had been willing to have sex relations with him only on rare occasions, and then seldom with real satisfaction to either of them. On most occasions when Frank suggested intercourse, she begged off because of a bad headache or being too tired. Usually for several days after such an episode they would either practically ignore each other or fight aggressively.

Several times Frank had suggested going together to see a marriage counselor, but Rose refused. Now he is just about at his wit's end. The last time they had an argument over sex, he really blew up—telling Rose that he had certain needs and, if she as his wife wasn't willing to meet them, he would find some other woman who would. Rose responded defiantly that he wouldn't dare, that if she ever found out he had gone to another woman she would disgrace him publicly and insist on a divorce.

Who is justified in this dispute? What seems to be the cause of their difficulty? Would more and better sex education for either of them have helped? What can they do now to help matters? What will be the probable effect on their marriage if Frank goes through with his threat? If he does nothing, just allowing things to go on as they have?

D. Gabe has experienced full sex relations with several girls. He has never really been in love but feels confident that when the time comes he will not regret what he has done. "I feel," he has said, "that it's better for me to have had this kind of opportunity before I meet the girl I'll some day marry. After all, how could I know otherwise what intercourse is supposed to be like or whether what I have with my wife is good? If I waited, I might never know what I had missed. This way I'll have a basis of comparison."

How valid is Gabe's argument? Suppose, on the basis of the comparison he mentioned, he decided later that his sex life with his wife was not as good as his previous adventures? With how many women would he have to participate in this kind of experience before he could be satisfied? Does his reasoning sound as if it would justify such comparisons only up to the point of his marriage?

E. As Helen approaches her wedding date, scheduled for a month hence, she finds herself becoming more and more apprehensive, especially about the sexual side of marriage. She is a virgin and glad of it but wishes she knew a little more about sex. Her parents have never really told her much; she had been too embarrassed to ask questions either of them or her married friends.

Under these circumstances she is really glad that Jeff, her groom, has had experience in such matters. She is confident she can depend upon him to teach her everything he knows. "How much more embarrassed I would be," she has thought to herself, "if neither of us knew anything. I would certainly never want Al to have intercourse with any other woman after we're married but I'm rather pleased that he already has."

How might Helen's apprehension and embarrassment have been prevented? Is she correct in believing that it is better for Jeff to teach her what he knows from experience than for the two of them to learn together? Why? How valuable will his previous experience be in their marriage?

F. Since Steven entered college and joined a fraternity, he found himself deeply troubled over ideas about sex he had previously taken for granted. Judging from the conversations of his fraternity brothers, he seemed to be just about the only one in the house who was still celibate.

The young biology instructor to whom he had gone for advice encouraged him to experience intercourse. "It isn't natural," he said, "to repress your sexual urges. Wherever we look in the animal kingdom, we see that the young male begins to have intercourse as soon as he is biologically ready for it. After all, we human beings are animals too. We can't fight nature, and the need to satisfy our sexual desires is a part of nature. A man who doesn't have intercourse before marriage builds up so strong a sex need that his wife will never be able to satisfy him. As a result, he is less likely to remain faithful after marriage than if he had indulged. So my advice to you is to stop trying to be the exception that proves the rule."

> How good was this advice? Why? Was the instructor correct in his comparison of men and animals? Is it true that satisfaction of our sexual desires is a part of nature? Were any factors of importance omitted by the instructor? Is it true that abstinence before marriage decreases the probability of faithfulness after marriage?

G. Aaron agrees that there is no justification for the double standard in sex behavior. Yet he disagrees with our discussion in this chapter. It is his contention that the single standard for both sexes should be a permissive one; that is to say, both men and women should be allowed to have whatever sex affairs they wish before marriage. He has, as a matter of fact, been urging this on his current girl friend. He says that, despite the lack of real love between them, they both feel physically aroused when they are together and he sees no reason why they should not meet each other's needs. Since neither of them has had intercourse before, there need be no fear of disease. Since they are both intelligent college graduates, they should be able to protect the girl against pregnancy. He concedes frankly that the two of them do not have enough in common culturally or emotionally to make marriage reasonable, but to him this is no reason they shouldn't give each other pleasure for the time being in the one area they do seem to share.

> How intelligent is Aaron's attitude? What are some of the possible or even probable consequences if his girl agrees? Which is preferable: a double standard or a single standard such as Aaron suggests? Why? Would he and his girl be more or less likely to marry each other if she acceded? What effect would the course of action he is urging have on a future marriage of either of them to someone else?

H. Judging from the conversation of his friends, Martin seems to be the only boy in the crowd who has not yet experienced intercourse. For some time now two of them have been urging him to go with them to a house of prostitution. Their argument is that this way no one gets hurt. There is no worry about having to marry a girl one doesn't love, no fear of giving a girl the impression that you want to become involved with her and no danger of contracting a venereal disease because certainly professional prostitutes know how to protect their own health. His friends are sure, as a matter of fact, that these girls get regular medical examinations.

How sure can Martin be that he is the only celibate among his friends? If he is, who is more mature—he or they? Who is more a man? How valid is each of the arguments given to Martin by his two friends? What other factors, not mentioned by them, should he take into consideration? Why?

I. "Unloving intercourse in marriage, though socially countenanced, is unethical whereas loving intercourse outside of marriage, though society still claims to disapprove of it, is right and proper." (This is a statement, not necessarily of the author's personal opinion, but expressing the view of those who support intercourse on the level of love.)

Would you mark the above statement (Borowitz, *Choosing a Sex Ethic,* p. 77) true or false? For what reasons?

J. Linda and Matthew have been dating for two years and have been engaged for eleven months. During all that time they have talked frequently about how far to go in their petting and at what point to stop. Neither has ever had intercourse; both have felt they wanted to save this for their married life together.

It is now just three weeks prior to their wedding. They have gone together for a weekend skiing trip and, after a day in the snow, a delicious dinner and a couple of drinks before a glowing fire, are ready to retire for the night. Linda is surprised to. hear herself suggesting to Matthew that they should spend the night together. "We've waited a long time," she says to him. "We know that we love each other, that we want to belong to each other for life. Is three weeks really going to make that much difference? Will a few words spoken by the rabbi and his name on a piece of paper change how we feel about each other? Why doesn't our love and our engagement make anything right now that will be right three weeks from now?"

What should they do? Why? Would the situation be any different if Matthew rather than Linda had made the suggestion? Is Linda correct in saying that a ceremony and signature are less important than their love for each other? Will their future happiness together be in any way affected by the decision they make now?

K. Three years ago Louise experienced the only sexual indiscretion of her life. She had been dating Charlie for nearly a year when one romantic night, before either of them realized what was happening, their petting had resulted in intercourse. It was an extremely distasteful episode for her, one which she resolved never to repeat. And she had kept her resolution with both of the boys she had dated since then, including Allan to whom she is now engaged. She has told him nothing of the earlier event nor of the fact that she had become pregnant but, with the help of a nurse she knew, had an abortion early in her pregnancy.

As the date of her wedding to Allan approaches, she finds herself increasingly troubled by a dilemma. Shall she tell him or not? If she does, she is afraid she may lose him. If she does not, will she be able to live with herself and to feel that she has been honest with her husband? Though she has been a calm kind of person most of her life, lately she hasn't been able to sleep well because of this worry.

What should Louise do? Why? What will be the probable consequences of keeping this episode to herself? Of telling it to Allan? Is there a perfect solution?

L. Andrew is the first boy who has seemed really interested in Beth. They have had half-a-dozen dates together and only now, in her senior year at high school, is she beginning to overcome the feelings of inferiority and rejection she felt in the past because she was so seldom asked out on dates.

But lately there has been trouble between them. Andrew has been insistent on petting. Beth has said it's all right for him to put his arm around her if he wants to and a good-night kiss is also permissible, but "nothing below the neck, Andrew, that's final!" His answer has been that Beth is being unfair. "What do you think this is," he has demanded, "the Middle Ages? For crying out loud, every guy I know messes around with his girl on dates. Am I supposed to be the only one with no rights?"

Their last argument on the subject took place two weeks ago. Since then, Andrew hasn't asked her for another date. Tonight, however, he called, and they are to be together again Saturday. Beth is positive the subject of petting will come up again. She hasn't changed her firm resolve but is afraid that, if she persists in refusing him, this may be the end of their relationship. To go back, after the fun of the last few months, to the lonely weekends she formerly experienced would be dreadful.

What should Beth do? Is Andrew being fair to her? Is she being fair to him? Will giving in to him assure her of his continued interest in dating her? Will persistence in refusing mean no more dates with him? If so, should she risk it? If she gives in to him, what is their future relationship apt to be like? If she does and they continue to see each other, what kind of marriage would they have?

14

"I thought I had made it quite clear, Rodney . . . my career comes first!"

New
trends
... and newer

There should be no need to argue at length that we live at a time of unprecedentedly rapid change. This is true in every area of experience and is at times so frightening that one competent commentator has labeled our reaction to it "future shock." We would be blind not to recognize that sex and marriage cannot be immune from the radical changes we confront generally. Indeed, we have already dealt with one aspect of this in talking earlier about the so–called sexual revolution. But there are other respects too in which we must reckon with the fact that marriage and the family as you are likely to know them a few years from now will probably differ a great deal from what they have been in the past.

One important indication that this will be so may be found in the women's liberation movement, a thrust to change the image and self–image of women in our society. Before turning in some detail to the aims of this movement, let's have a look at the status of women in Judaism. In doing so, it would not be fair to judge the attitudes and actions of our ancestors only by the standards of today. There are many respects, as we shall soon see, in which they did not give women all the credit and respect due them. Yet ancient Judaism was far superior in this respect to other cultures of the time. Aristotle, for example, called women "deficient males." All that a Moslem had to do to divorce his wife was to repeat three times before witnesses: "I hereby divorce you." The early Christian Church also denigrated the importance and role of women.

While the role of women in traditional Judaism was nowhere near what today's advocates of women's liberation would approve, it was noticeably superior to that of other contemporary civilizations. The ambivalence of the Jewish view can be traced all the way back to the story of creation in Genesis. As far as the origins of humanity are concerned, there are two such stories, one related in Genesis 1:26–31, the other in 2:18–24. According to the first account, man and woman were created simultaneously and equally: "And God created man in His image, in the image of God He created him; *male and female He created them.*" In the second story, woman is brought into being almost as an afterthought and for the comfort and convenience of man. After observing that "it is not good for man to be alone," God decides to "make a fitting helper for him. . . . So the Lord God cast a deep sleep upon the man and he slept; and He took one of his ribs and closed up the flesh at that spot. And the Lord God fashioned into a woman the rib that he had taken from the man, and He brought her to the man." In a similar vein, the first sin in the Garden of Eden is blamed primarily on woman. For this, her punishment is:

Yet your urge shall be for your husband,
And he shall rule over you.

Just as the two creation stories are inconsistent in their evaluation of women, so in following Jewish thought through subsequent centuries it is easy to find evidence on both sides of the question. The Talmud describes a woman who complained to Rabbi Judah that her husband had treated her abominably. The rabbi is reported to have responded: "Why are you different from a fish? You have no more right to complain against your husband's treatment than the fish has a right to object to the manner in which it has been cooked."[1] Not very flattering, to say the least!

There are other examples of the same sort. Rabbinic law prohibits a man from marrying a woman whom he has not seen lest he later find her repulsive. No such restriction was imposed on a woman, however, for "no matter how ugly and repelling the husband may turn out to be, she will surely be satisfied since to be married to a man, be he ever so loathsome, is better than to remain a spinster."[2]

Perhaps the most unacceptable of all such denigrations is the blessing pronounced every morning by traditionally observant Jewish males:

בָּרוּךְ אַתָּה יְיָ אֱלֹהֵינוּ מֶלֶךְ הָעוֹלָם שֶׁלֹּא עָשַׂנִי אִשָּׁה

Baruch Atah Adonai, Eloheinu Melech ha'olam, shelo asani ishah.
"Praised be the Eternal our God, Ruling Spirit of the universe, who did not make me a woman." It is quite probable that in origin these words reflected an assumption of male superiority, even arrogance. Before jumping to hasty conclusions, however, we should observe that this blessing bothered many of our medieval commentators who proceeded to mitigate its harshness. They said that the man who thanked God for making him a male was no more downgrading women than the כֹּהֵן kohen, the priest, who voiced gratitude for having been made a priest, meant to disparage others.

In both cases, we are told, the concept of מִצְוָה mitzvah—of special religious responsibility—is involved. For the faithful Jew a מִצְוָה mitzvah, while of course entailing extra obligation and burden, gives one the privilege of serving God in special ways. The priest expressed appreciation for the fact that he was permitted to perform מִצְווֹת *mitzvot* (pl. of *mitzvah*)be-yond those assigned to other Jews; this did not mean that he judged himself to be innately superior to them. Similarly, our rabbis insisted, men were grateful for the fact that they had to fulfill certain מִצְווֹת *mitzvot* of which women were absolved because of other important responsibilities. It would be unreal-istic to deny that there must have been men who, from time to time, misinterpreted this formula to imply male superiority. Judaism at its best, however, was almost as uncomfortable with any such notion as we are today.

So much so that during the Middle Ages, when many women began for the first time to read the entire morning service, the following blessing was prescribed for them while their menfolk recited their special words:

בָּרוּךְ אַתָּה יְיָ אֱלֹהֵינוּ מֶלֶךְ הָעוֹלָם שֶׁעָשַׂנִי כִּרְצוֹנוֹ

Baruch Atah Adonai, Eloheinu Melech ha'olam, she'asani kirtzono.
"Praised be the Eternal our God, Ruling Spirit of the universe, who has made me according to His will." If Judaism had been unequivocally antagonistic to women and their rights, either they would have been forbidden from full participation in public worship or no attempt would have been made to pro-vide alternate wording for them.

Evidence of the favorable attitude toward women to be found in our tradition is the fact that two books of our Bible are named after women, that the Matriarchs and Moses' sister Miriam are assigned major roles in the biblical narrative, that the Talmud enumerates forty–eight male and seven female prophets in the early stages of Jewish history.[3]

Regarding numerous incidents in the Torah, high praise is heaped by later commentators upon women. We are told that the faith of women during the Egyptian slavery exceeded that of men and that the Exodus from Egypt was granted as a reward for their righteousness.[4] According to an ancient *mid-rash,* before God gave the Torah in detail to the men at Sinai, He enunciated its basic principles to the women. Another *mid-rash* asserts that, when Aaron was about to make the Molten Calf, the women of Israel refused to contribute their golden jewelry for this purpose. It was only after the men had given theirs that Aaron was able to proceed. Later the women re-minded Moses of their virtue in this respect when he was at first reluctant to accept their gifts for the building of the wilderness sanctuary. Thus reminded, Moses acceded to their request and accepted their contributions.

When God decided in exasperation to destroy the Temple because of the people's repeated sins, tradition tells us that the Patriarchs, Moses and the prophets all interceded in vain. It was only after Rachel implored Him that He agreed eventually to bring His people back to the land they were about to lose.

In Judaism, woman's charity is judged to be more direct than man's,[5] her prayers are answered first[6] and she exercises the dominant moral influence on the family. To illustrate the latter truth, our rabbis told the following tale which the author has quoted previously.

> A pious couple lived together for ten years and, having no children, were divorced. The man married an impious woman and she transformed him into a man of wickedness. The pious woman married a man of wickedness and she transformed him into a man of goodness. Therefore the sages declare: "Woman determines man's behavior."[7]

I suppose that whether this be interpreted as privilege or burden depends, in the final analysis, on how important one judges the moral education of the family to be.

Women clearly suffered an inferior status in Jewish law and ritual observance. Yet, even here, much depends on the perspective and prejudice of the observer. Except for certain special cases, women were not accepted as witnesses in a trial[8] and did not inherit equally with their male siblings.[9] They were not expected to perform most of the daily religious duties or recite the many blessings assigned to men; they had to sit by themselves in a special section in the balcony of the synagogue. Here again, however, it is possible to interpret this kind of differentiation as either discrimination or privilege.

Most authorities on Judaism adopted the latter view. They agreed that it would be grossly unfair to hold women responsible for a complete schedule of duties which had to be performed at specific times during the day, thus conflicting with the needs and demands of their children. One modern observer summarizes this approach admirably in saying: "Not even an angel is given two missions simultaneously."[10]

If women were *prohibited* from performing the מִצְוֹת *mitzvot* incumbent upon men, that would be rank discrimination. The fact is, however, that they were *excused,* not *prohibited.* The distinction was clear to a medieval commentator:

> We do not prevent women from reciting the blessing over the *lulav* and the *sukah.* The fact that the Talmud says that women are free from positive commandments that are fixed by time means merely to specify that they are not in duty bound to obey those commandments, but, if a woman desires to fulfill these commandments, she may do so and we do not prevent her. . . .[11]

Even so brief a summary as this should not be concluded without reviewing our discovery in an earlier chapter that Judaism was sensitive to the sexual needs and rights of women long before other cultures had achieved this kind of insight. In this respect, the women's liberation movement now is still struggling for understandings accepted by our tradition long centuries ago.

It would be foolish to pretend that Jewish tradition extended full equality to women. Much improvement is still needed. In each period of history, however, our heritage treated women more fairly than other cultures of the time. And it includes insights which can still guide us as we strive for further justice on behalf of women.

And today?

Jewish thought is dynamic on this as on most other matters of importance. The institution of בַּת מִצְוָה *bat mitzvah* ceremonies can be cited as an example. True, in some congregations, there is an implied inferiority in the fact that girls celebrate their *bat mitzvah* rites at a different time and with a somewhat different format from that followed by their brothers. Elsewhere, the equality is complete; boys and girls celebrate בַּר מִצְוָה *bar mitzvah* and בַּת מִצְוָה *bat mitzvah* together on Shabbat morning, observing procedures which are identical.

Along with other religions, Judaism confronts a theological difficulty in that God is always referred to as He or Him. Where many ancient religions believed in female gods—conceived the Essence of all being, the Creative Force within all reality, to be womanly—we in the Western world have always assumed Divinity to be male. Almost inevitably, little children come to feel as a result that maleness is stronger, more powerful, more estimable than femaleness.

Is there any way in which this dilemma can be resolved? Should we refer to God both as He and She? As It?

In Reform and many Conservative congregations today women are counted in the מִנְיָן *minyan,* the quorum needed for a public worship service, and are called to the pulpit for עֲלִיּוֹת *aliyot* during the Torah service. Several rabbis have created rituals for welcoming a girl–child into the family shortly after her birth, parallel to the בְּרִית מִילָה *berit milah,* the circumcision ceremony, for boys. As this is being written, a half-dozen women have been ordained rabbis, several serve as cantors and quite a few are currently studying for both professions. In the early 1970s a poll conducted by the Union of American Hebrew Congregations revealed that 19 percent of congregational board members in Reform congregations were women, that five congregations had elected women as their president and twenty–eight had chosen them as vice president. While far from perfect equality, all this is evidence that contemporary Judaism is resolving whatever ambivalence afflicted the tradition by moving toward the aims and goals of the women's movement.

What, in brief, are those goals and aims? Basically, to eliminate all denigration and prejudice—both direct and subtle—against women in our society. A moment's reflection will show how pervasive this prejudice actually is. By and large, women are not hired proportionately for prestigious positions nor are they paid the same salaries as men for comparable work. A single woman, even if she is wealthy or earns a very high income, often has difficulty in obtaining a mortgage or other forms of credit. Men are often unaware of their prejudices against women. The first edition of this book was criticized in this respect by several of my female students; the suggestions made by one of them have been incorporated in this revision.

Much of the bias against women in our society can be traced to the notion that a woman is a defective or uncompleted man. Freud and his early followers spoke of "penis envy," the resentment of even very young girls that they lack an important and visible organ which their brothers and fathers possess. Even this view is recognized by many experts today as an example of male domination and arrogance. Why should a woman be considered inferior for lack of a penis any more than a man because he doesn't have a vagina, ovaries or fully developed breasts?

Indeed, many psychiatrists and psychologists are convinced that much that is irrational and prejudicial in male behavior can be attributed to "womb envy," to the fact that men feel inferior because they cannot become pregnant or give birth to a child. Women are not defective men. Men are not defective women. Those men and women are defective who refuse to accept themselves for what they are and to develop their unique potentialities.

Like every movement of protest, the cry for women's liberation can be extreme to the point of being ridiculous.

In early 1978 a Norwegian woman, an active feminist, refused to accept a blood transfusion from a male donor. This was scarcely less prejudiced than the bias of whites who have rejected transfusions of blood taken from blacks. When a prominent leader of the movement complains that "pregnancy is barbaric" or when women seem to express resentment or denial of the differences between men and themselves, one must be suspicious of their real motives. There are, after all, undeniable anatomical and physiological distinctions between females and males. In all probability, these cause emotional distinctions, too, though certainly not to the extreme degree emphasized in our culture. The legitimate aim of the women's liberation movement should be—without wishing such differences out of existence—to work for equal prestige and rights.

This has had and will have important consequences in marriage and family life. The sharp, almost unbridgeable distinction between the roles of men and women in our homes which prevailed until recently can no longer be maintained. Increasing numbers of women will have careers. Men will share—they already do—in the tasks of diapering and otherwise caring for babies, of marketing, of cooking, of house cleaning. Parents will no longer limit the play of little boys to erector sets, of little girls to dolls. Nor will they try to condition their sons to be independent and aggressive, their daughters to be submissive and docile.

Our culture has exaggerated and distorted the real differences which undoubtedly exist between the sexes. Many people have the foolish notion that it is inappropriate for a woman to seek a career, to enter politics, to demonstrate leadership skills outside her home; or for a man to show tenderness, to be sensitive and gentle, to cry when he is emotionally aroused. All this is nonsense. To the degree that it has helped erase such nonsense, the women's liberation movement has helped men also to remove blinders and shackles which have prevented them from being whole human beings.

We must be careful, however, lest women do what too many men have done in the past: use ambition and careers as an excuse to neglect their children. A woman who finds important work to do beyond her domestic responsibilities in order to fulfill herself and realize her potential is following a pattern which is wholesome and healthful. But a woman who frantically strives to be successful in public life as an escape from her husband, her children and her home is deceiving herself, pursuing a path which will yield no more happiness than the old way which she has properly rejected. When both husband and wife embark upon careers, they must share their home responsibilities in such manner that their children can enjoy the companionship of both parents and can look up to models of femininity and masculinity to help them grow into adulthood.

It has been suggested by some leaders of the women's liberation movement that married couples should so arrange their schedules that each can spend about half the week advancing a career, the other half taking care of their children and home. The fact must be faced, however, that only in a very limited number of jobs or professions is such an arrangement possible. The vast majority of husbands and wives will probably be unable to achieve so mathematically exact a division of domestic and external responsibilities.

Women sometimes make the mistake of contrasting the monotony and boredom of their chores to the apparent excitement of their husband's careers. Very few men, however, are so fortunate as to enjoy careers marked only by work they enjoy. The ideal—for both sexes—is to fulfill oneself with creative and exciting labor. Very few of us, however—in either sex—realize this ideal fully. Much of the work to be done by both men and women is drab and dull.

One additional word about working wives: One of the goals of the women's liberation movement has been to help females in our society in their search for self–identity. In the past, too many women found their identity only through their husbands, each "the wife of" a businessman, clergyman, physician or public official. When such a woman is widowed or divorced, she loses her identity. Just as most men need a vocation—a business or profession—to achieve self–identity, to know who they really are and to respect themselves, so many women sense the same requirement. The woman who is *only* a wife or mother during the early years of her marriage—however important these roles are and whatever success she attains in filling them—is inviting a painful vacuum into her life in later years when her children are grown and her husband is presumably at the height of his career. We have already referred to this in an earlier chapter.

Younger women can suffer this kind of gap in their lives, too. While their mates are rising in a career, becoming better known and more successful in their outside work, if the wives remain only at home—not growing, developing, expanding their minds and interests—the compatibility which existed between the two when they married can become dangerously diminished. After a while, they may find that all they really share aside from sex are the moments of crisis which come to their children.

When we spoke of compatibility in an earlier chapter, perhaps we should have included this kind of compatibility, too. A man who will feel uncomfortable about his wife's becoming successful in her career—possibly more successful than he is in his—has no business marrying a woman who wants very much to have a career. A woman should be as sure as possible before marrying that her future spouse's feelings about women's liberation are in agreement with her own. Any person who retains the stereotype that a husband should in every instance be stronger, more assertive, more dominant and successful than his wife had better be sure that these expectations jibe with those of a prospective mate.

The kibbutz experience in Israel has been instructive in defining the proper sex roles of men and women. When the kibbutzim were first founded, an effort was made to eliminate differences in work standards between men and women. They shared equally in all tasks: kitchen and housework, rearing of children, teaching, tractor work, heavy labor and so on. In the course of time, however, an interesting change took place. The women discovered that certain types of labor were physically too difficult for them. In addition, many menstruating women found it necessary to take a day or two off during their periods. And of course pregnant women had to take time off before and after delivering their babies. As a consequence, without consciously planning it so, little by little men and women began to assume the same kinds of tasks they had always performed in the past. There was, however, one exception: Some of the women were less happy than they had been before entering the kibbutz because, instead of performing a variety of household duties during the day, the organization of kibbutz life made it necessary for each to spend the entire day on one job which soon bored her.

Drs. Katchadourian and Lunde summarized the kibbutz experience regarding women's liberation in these words:

> The traditional roles of wife and mother cannot simply be abolished by decree. Despite technological advances, someone must still prepare food, care for children and so forth. It seems unfortunate that the values and rewards of such activities, particularly child rearing, have been awarded low status and prestige in our society. Furthermore, the value of many of the more public achievements of men has often been overrated whereas the importance of the father's role in the raising of children has been sorely neglected. Is flying to the moon really a greater achievement than raising a child in an atmosphere of loving concern? Which requires greater skills and patience? Which, in the long run, is most rewarding to the participants?[12]

Does the experience of women in the kibbutz mean that the old roles of men and women were correct after all? What differences are there in this respect between the kibbutz and our families? Can women take care of children better than men can? Are men basically more capable than women in executive positions? In business? As physicians or attorneys?

We ought not leave this subject without a further word of caution. There is nothing inferior or abnormal about a woman who prefers to follow the more traditional role which has historically characterized her sex—to be most essentially a wife, a homemaker, a mother. She has every right to make such a choice voluntarily. What we must resolutely reject is forcing women into that role, whether they want it or not.

Two examples can help us here. The story is told of a nineteenth-century chasidic rabbi who resolved to fast and stay awake a thousand nights studying Torah. His wife stayed awake with him, holding a candle so that he could see to study. One wonders whether she was not just serving as a martyr, not really fulfilling herself at all.

On the other hand, Mrs. Albert Schweitzer—wife of the renowned physician, theologian, and musician—once said: "It has been the joy and the pride of my life to follow and assist him in all his activities, and my one regret that failing strength prevented me from keeping pace with him." It is entirely possible for a husband and wife to share so fully in their joint interests and careers that both live creatively together.

Back to you

The women's liberation movement has also had an indirect effect on dating, a matter which is of more immediate concern to you. The roles of boys and girls in a dating situation are not as differentiated as they were formerly. A generation ago it was unheard of for a young couple to go "Dutch treat" on a date, that is, share the cost. The boy was always expected to pay for everything. Quite frequently today the cost is shared. Girls of high school and college age also seem to be more assertive, expressing their preference on places to go instead of leaving the decision entirely up to their male companions. This is all to the good. Incidentally, the women's movement has probably also had something to do with unisex clothing, with the fact that today, with boys and girls wearing similar clothing and hair styles, it is sometimes almost impossible at a quick glance to distinguish one sex from the other. Where the wearing of such attire comes from fear of acknowledging one's own sexuality, a desire to deny or repress very real sexual differences, it can be unwholesome.

While speaking of dating—though this will be a digression from the main topic of our chapter—a few words about dating behavior in general should be added.

There is a tendency for each young person to think he or she is the only one who feels somewhat clumsy and awkward in asking for or accepting a date. The fact is that such inner lack of confidence and poise is perfectly normal—"standard operating procedure," so to speak, for adolescent boys and girls. Many an engaged or married couple enjoy hearty laughter together in later years when comparing notes on their respective feelings during the early weeks or months of their dating experience. Each felt uncertain and insecure compared to what was assumed to be the assurance and complete confidence of the other. They later realized that they were equally awkward but saw this only in themselves. With experience in dating one develops greater security and poise.

One reason for the trepidation which often precedes a date is that the individual isn't quite sure of just what is expected. A few years ago, about eight thousand high school students were surveyed in an attempt to ascertain the qualities most desirable in a prospective date. Both boys and girls agreed overwhelmingly that they enjoyed most spending an evening with someone who is:

- physically and mentally fit,
- dependable and trustworthy,
- careful of personal appearance and manners,
- clean in speech and action,
- pleasant in disposition, with a sense of humor,
- considerate of others and
- able to act maturely, not childishly.

What are the traits, in the boys they had dated, of which girls in this survey complained most frequently?

1. Vulgar action and speech
2. Too anxious to neck and pet
3. Reluctant to give compliments
4. Careless manners and dress
5. Disrespect of the opposite sex.

And what were the complaints voiced most often by boys? That the girls they had dated were

1. too self–conscious and shy
2. too sensitive, too easily hurt
3. emotionally cold
4. too possessive
5. acting childish and silly.[13]

There is a temptation to wonder what connection there may be, if any, between the second complaint of the girls and the third expressed by the boys. What do you think? In any event, each sex, when confronted with the list compiled by the other, was in general agreement that the criticisms were fair.

In the years since this study on dating preferences was made, there have been significant changes. Most dating today seems to be much less formal than it was then. Certainly both language and apparel have changed. It might be a good idea, therefore, to revise the lists given above.

What are the qualities you like in a dating partner? To what characteristics do you particularly object? Do you prefer dating just with your partner or with one or more other couples? Why?

Since it is easier to agree in theory than to take concrete steps to improve the impression one gives on a date, let's try now to translate these valuable generalities into a few specific suggestions for your future dates.

Simple courtesy

It helps considerably if, at the very beginning, a boy asks for a date in a manner which indicates that he would really very much like to spend an evening with the girl he is inviting. If he has a specific place or occasion in mind, it should be mentioned; then the girl has all the facts on which to base her answer. He should, as much as possible, avoid asking her at the last minute, as if it were an afterthought or a last desperate try after having been turned down by someone else. If, for a legitimate reason, he was unable to make the invitation sooner, it would be wise to say why, honestly. When he has no particular party or program in mind and just wants to spend an enjoyable evening with a girl whom he likes, it will make things much more pleasant if he discusses with her what she might like to do or where she prefers to go.

Thus far, all the responsibility for courtesy seems to rest on the boy. Obviously, however, the girl's obligations are no less important. She owes it to the boy who has invited her to give him an answer as promptly as possible. If she must wait to consult her parents or find out whether or not tentative family plans are confirmed, she should tell him so and promise him an answer by a specific time. He is entitled to a direct *yes* or *no* answer at the earliest possible moment. It is unforgivable to keep a boy dangling in order to see whether a better offer turns up for that night, or to break a date already made in favor of one which seems more attractive. If the answer is yes, it should be given in a manner and voice indicating the girl really looks forward to spending the evening with him. If the answer is no, it should be as polite and considerate as possible. The only excuse for not telling the truth is that it might unnecessarily hurt someone. If the real reason a girl turns down a date is that she finds the fellow an insufferable boor or his company boring, kindness requires that she try not to be so specifically truthful as to hurt his feelings. A tactful *white lie* to spare another person may at times be justified; when it is meant to deceive or take oneself off the spot, it is never warranted.

Another dating area which calls for mutual consideration is the matter of money. How much should a boy be expected to spend on a date? That will depend, of course, on a number of things: on the occasion, on his overall financial condition, on his available cash at the moment. When two people know each other well and have dated before, they can discuss these things without embarrassment. When their relationship is not that close, the invitation itself will often provide a clue to how much the boy expects to spend. A bid to the senior prom obviously involves spending more money than an evening at the local movie. A girl who is asked out for dinner or taken for refreshments on the way home can estimate how much she is expected to spend, by the kind of place to which they have gone, and by waiting to see what the boy orders. If the choice of place is left up to her, she can tactfully suggest several at different price ranges, letting him make the final decision.

Sometimes, when a boy and girl know each other well and have dated frequently, they may wish to split the cost of an expensive date. No hard–and–fast rule can be made on this. If the two people involved feel comfortable about such an arrangement, there is no reason not to make it.

In other words, two people on a date should have mutual consideration and respect for each other as people. Neither one should just *use* the other. What we said earlier about the difference between I–It and I–Thou relationships applies to dating, too. A girl has no right to accept a date from a fellow whom she neither respects nor likes, just as a way of getting to a place or event she finds attractive. A boy should not date a girl whom he does not respect or like, just because it flatters his ego to be seen with her or in the hope of "making out."

Always parents

Often, dating creates tensions, not just between the two people most directly concerned, but also between one or the other of them and his or her parents. One way to reduce, if not altogether eliminate, such tension is to be honest with parents. True, some parents are unreasonable in their expectations, but most of them will respond with honesty and considerateness if they are approached in this spirit from the start. Parents have a right to know whom their child is dating and to meet the dating partners. This is obviously a problem more frequently involving the parents of the girl than of the boy. When a fellow comes to the home of his date for the first time, he should be introduced to her parents. A few minutes in which to get acquainted make a good prelude for the rest of the evening— but *a few minutes,* not longer; he didn't come to spend the evening with her parents!

Sometimes parents will strongly object to a particular boy or girl their daughter or son is dating. There is no sure and certain formula for such disagreements. Parents are not always right, but neither are they always wrong. Adolescent boys and girls are not always wrong, but neither are they always right. Each has an obligation to listen to what the other has to say, as calmly and objectively as possible. Remember: If your parents are right in objecting to a particular date, it is you who stand to lose most by defying them just for the sake of asserting your own will. And if they are wrong, your best chance of convincing them in the long run is by patient listening and courteous response.

How about parents who refuse to leave the room or the house when their son or daughter is entertaining either a single date or several couples? There would appear to be a deplorable lack of trust in any parent who insists on remaining in the same room with a dating high school student. But the fault could be on either side: The student could have shown by previous irresponsible conduct that he or she hasn't earned such trust; or the parent could be too strict. Most parents will have enough confidence in their children at this age to give them the privacy of a room in which to entertain a friend or friends.

The same thing does not apply, however, to vacating the house. There is no reason why parents should be expected to become exiles whenever a stay–at–home date is planned. A responsible son or daughter will be happy to have mom and dad in the house, perhaps even in the same room for part of the evening. But the privilege should not be abused. Thoughtful parents will act their age and allow young people as much freedom as they have shown a mature capacity to use.

Curfew can be a troublesome problem. The hour which is reasonable for a date to end depends on the age and maturity of the individuals involved, as well as on the occasion. There are always a few special occasions during the year when parents can afford to be flexible about time limits. The probability that your parents will understand this depends in part on how reasonable and cooperative you have generally been.

When youngsters play each other off against their parents—each insisting that *everybody else is permitted to stay out later* when in point of fact *everybody else* is saying the same thing—they are not being fair. When parents persist in applying to a high school senior a curfew appropriate for a fourteen–year–old, they also are less than just. In some communities parents and young people have cooperated to establish a schedule of curfews for various occasions. Whether on this basis, or just privately with your own parents, it is always wise to have a clear understanding of the time limit for each date. Both partners to the date should know their respective curfews. If unforeseeable and unavoidable circumstances prevent your getting home on time, every effort should be made to telephone your parents in order to spare them unnecessary worry. When two people have different curfews, the one with the later limit should be courteous enough to abide by the earlier time.

Another frequent bone of contention between parents and their adolescent offspring is the use of the family car. On this point we shall try to avoid either elaborating on the obvious or preaching a sermon. A car is not a toy; it is power. Like all power, it can be used for enormous good or immense evil. It can increase your pleasure in dating or it can kill or maim you and your passengers. This is not just theory. Almost every weekend in a large city the morning papers bear tragic testimony to some young person who knew *intellectually* that a car required extreme care but who was not *emotionally* equal to such responsibility. If you drive carelessly or too fast, if you use the car as a place for sex activities you would be ashamed to have your parents know of, you aren't being fair to them. If you have demonstrated a capacity for responsible behavior in other respects and in previous use of the car, yet your parents refuse to let you use it on dates (consistent with the needs of the rest of the family) they aren't being fair to you. Again, the answer to tension is mutual responsibility and respect.

We have already referred to the fact that alcoholic drinks lower one's self–control. They also slow down our reflexes—those speedy, almost–automatic reactions which we need in emergencies. A frightening proportion of serious collisions is due to the fact that a driver had been drinking. Each drink decreases the ability of even the most skilled driver to control the car. The person who values life will neither drive within an hour of having consumed any alcohol nor ride in a car if the driver has been drinking.

A few details about dating remain. There is, for example, the question of how frequently it is desirable for an individual to have dates. While no one answer will cover every person or every situation, as close as we can expect to come to, a general rule is to say: as often as is enjoyable and does not interfere with the health of the individual or with other commitments and responsibilities. It would be naive to expect parents and children always to agree on what that means specifically. But we repeat here, as we have said elsewhere: Your parents will be more inclined to see your point of view on this if you have shown yourself to be reasonable and responsible in other respects; you will be more moved to consider their point of view if they have been generally disposed to treat you with consideration. In most families these problems can be worked out without too much strain. If not, it often helps to call in someone whom both parents and youngsters can trust—an older, impartial relative—a camp counselor or teacher—perhaps your rabbi or doctor.

How about blind dates? They can be either good or bad. You should know the person who is arranging such a date; he or she should know both you and your prospective dating partner. Even then, it is wise for the first encounter to be at an informal house party or on a double or triple date. After that, you have a better basis on which to judge a person. And, of course, parents are just as entitled in the case of a blind date—perhaps even more so—to meet the unknown person as the evening begins.

A practical suggestion: If you and your parents have experienced trouble with regard to your dating pattern, it might be a good idea for you to read and discuss this chapter together.

No one else

Before we leave the subject of dating, one more very serious problem deserves our attention. A relatively recent phenomenon in the life of American young people is the practice of "going steady." We are aware of the fact that grammatically, the phrase should be "going steadily," but that seems to have acquired a somewhat different meaning—one degree less, we are told, than "going steady," which is one degree less than being pinned, which is one degree less than being engaged. So, in the interests of clear communication, we shall be deliberately ungrammatical. By "going steady" we mean the practice of a boy and girl dating each other exclusively—no dates with anyone else.

There are rather obvious reasons for the growth of this practice. The boy and girl involved may just discover they enjoy being with each other more than dating others. They may like the fact that they can save time and money because, not being new to each other, it is unnecessary to make an impression by going to fancy places. They may feel more secure knowing they can count on each other for dates rather than the boy's risking being turned down by other girls and the girl's waiting in vain for a boy to call her.

There are dangers involved, however, in going steady. When we talked in an earlier chapter about the stages of growth toward love, we mentioned the level on which one becomes quite generally interested in members of the opposite sex before narrowing oneself down to just one individual. To go steady too soon means either to detour around this development or to cut it short too quickly. It denies one the much needed opportunity to test the individual's ability to relate to different kinds of personalities before settling down with one alone.

Going steady also exposes young people to the risk of drifting, almost by inertia, into the wrong kind of marriage. After a boy and girl have dated each other exclusively for a long while, they are tempted to stop asking questions and to take each other and their relationship for granted. Even if they begin to develop doubts about each other, the boy may be reluctant to break off for fear that the girl, having been taken out of social circulation for so long a time, will be hurt more than he. A final danger is that a couple who spend all their dating time together increase the temptation to go farther than they intend sexually than if each is dating a variety of partners. All of which means that, while going steady has certain obvious advantages, there is a price to be paid too. Often in the long run that price by far outweighs what is gained.

So much for dating. Your ability to handle the normal problems of dating in general is a test of your maturity and of your readiness for the next stage, dating one particular boy or girl to the exclusion of all others. That, in turn, is the testing ground for the next step, engagement. And only one who has shown the ability to cope with the challenges and tensions of an engagement is ready for marriage.

Finally

Turning back to the main concerns of this chapter—new trends and newer—a few more items should be covered before we conclude. Because of the widespread unhappiness they have seen among their married friends and the rapidly increased rate of divorce, some people seem ready to give up on marriage. A few have proposed substitutes, such as communes, group marriage, term marriage, two–stage marriage, mate swapping and "swinging." Some communes resemble Israel's kibbutzim; some involve the sharing of sexual mates, while others are as sexually monogamous as conventional marriages. Group marriages are those in which two or more couples unite, sharing sexual activity freely with all in the group. Term marriage refers to the proposal that initially a couple should agree to marry for a specified number of years—one, three, five, or whatever total is agreeable. If, at the end of that period, they no longer wish to remain together, there would be no legal obstacle or financial penalty involved in their separating. If both agree that the trial has been successful, they could renew their relationship permanently or for another specified time span.

Margaret Mead, the well–known anthropologist, has proposed a two–stage marriage. Couples would at first agree to live together tentatively and to have no children. Separation during this stage would be simple and easy, requiring no further financial or legal responsibility of either party for the other. Before such a couple conceived a child, they would move to stage–two marriage, which would be the equivalent of marriage as we know it now.

Mate swapping means that, for purposes of sexual variety, two or more couples agree openly to have intercourse with each other's spouses. The term "swinging" refers to a group of individuals—single or married—who get together on a specific occasion with the intent of having an orgy, of experimenting sexually, then mating off with anyone in the group who is agreeable.

Some of these cure–alls for the ills of marriage are not so new as their supporters may think. The Talmud, for example, condemns those who "ate and drank in company, put their couches together, exchanged wives and contaminated their couches with alien semen."[14] What may be new is that people are writing and talking about such forms of behavior more openly than they did in the past.

Though enthusiasts can be found to support any of these radical forms of behavior, there is reason to doubt whether any of them can replace marriage. By reviewing our earlier comments about the family and about the highest meanings of sex in human life, it isn't too difficult to conclude that none of the experiments described above is likely to meet our most basic human needs or give us more happiness in the long run than a good marriage.

My own opinion, after reading a great deal about these suggestions, is that it is not marriage that has failed, but men and women who marry too hastily, too thoughtlessly or too much on impulse. Judging only from newspaper reports and statistics of divorce, it is easy to conclude that happy marriages don't exist anymore. Such a conclusion, in my judgment, would be premature and grossly inaccurate. Couples who are happily married are seldom described in the press nor are they likely to be among the respondents to surveys and questionnaires. I do not mean to minimize the many failures in marriage. Indeed, a major purpose of this book is to prevent such failures for its young readers. But I remain convinced that—given reasonably mature individuals who are adequately compatible with each other, whose expectations are realistic and who are willing to put as much effort into their life together as they give to their vocations and similar enterprises—marriage still offers us our best hope to satisfy human need and fulfill human expectations.

One of many pieces of evidence which attest to the fact that it is people who fail, not marriage as an institution, comes from a study of "swinging" done by a couple who are generally favorable to this kind of sexual experimentation. Yet their research shows that, of "swinging" couples in their first marriage, 83 percent had married between the ages of seventeen and twenty–one, 9 percent between the ages of fifteen and seventeen.[15] Quite probably the only thing such couples really had in common was sex; and, when this is the one major bond, it is almost inevitable that sooner or later one or both partners will restlessly seek erotic variety. After carefully studying the women involved in "swinging" groups, the authors conclude:

> In general, these were bored, often frustrated women who lacked the ability to generate joy and stimulation with themselves or from their world.[16]

We would be remiss in not recognizing that the world in which we live today has also had an impact on marriage. In an earlier chapter we noted that the tensions, fears and frustrations of our social order impel more than a few young people toward early marriage for relief or escape. These social conditions continue to haunt them even after they are wedded. Couples do not live in a nest, isolated from the larger world. Political corruption, economic insecurity, frequent moves from city to city at the direction of an employer, periodic military conflicts, doubts as to whether human life is governed by any purpose or value—all these and a host of additional pressures threaten our individual well–being and the stability of our marriages. Two persons coupled in a good marriage provide solace and strength for each other when life seems almost too much for them. A man and woman who should never have married in the first place use their mates as scapegoats for the relief of intolerable tensions.

Much depends also on the expectations people bring to their marriages. Where either partner is seeking a parent–substitute, an adult mommy or daddy who will soothe all pains, salve all hurts, solve all problems—as our real parents seemed to do for us when we were infants—the prognosis cannot be good. If either uses the other, consciously or unconsciously, as a means of meeting personal needs, failing to see marriage as a symbiotic relationship in which the needs of both must be mutually satisfied, the result will most probably be bad.

Too many marriages fail. I would venture a prediction, however, that most men and women who have failed in marriage will, in the long run, be no more successful in group marriages or communes, with term marriages or "swinging" parties. I still believe that the right kind of marriage, involving properly matched individuals, offers us—and our children—the best prospect for happiness.

In a previous chapter we turned our attention to the problems confronting children of a divorced couple. The great increase in recent years of our divorce rates, a small but probably growing number of unmarried persons who wish to be parents and the loss of a mate—all these have combined to expand the number of single–parent homes in the United States today. One rabbi has told me that close to a quarter of the students in his religious school live in such homes.

If—for any of the reasons detailed above—you happen to come from a single–parent home, you don't need to be told that there are problems. All other things being equal, it is best for a child to live in the presence of two parents, to have constant contact with both male and female models to aid in his or her own sexual development. The absence of one parent, however, need not be a catastrophe. A wise, mature, loving mother or father can do much to compensate for the absence of a father or mother in the home. So can understanding relatives and friends. It is more than possible for the child of a single-parent home to receive a kind and quantity of love which will enable him/her to become fully and healthfully developed as an adult. If these remarks fit you and you feel the lack of living with both your parents, why not find someone—your rabbi, physician, teacher, camp counselor, friend—with whom you can openly and confidentially talk about your anxieties?

How realistic?

From a book by two writers who recognize how widespread bad marriages are in the United States, I have selected and adapted the following as some of the assumptions and expectations people often bring to their marriages.[17] Which are realistic? Which are wishful thinking? Are there others you think should be added?

- Marriage means total commitment of two people to each other.
- In marriage each partner is individually responsible.
- Husbands and wives should satisfy all of each other's needs.
- Husbands and wives belong to each other.
- There is never serious conflict in a good marriage.
- If either husband or wife feels sexually attracted to another person, this means their marriage is not good.
- Sexual fidelity is a true measure of love.
- The ultimate goal of marriage is to have a child or children.
- Sacrifice is a true test of love.
- The less two people change after they marry, the greater is the probability of their continuing to love each other.

Close to home

How would you evaluate your parents' marriage? In what respects have they succeeded? In what ways have they failed? How much do you really know about their marriage? Would you be satisfied to have a similar marriage yourself?

For instance

A. Richard has invited some business associates for dinner. Before his marriage to Gwen, while working for two years in the Paris branch of his firm, he learned to cook a few French specialties. He would like to prepare and serve one of them to his friends, but Gwen complains: "How will it make me look if you cook dinner? Our guests will think I am incompetent." Though Richard really enjoys cooking, for the sake of marital peace he gives in. His creativity is squelched, Gwen's image is preserved and the guests get roast lamb.[18]

Who was right and who wrong in this incident? After reading it, what do you know about Richard and Gwen? About their marriage?

B. Ann has been married for ten years to an advertising executive who has few interests outside his job. She feels frustrated because of Fred's objections to her taking singing lessons. "Because Fred couldn't stand to hear me practice, I was always self–conscious about singing. He complained all the time—I think he would have complained even if I had sung like Leontyne Price. Not only that, but he objected to my rehearsing evenings with the little theater group. Why? He thought that as a wife I should be at home with him all the time. He didn't like to be alone. Well, I can tell you it was certainly *complimentary* to me that he wanted me around all the time. But how many compliments do I need? I can't grow on them."[19]

What justification is there, if any, for Fred's feelings? For Ann's? Do you think Fred would have been satisfied if Ann did all her practicing during the day while he was at the office? If the little theater group held all its rehearsals in the afternoon? What solution would you suggest?

C. Fran wants to "do her thing." She finds marriage humiliating and confining. The fact that Greg spends his days doing fascinating things, meeting interesting people and advancing himself in his vocation, while she has to spend so many hours cleaning the house and caring for their children, bothers her a great deal.

On his part, Greg doesn't object to Fran's pursuing a hobby or even some kind of part–time work if she wishes to. But he insists that her first responsibilities must be to maintain their household and see to their kids. He would like to be able to help her in these tasks, but his work requires him to be out of the house at least ten hours every day, and he is dead tired when he gets back in time for dinner.

Fran says: "Thanks a bunch. All you're doing is giving me the privilege of taking on a third job after I run myself ragged on what you think should be my first two."

Things have finally reached the point where Fran has asked

for a divorce. She intends to adopt a career, the only way she feels she can fulfill herself as a woman. She will either get someone to take care of the children during the day or will send them to a day care center. "No more of this slavery called marriage for me," she says. "From now on, I'm going to be my own person!"

> Should Fran and Greg have married in the first place? Is it true that being a housewife and mother is "humiliating and confining"? Can one have a career and be a good mother? What solution can you suggest for this couple?

D. Suppose, in the case of Fran and Greg above, Greg were to say: "Okay, you have a point. From now on, I'll go to the office every day until one o'clock while you stay home. From one o'clock on, I'll take care of the children and the house while you do whatever kind of outside work you want to do. On weekends, each of us will be responsible for the domestic front one day."

> Does this strike you as a sensible solution? Why? How would it affect their marriage? Their economic situation? Their children?

E. Kevin and Amy are in their final year of graduate study— he as an engineer, she as a social worker. They are both applying in various parts of the country for positions. Among the possible courses of action they have discussed are the following: (1) he will locate first, then she will narrow her search to the same city; (2) she will take a position first, after which he will consider offers only in the same area; (3) whichever one receives the most promising and lucrative opportunity will take it, the other accommodating to that priority; (4) the first one to receive a viable choice will accept it, then the other will consider offers only in that community and (5) each will take the most attractive opportunity he or she receives, they will live apart for a year, commute to spend as much time as they can together and later try to find a permanent solution.

Which of these proposals seems best to you? Why? What are the probable consequences of each solution? Can the needs of both Kevin and Amy be met?

F. Proverbs, chapter 31, is read on Shabbat evening traditionally by observant Jewish husbands in praise of their wives. Read it carefully, then evaluate it as a tribute to women.

For what does it praise them? What does it fail to say? Do you think it should still be a part of Shabbat observance in Jewish homes? Why? Should it be accepted by the women's liberation movement? Why?

15

"You know what I wish? I wish I belonged to a species that got a new mate every season!"

The
stakes
are high

Let us examine, now, the question of mixed marriages. This term refers to any marital partnership in which husband and wife come from different backgrounds, either racially or religiously: Black and White, Protestant and Catholic, Caucasian and Oriental, Christian and Jew. For present purposes we shall limit ourselves largely to the last of these, marriages in which one partner is Jewish and the other is not. If one of them converts before marriage to the religion of the other, this is no longer considered a case of mixed marriage.

The main stream of Jewish tradition has always been opposed to mixed marriage. We see this even as long ago as in Bible days. When Abraham sent his faithful servant to find a wife for his son Isaac, he warned him: ". . . thou shalt not take a wife for my son of the daughters of the Canaanites, among whom I dwell. But thou shalt go unto my country, and to my kindred, and take a wife for my son. . . ."

Since Abraham gave no reason for this injunction, we can only guess about his motivation. The reasons become clear, however, when his preference is embodied as law in the book of Deuteronomy; there the reason is stated explicitly. The ancient Jewish people is told that when they come to the land which God has promised them and become acquainted with its inhabitants—"neither shalt thou make marriages with them: thy daughter thou shalt not give unto his son, nor his daughter shalt thou take unto thy son. For he will turn away thy son from following Me, that they may serve other gods."

From the very beginning, then, Jewish opposition to mixed marriage was based not on any notion of racial superiority but rather on realistic recognition of the fact that such matches posed an ominous threat to the survival of the Jewish people and its faith. Even as water always seeks the lowest level, the members of a small minority group intermarrying with the majority almost inevitably become assimilated, to the point of losing their original identity.

That this was indeed the biblical motivation for resisting mixed marriage is evident in two other books of the Bible. In the book of Ezra, general opposition to such marriages is voiced in the strongest possible terms, and those Jews who had already married Gentile wives were ordered to divorce them at once. This seems extraordinarily cruel, does it not? It reflects, however, a time of grave emergency. The Jewish people had just returned to Palestine from Babylonian exile. Ezra, their leader, found that so many of them had intermarried, and their attachment to people and faith was so weak that they were confronted with the very real, imminent danger of total disappearance. Therefore, he had to take stringent steps in an effort to reverse the tide and to insure Jewish survival.

The second biblical book may seem to contradict the emphasis of Ezra, until we inquire into its background. We refer here to the book of Ruth. Its heroine was a Moabite girl who married a Jewish man. There is no opposition to their marriage voiced in the book. In fact, Ruth became so cherished a figure in Jewish lore that she is believed to have been the ancestor of King David himself. A careful reading of her story will disclose three important differences from the situation facing Ezra. First, this is an instance of only *one* mixed marriage; not of so many that it became a prevailing pattern. Second, Ruth lived in a time when the Jewish people was not threatened by the possibility of total assimilation. And third, she embraced Judaism—following it faithfully during the lifetime of her husband and after his death. Her second husband too was a loyal Jew. Here, then, we see with utmost clarity that Judaism has not opposed mixed marriage out of sheer stubbornness, or because of a sense of racial superiority or pride, but because intermarriage jeopardizes Jewish survival.

Do our circumstances today resemble more closely those of Ezra or of Ruth? Unfortunately, the former. All studies of mixed marriage in the United States agree that, in the past generation, it has increased considerably. Research in the city of greater Washington showed that the rate of such marriages among Jews in the late 1950s reached 13.1 percent. As alarming as this statistic is, it becomes even more threatening when we consider that it represented an average of the *entire* Jewish community, and that *among third-generation Jews in Washington the rate had already reached 17.9 percent.* It was discovered, moreover, that in at least 70 percent of mixed–marriage families in Washington the children were not identified in any way with the Jewish people![1]

While the figures themselves undoubtedly vary from community to community, and there is still much to learn on this subject, there can be no doubt that the Washington pattern prevails throughout the country: the rate of mixed marriage is increasing, and the vast majority of children born of such marriages is lost to the Jewish people and Judaism. By 1980 the estimated rate of mixed marriage among Jews in some areas of the United States was as high as 40 percent! This becomes a matter of greater concern in light of the fact that the Jewish proportion of the total population in the United States has been steadily declining. In 1937 we were 3.7 percent of the whole, in 1963 only 2.9 percent. If present trends continue, it is estimated that by the year 2000 no more than 1.6 percent of the population will be Jews. Intermarriage is beyond doubt one of the factors accounting for this rapid decrease. Rabbi David Einhorn, one of the early leaders of American Reform Judaism, was more prophetic than he himself may have known when he wrote, nearly a century ago: ". . . intermarriage drives a nail in the coffin of Judaism."

But why Christians?

All this helps explain why Jews have been so strongly and at times bitterly opposed to mixed marriages. The interesting thing, however, is that Christians—who do not confront the same danger of group disappearance—are almost equally averse to it. In 1956 the General Conference of the Methodist Church declared that "recent research has emphasized the importance of common cultural and religious backgrounds as the foundation of successful marriage. It is important that Protestant youth discuss this problem with their ministers before it is too late. Ministers are urged to discuss with both youth and parents the likelihood of failure in mixed marriages."[2] Three years later the Lutheran Church Missouri Synod adopted a statement affirming that "religious agreement between a husband and wife is undoubtedly one of the major factors in securing that peace and harmony that makes possible the normal functions and development of Christian family life."[3]

These statements, so typical of many others that could be quoted from both Protestant and Catholic sources, indicate that another reason for opposition to mixed marriage is the decreased probability of happiness and success. It will be remembered from earlier chapters, that the more two individuals share common cultural background and values, the greater will be the odds favoring a happy marriage. In the next chapter we shall see that a shared religious experience can be one of the strongest positive factors producing marital happiness. In mixed marriages this positive possibility becomes, instead, a destructive one. This does not mean that every mixed marriage is doomed to failure, or that every marriage within a given religious group can count on success. What it does mean is that, in the delicate balance which determines the plus or minus of each match, mixed religious backgrounds are a serious hazard which frequently makes the difference.

The facts reveal this to be true. Whatever statistics we have indicate the divorce rate to be between three and four times higher among mixed–marriage couples than among others. In one of the earliest authentic scientific studies of marriage, Burgess and Cottrell concluded that the chance for success in marriage is eleven times greater where husband and wife agree on all religious matters than where they differ.

In an earlier chapter we made passing reference to an investigation made by the American Youth Commission. The following table, taken from that study, reflects the number of young people in several categories who were found to come from broken homes.

Both parents Jewish	4.6% from broken homes
Both parents Catholic	6.4% from broken homes
Both parents Protestant	6.8% from broken homes
Parents from mixed religions	15.2% from broken homes
Parents with no religion	16.7% from broken homes

For anyone who truly understands the meaning of marriage, this should not be difficult to understand. It must be remembered—with reference to Judaism perhaps even more than other religious traditions—that religion is more than just theological belief. It also involves attitudes toward the meaning of life, frames of reference regarding sex, patterns of family behavior, idioms and idiosyncracies of language, matters of food and holiday observance, and similar items. A Jew who is accustomed to celebrating Chanukah and Passover would find it extremely difficult to observe Christmas and Easter instead. A Christian who had always taken Communion in church might miss such a tradition painfully. There are many subtle yet vital patterns of each person's life—no less imperative for the fact that they may be taken for granted—the absence or disruption of which can pose a serious threat to personal security. Mixed marriage inevitably involves many of these.

There are also important differences in life–style and values between most Christians and most Jews. These include quite opposite evaluations of sex in general, of birth control and abortion in particular—differences which we have already discussed in detail. Fewer Jews than Christians indulge in premarital and extramarital sexual intercourse. As interesting as these divergencies are in theory, they can become more compelling and disturbing in a specific mixed marriage.

Typical of the conclusions reached by most experts on marriage, after careful study and observation, is the following, written by Dr. Clarence Leuba, professor of Psychology at Antioch College:

> In every marriage there are bound to be some outstanding differences in interests, attitudes and beliefs; but a marriage cannot stand too many of them. . . . Cultural, religious or racial differences are of this sort; they are likely to have far–reaching effects on marital adjustments. . . . Where the marriage partners come from different religions, economic, political or social backgrounds, there are endless possible sources of irritation.[4]

Heart of the problem

The point of greatest possible dispute in mixed marriage is the future of a couple's children. This is also the most serious source of grief. A child's most desperate need is the security of knowing where he or she belongs. Children born to a couple of mixed religious background are not likely to know this security. They will probably be made to suffer certain disadvantages by virtue of the fact that one parent is Jewish— wondering all the while why they cannot be identified instead with the other who is not Jewish—oblivious to the positive pride which comes from knowledge of Judaism and which can serve as an effective antidote to painful prejudice.

I remember a woman who came to me some years ago, insisting that I convert her to Judaism before she would be willing to marry her Jewish suitor. Her vehemence elicited considerable curiosity about her motives. After insistent questioning, she finally responded: "Rabbi, I am myself the product of a mixed Catholic–Protestant marriage. I know in my own blood and bones the terrible uncertainty and perplexity which afflict such a child. Under no circumstances would I ever cause such pain to any child of mine. This is why I insist that my marriage must be based on a religiously unified home!"

In addition to the insecurity already discussed, where religious unity is not achieved, there is also a probability that somewhere along the line the children will become ropes in a tug–of–war; if not between their parents, then perhaps between competing grandparents. It is extremely difficult for two families of divergent religious loyalties not to press their respective points of view, however subtly, upon their children. The love between husband and wife must be extremely strong and almost superhumanly mature to survive such potential competition. This is often the straw that breaks the camel's back of marital happiness. And the result—more often than we would like to contemplate or admit—is a confused, neurotic child.

Sometimes even intelligent parents deceive themselves on this score. While they act as if all the problems posed by interfaith marriage have been solved, their children reveal the truth; in erratic behavior when they are young, or in confidential conversation with trusted advisors when they reach high school or college age. It is not uncommon for a clergyman, psychiatrist, or college professor to hear from the children of such marriages that they detected the religious differences between their parents, and felt a subtle but devastating war being waged through and over themselves.

It is not only intermarried parents who often use their children as pawns in working out their own unresolved religious conflicts; children too have been known to play their parents off, one against the other. Several rabbis have, in recent years, been confronted with students of junior high school age who refused to continue their religious education. Their justification was that with only one parent being Jewish, they had the right to opt for the parent who was Christian. The problem is serious and disruptive enough when it is thus expressed on a conscious level. It becomes ever so much more explosive when repressed to the level of the unconscious, where it can cause many kinds of emotional distress.

Neat intellectual solutions agreed upon in theory before the wedding often fail to stand up before the stubborn realities of daily life. Two young people romantically involved with each other, no matter how sensitive or perceptive they may be, cannot possibly know what it will be like one day to behold their own precious child, fruit of their bodies and their love. To agree in advance that a child will be reared in no religious tradition, or in that of one's mate, may seem like such a simple thing at the time. But when the child snuggles in one's arms, suddenly the problem is emotional too, not intellectual alone. Circumcision and Bar or Bat Mitzvah and Confirmation for the Jew—Baptism and Communion for the Christian—there is no way of preparing a couple ahead of time for what these rituals can mean later in the life of their child.

I have had two unforgettable experiences which bear on this point. Late one night I sat for several hours with a Jewish father and Protestant mother who had asked for help with the problem of religious education for their children. The discussion had been neither pleasant nor productive. As the couple was about to leave, I asked one last question: "If you had known sixteen years ago what you know now . . ." I began. I never had a chance to finish the question. The wife turned to me and shouted almost viciously, "If I had known then even half of what I know tonight, I would never have married him!" This, if you please, in the presence of her startled husband! The disappointment and hatred so evident in her voice bespoke a frustration which was pathetic.

The other experience involved a Lutheran father who asked one day for an appointment. Sitting across my desk, he recounted the following story: He had been born a Jew. Religion had meant so little to him that twenty years before, at the time of his marriage, he had glibly agreed to have his children follow the Lutheran faith of their mother. Throughout the years this had not seemed to pose any problems of grave consequence. But now he had come to see a rabbi because his son was six months short of thirteen. "Rabbi," he blurted out between tears, "it has suddenly come to me that this boy will be the first son in my family for centuries not to celebrate a Bar Mitzvah. I haven't been able to sleep for weeks since that thought first occurred to me." And the man wept—almost like a hurt child.

Had you been the rabbi in the two incidents described above, what would you have said or done? What would you have done if you were the husband in the first case? In Greece there is almost no intermarriage because it is forbidden by state law. Would this be a good solution for us in the United States? Why?

Are you the son or daughter of a mixed–marriage couple? Are some of your friends? (Remember: once a conversion has taken place, the marriage is no longer a mixed one.) If so, you may already know from personal experience what I have attempted to describe here in theory. Yet there is something else too which you ought to know. The very facts that you are studying in a Jewish school, that your parents are members of a temple, shows that one of the important objections to mixed marriage doesn't apply in your case. There would seem to be no danger that Judaism will become extinct in the case of your family.

Does the second major argument against mixed marriage apply to you? Are your parents happily and successfully married despite the original religious difference between them? You are better qualified to answer than I—perhaps better than anyone on earth. You should also be aware of the fact that—regardless of whether your originally–Christian parent did or did not convert to Judaism—you are accepted fully by your rabbi, your teachers and your classmates. In Reform Judaism the offspring of a religiously mixed couple, if he or she celebrates Bar/Bat Mitzvah and/or Confirmation, is considered to be in every respect a Jew, without personally undergoing formal conversion.

How does one convey the truth about mixed marriage to a couple already in love and contemplating marriage? It isn't easy—it may even be impossible. This is where the more immediate problem of dating with non–Jews enters the picture. In our earlier discussion on dating we intentionally deferred this; it can best be considered here, in connection with the whole issue of mixed marriage.

Are you free tonight?

There is nothing morally wrong in a Jew's dating a non–Jew. It can be, however, explosively dangerous. No one decides in advance when and with whom one will fall in love. The more you grow accustomed to dating Gentiles, the greater is the possibility that when love arrives on the scene, the other member of the cast will be of a faith different from your own. You may be inclined to protest at once that you are still in high school and not likely to be choosing your permanent mate this month or next. True, but the matter is not so simple.

For one thing, there are couples who establish a romantic relationship in high school which persists through the years to the point of marriage. One can never be sure. It is still more likely that boys or girls who establish a general pattern of dating Gentiles in high school will continue that dating pattern in college too. In this connection it would be wise for young people who seem to prefer non-Jews to Jews as dating partners to ask themselves why. Earlier, we mentioned that one's choice of a mate can in some instances be a rebellion against parents. This is especially possible when the mate—or dating partner— is of a faith different from one's own. Such a choice is often the best device at hand—no less effective when adopted un- consciously—for hitting out at one's parents. Or it can be the expression of bitter resentment against being a Jew. In either case, the motive is not a healthy one, and the prognosis for a good marriage is far from encouraging.

Several studies have been made of the type of personality apt to marry out of the group or faith. They show in this category a disproportionate number of people who are "unor- ganized or demoralized . . . detached . . . rebellious . . . marginal . . ." This, of course, does not mean that every person contem- plating a mixed marriage fits these descriptions; only that more individuals of this type than of others will eventually enter into such marital partnerships. Very often the compulsion to marry outside one's group is a symptom of general personality disorder or inadequacy.[5]

The path of wisdom then—if one wishes not to rule out completely the dating of Gentiles—is to keep these contacts on as casual a basis as possible. Let these dates be interspersed infrequently in a dating pattern which is mostly with Jewish partners. And let the first symptoms of any affection exceeding simple friendship be a warning signal that danger lies ahead!

One of our most frequent errors—in life generally, when choosing a mate particularly, with reference to mixed marriage most especially—is drifting with the wind. Establishing no ultimate policy or aim; just inviting events themselves to take over; allowing a long series of apparently unimportant small decisions to box us in so that, in the end, a large choice we never consciously confronted has already been made for us. I cannot urge too vigorously the extreme importance of planning in advance what we hope to achieve, then governing our daily decisions accordingly. It is too late to grapple with the issue of intermarriage only after one is in love with a non–Jew. Hence the urgency of defining your goals before establishing a dating pattern which can lead to frustration and anguish.

This brings us back to mixed marriage. What if the prospective bride and groom happen to be people to whom religion seems not to have much meaning? Can they then afford to disregard the precautions recommended in this discussion? Not if they are wise. The fact that religion is of relatively minor importance in the life of a young man or woman in their twenties is no guarantee that it will be unimportant in their thirties or forties. Religion generally means more to young parents than to adolescent or immediately postadolescent men and women. To establish a household and family on the premise of religious neutrality or indifference is to deny, from the start, a precious area of sharing which can bring immeasurable happiness to a married couple and their children.

Often, young people of an age to date or marry accuse their parents of bigotry when they hear them voice objections to intermarriage. "You're a hypocrite!" one college student hurled at his mother and father. "All my life you've preached to me about democracy and equal rights. You encouraged me to make friends in all races and religions. Now that I want to marry a non-Jewish girl, you suddenly change your tune."

Were his parents really hypocrites? I think not. To support equal opportunity for everyone doesn't imply that everyone is necessarily calculated to be a good mate for one's child. If I am convinced that a particular person—or kind of person—represents too great a gamble for marital happiness, or poses a threat to Jewish survival within my own family, I can simultaneously oppose the marriage of my son or daughter to that person, without in any way demeaning them or diminishing my struggle for equal rights on their behalf.

Just in case

Suppose that, despite the truth of everything that has been said, two people—only one of them Jewish—find themselves in love, determined to marry? What course should they follow? The first essential is to resist the inevitable temptation to say: "We're different!" Almost every couple in this situation responds in some such manner; the tragedy is that they honestly believe themselves to be capable of surmounting all the difficulties and obstacles of which they are at least intellectually aware. Yet an alarmingly high proportion of these couples learn later through the bitterest kind of personal disappointment that in fact they were not different.

There is a maximum weight which every beam, even the strongest, can carry. If more than its maximum is piled on, the beam will crack and break. There is also a maximum strain which any individual or couple can tolerate, a point at which their marriage must fail because the weight they have attempted to carry exceeds the strength of their love. Mixed religious background constitutes one of the heaviest burdens for any couple to carry. Those who blithely dismiss the experience of others, who proceed with their plans to marry because of a naive confidence that they will surely succeed where so many others have failed, do themselves a great disfavor. Bishop Pike of the Episcopal Church compared them to one who would purchase a ticket for a trip by plane on the assurance of the agent that "once in a while a plane gets through." The very first practical course for such a couple is to consider seriously the additional problems their marriage will have to carry, and to measure with impeccable honesty the quality of the love they possess.

To do this properly requires time. Here we would remind you of what was said many pages back about the test of time being our most valid way of distinguishing infatuation from love. If this is true of the average couple, it is very much truer of the couple contemplating a mixed marriage. Their engagement needs to be both longer and more searching. To succeed, they must try to be even more confident than others that they are sufficiently compatible and mature.

Such a couple would also do well to inquire scrupulously into their motives. A young man or woman who has experienced unusual difficulty with a parent or a home situation, who has been perceptibly unhappy on the job, who has followed a consistent pattern of dating members of other faiths: this person should be extremely cautious about the real, unconscious motivations which drive him or her toward so precarious an experiment. A marriage undertaken as a weapon to punish a parent, or to strike back at an unkind fate, or to achieve a spurious sense of superiority is almost certainly bound to fail.

If the most rigorous kind of investigation over a protracted period of time leaves a couple still convinced that they wish to proceed with a mixed marriage, they should then give serious consideration to the possibility of the non–Jew's converting to Judaism. Such conversions should not take place merely as expedient devices, only to assuage antagonistic relatives or induce a rabbi to officiate at the wedding. They are valid only after a respectable course of study which convinces the prospective convert that he or she can truthfully accept Judaism as the religious civilization and faith by which they will live their lives. In most large cities today local rabbis cooperate with either the Union of American Hebrew Congregations or the United Synagogue of America in conducting regular classes for this purpose. Obviously, conversion cannot change the past background or preferences of any individual. But if it is undertaken with sincerity, it can at least offer the couple the best possible chance for happiness in a home which is religiously unified, rather than divided. And, most important of all, it can provide in advance a setting of harmony in which children will one day be able to find the security and confidence they so desperately need.

Why do I suggest only that the non–Jew consider conversion to Judaism? First of all, because I am a Jew, anxious and concerned for the survival of Judaism. Second, because most intermarried couples find, whether they plan it so or not, that they are accepted more warmly by their Jewish than their Gentile friends. A majority of these couples seem to end up as Jews socially, even if not religiously. As far as anti–Semites are concerned, the couple and their children are considered Jews even if they prefer not to be. How much better then, especially for the children, to be Jews because they want to be, because they feel gratification and pride in following the Jewish way of life.

Some of the problems involved in mixed marriage must at times be faced in lesser degree by a Jew who is marrying a person from another branch of Judaism. A Reform Jewish girl, for example, in love with an Orthodox boy who insists on a kosher home, must also expect major problems of adjustment. These cannot compare in severity, however, to the vexing obstacles in the path of those who cross major religious lines in their choice of a mate.

Our ancestors were not wrong in their opposition to mixed marriage. They knew that the survival of Judaism as well as the probability of happiness are both enhanced by marriages in which both partners are Jewish.

No easy solution

My telephone rang insistently. A good friend was calling to tell me of her daughter's engagement and wedding plans. Of course I congratulated her. She asked me to consult my calendar for a date and time, assuming that as her rabbi and a family friend I would officiate. Only after we had completed all the arrangements did she mention—almost as an afterthought—that her future son–in–law was not Jewish.

Should I officiate at the wedding? My love for the bride and her family encouraged me to say *yes*. My responsibilities as a rabbi forced me to refuse.

No Orthodox or Conservative rabbi will officiate at a mixed–marriage wedding ceremony. Neither will the great majority—perhaps two–thirds or more—of Reform rabbis, though a minority will. I stand with the majority in believing that—as a rabbi—I have a right to officiate only where two Jews are involved and the prospect for Jewish survival is good. I cannot and must not forget the statistics about Jewish identity given earlier in this chapter. My obligation as a rabbi is to maximize, not minimize the probability that there will be a viable Jewish community in the United States five hundred years from now.

I am aware also of the fact that all too often the couple asking a rabbi to officiate at a mixed marriage is actually "using" him or her—either to give the appearance that theirs is a valid Jewish marriage . . . or to appease their guilt . . . or to mollify unhappy parents or grandparents. My Judaism is too precious to me to allow my complicity in such a ploy. Like the overwhelming majority of American rabbis, therefore, I am always willing to meet with such couples if they wish, to discuss with them the very real problems they will most probably face, to help them in any way I can, consistent with my principles and conscience. And I accept them as a couple—as friends and members of my congregation if they so desire—regardless of how or by whom they are married. As a rabbi, I owe them no less than that. They, in turn, owe me respect for my integrity and understanding of my position.

A final word for this chapter: if you are interested in reading more about mixed marriage, I recommend an excellent booklet by Rabbi Sanford Seltzer, *Jews and Non–Jews Falling in Love,* published in 1976 by the Union of American Hebrew Congregations.

For instance

A. Alison and John are aware of the fact that, because she is a Protestant and he a Jew, they must expect more than the average number of problems in their marriage. They have discussed this at length with their parents, her minister and his rabbi. They have also seen the statistics of failure and divorce among couples who have intermarried.

While not discounting this evidence entirely, they are inclined to minimize its importance for themselves. They have called their parents' attention to the fact that a divorce rate three or four times higher in cases of mixed marriage still leaves a large number of matches which succeed. Their love, they are confident, will enable them to solve whatever problems they may have to face. They feel this way particularly because of the many other cultural and spiritual values they share. Their parents have not been particularly impressed by the couple's insistence that they might have fallen in love with someone in their own religious group with whom they would have had less in common than they have with each other.

Is it true that individuals in the same religious group can be incompatible in many important cultural and spiritual respects? Can John and Alison be sure they are viewing their prospects objectively? Is their evaluation of the statistical evidence dependable? If they are determined to marry, what steps would it be wise for them to take in preparation for that event?

B. Janet has been a Reform Jew all her life. Both of her parents were confirmed in Reform temples and have sent their children to a Reform religious school. Janet has now come to her rabbi, disturbed over the fact that in the past few months she has become very much interested in an Orthodox Jewish boy.

They get along well together and have a good time on their dates. Janet is slightly uncomfortable about going into a restaurant with Eric because he keeps kosher and will eat nothing except cottage cheese or fruit salad. While he doesn't object to her having whatever she wants, she feels uneasy about eating meat in his presence. The one time that she accompanied him to a religious service in his synagogue she was upset by the fact that she couldn't sit with him and didn't understand the service. The one time he went with her on a Friday night to her temple, he tried to be polite but could barely conceal his feeling that this wasn't even a Jewish service. They have not yet become serious enough to talk about the kind of home they would have if they were married, but Janet knows he would insist on its being kosher. This bothers her on two grounds: she doesn't see why any modern Jew should want to keep kosher, and she wouldn't begin to know how to keep such a home.

She has come to her rabbi because she has never felt so close to any of the boys she has dated; she has little doubt that if she and Eric continue to date, their relationship might well develop into love. What she has asked the rabbi is whether or not, under the circumstances, she should continue to accept Eric's invitations and thereby perhaps complicate her life.

What advice do you think the rabbi should give Janet? What could she do to bridge the religious gap between Eric and herself? What could he do? Is there any possibility of their being able in the future to worship together with inspiration for both? Wouldn't it be hypocritical for Janet to keep a kosher home? Is their problem more or less serious than if one of them were a Christian? From a religious point of view, what, if anything, do they have in common?

C. Having just talked to Rabbi L., Carla and Lew are deeply unhappy and disturbed. They had invited Carla's rabbi to officiate at their wedding and he had refused. Though Rabbi L. had been polite and had tried patiently to explain his reasons, still they both felt, when they left his study, as if they had been slapped in the face.

The rabbi had told them that if they were both Jewish, it would have been a pleasure for him to accept the invitation. The fact that Lew was Christian made such acceptance on his part impossible. He said there were two reasons for this. First, he was a rabbi, committed to the survival of Judaism, and felt he could not in good conscience bring the sanction of his position and the synagogue to a marriage which in all likelihood would lead to the disappearance of the family from Jewish life. In the second place, he was so convinced of the probable failure of such a marriage that he felt he was doing the couple a favor by refusing to officiate unless Lew was first converted to Judaism. Rabbi L. went to great lengths to explain that his attitude was not based on any Jewish superiority complex and that he and his congregation would accept the marriage as valid even if it were performed by a judge. He also called their attention to the fact that the Central Conference of American Rabbis, of which he is a member, has officially called upon all Reform rabbis to refrain from officiating at mixed–marriage ceremonies.

Lew says he cannot escape the feeling that Rabbi L. considers him a second–class citizen. His own Unitarian minister was willing to officiate; why should a rabbi be so narrow?

Do you agree that Rabbi L.'s point of view was narrow? Why might it be easier for a Unitarian minister to officiate at such a wedding than for a rabbi? What else might Rabbi L. have suggested to them? Had he in fact rejected the couple? Is there any justification for his saying that he could not officiate but would accept them after their marriage if they then wanted to join his congregation?

D. Nancy simply cannot understand her parents. From her earliest childhood they had encouraged her to accept all kinds of people as friends, regardless of their color or faith. They themselves had been very active in many civil rights organizations and interfaith projects. Nancy had been encouraged to do the same.

Yet now her parents are frightened and angry over the fact that she wants to marry a Christian. "You just don't make sense!" she has insisted. "You aren't in the least consistent! All my life you teach me democratic acceptance of everyone, yet now you want me to retreat from my high ideals. If all human beings are equal, then why isn't Mark good enough to be my husband?"

In addition to her unhappiness and anger, Nancy is puzzled by the fact that up to now her parents have never been particularly diligent in their Jewish loyalties. They have been members of a congregation, but attended services only on the High Holy Days and never enrolled either Nancy or her sister in the religious school. This too seems utterly inconsistent with their present disturbance over the possibility of having a non–Jewish son–in–law.

Can you explain this last apparent inconsistency in the conduct of Nancy's parents? Are they in fact retreating from their former democratic idealism? Does one who is opposed to mixed marriage have a right to be active in civil rights causes and interfaith organizations? Why? What might Nancy and her parents do, respectively, to resolve the impasse?

E. Neither Derrick nor Norma had ever been particularly religious. It had been years since he had seen the inside of a church or she a synagogue. They were certain, therefore, that the religious difference between them would never be more than a technicality. They felt no sense of deprivation or loss over the fact that they were married by a justice of the peace.

Derrick began to change after their first boy was born. In the beginning, the difference was subtle. He would occasionally attend church services on a Sunday morning, but would never mention it to Selma, either before or after. Within two years, however, he went to church every week without fail. Then he enrolled in a Monday night Bible class and began to bring missionary tracts home.

Norma resented this. She was never quite sure whether it was genuine conviction that moved her or just an unreasoning need to strike back at her husband, but she started to observe a few of the traditional Jewish rituals in their home. Their boy was sent to Hebrew School when he was old enough.

It was the talk of Bar Mitzvah which really brought things to a head. Norma insisted on it, Derrick threatened that he wouldn't attend if it were held, and the boy felt trapped between his warring parents. At this point the child developed so many symptoms of tension that he was referred by his school for psychiatric help.

Does this sound like a real or a manufactured story? How would you recommend that the impasse be resolved? Should there be a Bar Mitzvah? Could both parents be satisfied by celebrating Bar Mitzvah in a synagogue and Confirmation in Derrick's church? Can we learn anything from this case?

16

"It would never work, Freddie. I've evolved and you haven't."

How important is religion?

At several points in previous chapters, when reference was made to the fact that religion has been found to be an element of importance in the wise choosing of a mate and in working toward happiness in marriage, we indicated that a full discussion would be temporarily deferred. We are now ready for that discussion.

Almost everyone recognizes the important connection between religion and marriage. Even those who do not look upon themselves as particularly religious or devout are usually anxious to have a rabbi or other clergyman officiate at their wedding. And large numbers of individuals who seldom attend synagogue services of a public nature still wish to have their wedding ceremonies solemnized in a sanctuary.

It would almost seem as if many people understand by instinct a truth which can be demonstrated by experience. The fact is that the marriages of religious people *do* tend to be more successful than those of the irreligious. The American Youth Commission study mentioned in a previous chapter showed that, while only 4.6 percent of the students born to Jewish parents came from broken homes, among those whose parents had no religion the proportion from broken homes was 16.7 percent!

> Can you offer any immediate explanation for these figures? Why should Jewish marriages be the most successful? Does this tie in with any of our conclusions in the first few chapters of this book? Why should Catholic marriages seem to be more stable than Protestant marriages? Why should those with no religious background appear to be the least successful? Is this due to the influence of religion, or to the fact that religious persons are likely to possess some of the other personality values and traits which are conducive to a successful marriage?

There are other statistics and studies which confirm these impressions. Bishop Pike, for example, has mentioned surveys which show two–and–a–quarter times the divorce rate among couples who are not connected with either synagogue or church or who worship separately, compared to those who actively share a common religious tradition.[1] Other research indicates that a high happiness score in marriage tends to be found together with a high rating in religiousness.[2] A survey, some years back, at the University of Southern California showed that among couples belonging to the same church 68 percent of the men were happily married; in a comparable group where neither husband nor wife was a church member only 31 percent of the men were catalogued as happy in their marriages.[3]

The Oklahoma City Family Clinic came to similar conclusions. In attempting to reconcile 250 couples who were experiencing marital difficulties, the clinic staff discovered that only 3 couples were attending church when they first came for help. A very high rate of success was achieved in working with these people. It was discovered that participation together in church activities made reconciliation "almost a certainty."[4]

Why should this be so? It is commonly known that the more two people share in terms of cultural background, the greater is the probability they will have a successful marriage. If this is true with reference to such cultural interests as reading, music and art—how much truer in so significant a cultural area as religion! After all, two persons who share a quest for the essential meaning of life, who strive to comprehend whether or not their love reflects an immeasurable Source of Love in the universe—two such as these have touched as deeply in their sharing as is humanly possible. They are likely to forge between them far more durable bonds of unity than two whose sharing is limited only to humanly created culture.

Dr. James A. Peterson has understood this and expressed it well:

> Religious values, when sincerely believed and made a pivotal part of one's aspirations, must contribute to marital adjustment because these are the very values that are most necessary for it. . . . It matters in marriage whether a couple reach upward in their common interests toward that which is creative and lofty or whether they are content with that which is tawdry and inconsequential.[5]

It matters especially in Judaism. Hence the very beautiful poetry of the Jewish marriage ceremony. Hence also such statements of Judaism as that in the Midrash: "No man without a woman, nor a woman without a man, nor both of them without God."[6]

Our ancient rabbis used an interesting play on words to emphasize that the relationship between husband and wife should be sacred; which means, really, that religion should play an important role in marriage. You may already know that the Hebrew word for man is אִישׁ *ish,* while that for woman is אִשָּׁה *ishah.* The first of these words contains the letter י , which is missing from the second; the second contains the letter ה , which is not to be found in the first. These two letters together spell out a Hebrew abbreviation for God. If they are removed from the words *man* and *woman,* what we have left in each case is the word אֵשׁ *esh,* meaning fire. From this, our rabbis deduced that when God is removed from the relationship between man and woman, nothing but consuming fire remains. Only if God is present in all they experience together, is it possible for their marriage to be truly human.[7]

Thus did the ancient teachers of Judaism express their understanding of how important religious faith is to marriage. There are many kinds of experience through which a sensitive person can become aware of God and feel a close personal relationship to Him. We sense God in the beauty of the universe . . . in a mysterious feeling of kinship between ourselves and the rest of nature . . . in our yearnings after moral improvement . . . in the excitement of discovering a new truth . . . in our intuitive recognition of cosmic purpose to which, if we will, we can contribute.

But in the love of husband and wife for each other—more than in any other kind of experience or emotion accessible to human beings—men and women come close to the divine spirit which permeates the entire universe. And in the love act which unites both their bodies and their souls, through which they initiate a new life—more than in anything else they do—a husband and wife become creative partners of God. Two individuals who are unaware of this share less in life and are therefore less firmly bound to each other than those who do.

Professor Magoun must have had this in mind when he wrote: "The child who cannot find God in his parents will not have an easy time finding God anywhere. The parent who cannot see God in the face of his child has never known God."[8]

In more practical terms too

There is another level too on which religion can add much to a marriage. This is in terms of visible practice rather than speculative belief. We often say that Judaism is a way of life, even more than a system of belief. Our Jewish way of life can affect the daily lives of husbands and wives in two ways. First, if they are aware of the ideals of sex, love and marriage which our people and faith have evolved, they can enrich their relationship by undertaking to implement these ideals in their own lives. Husbands and wives who try to treat each other with the tenderness and compassion recommended by Judaism will have a far sweeter, more loving life together than those who, though born Jews, know nothing of these values.

There is often a gap between our intellectual understanding of ideals and our emotional acceptance of them. Many of our attitudes and much of our behavior in life are motivated by experiences of earliest childhood. When these experiences were particularly painful, they were pushed down into the unconscious part of our minds. Though we are unable to remember them, they continue to influence how we feel and what we do. This helps explain why we sometimes do or say things which are the opposite of what we intended, or which seem strange even to ourselves. It accounts, too, for the fact that even a person who understands and appreciates the ideals of Judaism concerning love and marriage may not always be able to apply those ideals effectively in his or her own life.

Most of us are able, most of the time, to live comfortably without exploring our unconscious. We manage to keep our intentions and performance close enough in line to maintain good health and self–respect. A person who is unable to accomplish this may need the professional help of a psychiatrist. Often a good guidance counselor at school, or a physician or rabbi who has psychological knowledge and insight, can either supply the necessary assistance or can tell whether psychiatric aid is needed.

It is important to remember, however, that in most cases our conduct is motivated not only by the unconscious pushing us, so to speak, from below, but also by our values and ideals, pulling us upward from above. Thus the marriage goals of Judaism can exert a most beneficient effect on our lives.

The second practical realm in which Judaism can supplement the lives of married couples is that of ritual. In modern life we sometimes tend to minimize the great importance of ritual. As human beings have developed out of animal life in the direction of greater spiritual comprehension and capacity, they have also—both consciously and unconsciously—sought to express symbolically the values and concerns which mean most to them. A valid ritual is a poetic symbol, through which we attempt to express something which words alone may be unable to communicate.

Shaking hands is a ritual. Though we have long outgrown the probable original reason for this custom—a desire to show the other person that one is not carrying a concealed weapon in his or her closed hand—it still symbolizes our openness to friendship, our desire to accept others as we would like them to accept us. Saluting the flag is a ritual. If performed properly, it can say and demonstrate more about our feelings toward our nation than many words. Putting candles on a birthday cake or giving gifts to mark an occasion—these too are rituals which enrich our lives.

As the final draft of this chapter was being prepared, a new president of the United States was inaugurated. If, as a nation, we had wanted to be coldly practical, all that was necessary was that the chief justice of the Supreme Court swear in the new president and vice-president privately in his office. Instead, an elaborate ritual was performed. Members of the Cabinet and Congress entered in an impressive processional. Clergymen of four faiths offered prayers. The United States Marine Corps Band played. In the afternoon there was a magnificent parade, which was reviewed by the president and other officials from a specially constructed stand. All this was ritual, and the nation watched it on television.

In poetic, dramatic style the ideals of the American people were symbolized. The movements and motions said more than even the most eloquent words could have captured.

After witnessing another public ritual, James Reston summarized its value. Calling attention to the fact that we were perhaps becoming too practical, he wrote that the rich ritual of the preceding day "reminded Washington of the imponderables of life. It suggested that sentiment and history, that ideas and philosophy, are also powerful. . . . The ceremony, for a few hours, brought . . . the past and the present together, and made men here wonder whether, in this computerized modern world, they were not casting aside something from the older world that was essential to the future."[9]

This role of ritual in group life is duplicated in our personal lives. It serves as a bridge from the past—across the present—to the future. It reminds us of the imponderables, the spiritual values by which our actions should be guided. We Jews are especially fortunate because our faith provides us with a rich treasury of beautiful ritual. The most important moments and emotions in life—birth, growth, adolescence, love, marriage and death—are enhanced by rituals which grow out of our people's past and express our hopes for the future.

The sharing of rituals—precisely because they are poetic symbols appealing to the emotions—can do more to bring husband and wife together than any intellectual sharing. And the most productive rituals of all for a Jew are those through which his ancestors, for centuries, have expressed their loftiest ideals. The Jewish bride and groom associate themselves with these ideals and with the men and women who developed them when—standing before the rabbi at their wedding—they repeat words and enact a drama in which every Jewish bride and groom for hundreds of years have participated. In a sense they thereby invite all Jews alive today and all Jews of the past to share in their life together, to give it the richness and strength they would be unable to evoke by themselves.

From time to time I hear young couples asking why a special ceremony is needed to celebrate their love. "What does a piece of paper add to the way we feel about each other?" Not all pieces of paper are identical. The wrapper of a candy bar is a piece of paper. So are a piece of Kleenex . . . an Israel Bond . . . this page . . . the Constitution of the United States . . . a Bible verse . . . a treasured family photograph . . . a love letter. The piece of paper on which your כְּתוּבָה *ketubah* or marriage certificate is printed is important only as it finalizes the dramatic ceremony which symbolizes the most significant partnership in which you will ever participate. If your marriage comes even close to the high ideals of Judaism, if it even approximates the rich relationship it can and should be, then it is worth celebrating and remembering. If, on the other hand, it is just a casual agreement, an interim experiment, a temporary trial, then it isn't worth either a special ceremony or a "piece of paper."

After the honeymoon is ended and a couple commence living a normal life in their home, each Jewish ritual they perform together brings them closer to each other and to a rich part of their background. The couple who light their candles and chant קִדּוּשׁ *Kiddush* each שַׁבָּת *Shabbat,* who commence every meal with הַמּוֹצִיא *Hamotzi* thanking God for their food, who participate in a סֵדֶר *Seder* on פֶּסַח *Pesach,* who kindle the lights of חֲנוּכָּה *Chanukah* and attend religious services regularly and enjoy Jewish music and literature together—this couple makes use of an asset in their marriage which they would be utterly foolish to ignore or neglect. It is true, of course, that the performance of these rituals contributes greatly to the survival of the Jewish people and of Judaism. It is no less true, however, that they add an experience of indescribable beauty and deep meaning to a Jewish marriage.

If we do not go into greater detail here regarding the ritual wealth of Judaism, this is because we assume you are already familiar with much of it from your previous studies and from your home life. Suffice it to say that the Shabbat and every Jewish holiday have something important to add to our lives, both as human beings and as Jews. The book by Rabbi Ira Eisenstein listed in the notes for this chapter can help you to understand this.[10] But it is not enough to be just intellectually aware of what our holidays mean; only the Jewish couple who *live* their holidays, who dramatize them in their home through the appropriate rituals, can benefit from them fully.

A special word is in order here concerning *Shabbat.* Jewish tradition has wisely evaluated שַׁבָּת *Shabbat* as second in importance only to יוֹם כִּפּוּר *Yom Kippur.* The husband and wife who deliberately set aside one full day a week for spiritual companionship and enrichment, for sharing an active pursuit of the true, the beautiful and the good—such a couple bind themselves closer to each other and to Jewish tradition. Their chance to become finer human beings and to enjoy a more wonderful marriage is greatly increased.

All this becomes more probable if, from the beginning of their marriage, a couple are affiliated with a synagogue. Most congregations today have clubs as well as lower dues for newlyweds. To join a congregation, to attend its religious services regularly, to expand your knowledge of Judaism through its adult study program—these are among the most positive ways to enhance your marriage with religion. One of the chasidic rabbis expressed with rare beauty the importance of religion and ritual for Jewish marriage:

It was said that the Berditschever's wife excelled even the rabbi himself in holiness. Once she was overheard saying: "O Lord, may I be worthy that my Levi Isaac may have the same holy thoughts when he says grace over the bread that I have when I form the loaves."[11]

For instance

A. Burt and Debbie, who have been engaged for six months and are to be married in three weeks, have much in common but differ widely in their attitudes toward religion. Debbie has been close to her temple since the year of her Confirmation. She graduated from the temple high school department, served for a while as a student teacher in the religious school and attends services at least three times a month. Burt, on the other hand, has felt no particular attachment to the synagogue or Judaism since his Bar Mitzvah.

They have discussed in some depth the role religion is to play in their life with each other. Burt has no objection to his wife's continuing her work and attendance at the temple, but sees no reason why he should be expected to follow a pattern of conduct which has no meaning for him. He feels that it isn't necessary for the two of them to be exactly alike in their loyalties and preferences, that neither should try to make the other over. He is therefore willing to cooperate in permitting Debbie to go to temple every Friday night, if she wishes, and has agreed to have their children eventually enrolled in the religious school, if that remains her preference. He just doesn't want to be bothered, however, with doing these things himself.

Is Burt right in asserting that husband and wife should not try to remake each other? Does this mean they each should retain only the interests they had before they met? What are the probable consequences in their marriage, if Debbie and Burt remain unchanged in their views of religion? What could either do to improve the situation? Are they likely to face the same problem in areas other than religion?

B. Charlotte and Gerald were very much impressed by the rabbi's emphasis on the importance of a Jewish home when they met with him for a premarital conference. Though neither of them came from an observant Jewish home, they understand the value of rituals and symbols, especially for children.

They have agreed, therefore, that after their first child has been born and reaches school age, they will begin to practice some of the rituals and ceremonies of Judaism in their home. They see no useful purpose, however, in starting to do that immediately after marriage. Neither of them is accustomed to this; they feel, therefore, that they would be self-conscious— just the two of them in their little apartment doing such things as lighting candles and chanting קִדּוּשׁ *Kiddush* for שַׁבָּת *Shabbat.*

> Are Charlotte and Gerald wise in their decision? Is the value of ritual chiefly for children? How long is it apt to be from the time of their wedding until their first child reaches the age they anticipate? What do you think will happen to their intentions in the meantime? Would it make any difference to their children whether their parents had performed these rituals before their birth or began just for their sake?

C. To Sharon there has always seemed to be something both primitive and confining about religious ritual. Her college courses in anthropology had shown her how many of the rituals her parents observed had originated in primitive superstition. She had learned, for example, that the origin of Chanukah candles was probably to be found in the huge bonfires kindled by primitives as the winter solstice approached, because, as the days grew frighteningly shorter, they feared the sun would vanish unless they coaxed it to remain by lighting magic fires.

She was determined not to expose her children to such ancient ideas. She would introduce them to the highest ethical ideals of Judaism, but none of this ritual nonsense!

She objected also because she felt that ritual tends to keep us isolated in our own narrow little compartments. If Jews would relinquish their rituals and Christians would give up theirs, she felt that greater brotherhood would prevail between them.

Does Sharon have good grounds for her objections to ritual? Is she correct about the origins of many ceremonies in Judaism? About rituals keeping people apart from each other? Will her marriage gain or lose by her attitude? Will her children gain or lose? Why?

D. Yvette and Bernie, who have just come from their premarital conference with the rabbi, don't deny the importance of the statistics given at the beginning of this chapter. They feel very strongly, however, that religion can be an important positive factor in marriage only for two individuals who feel religious.

As for themselves, they are both atheists. Their college courses in philosophy have convinced them there is no God. They felt it would have been impolite to argue with the rabbi, but in later private conversation they agreed that it would be dishonest and artificial for them to attempt to utilize the beliefs and practices of Judaism to improve their marriage, when neither of them is religious at heart.

Do you agree with their conclusions? Why? Were they correct in not arguing with the rabbi? Can an atheist honestly practice the rituals of Judaism? Are Yvette and Bernie justified or wise in rejecting the theme of this chapter because of their feelings about religion?

Epilogue: and so—

We reach the end of this volume. But not by any means the end of your thinking about marriage. These are thoughts which should continue to occupy you for the rest of your life, first in hopeful anticipation of your own marriage, then in intelligent preparation for your children's. I hope that this book has been of interest and value to you and that you will want to reread parts of it more than once in the future.

I have tried to alert you to the most important ingredients of a good marriage: the meaning of love . . . the importance of the family . . . criteria by which to make an intelligent choice of mate . . . factors which lead to marital happiness . . . the role of sex, both before and during marriage . . . the problems of intermarriage . . . the significance of religion . . . and above all, the immense contribution which Jewish tradition and thought add to your future joy as a husband or wife.

There is an element of risk in every marriage. No bride and groom have a guarantee that their life together will be happy. The delicate ratio between the strength of their love and the weight of their burdens is one which cannot be measured with mathematical precision. The more deliberately they attempt to temper, with sober rational thought, the overwhelming emotion which attracts them to each other, the more hopeful their future will be.

You are not making your choice of a mate now. But you are shaping your personality and values; you are acquiring new knowledge and forming new attitudes; you are making other important decisions every day—all of which will eventually add up to your choice of a mate when the proper time comes. There is always a strong bond between the present and the future. What you do today helps determine what you will be and do tomorrow. Each important decision you make is like another number placed in a long column for addition. You have a considerable amount of freedom to choose what each number is to be. Once the numbers have been listed, however, once the choices made, what you are at any given moment is their sum total. No number can be erased. They can be counteracted by later subtractions, but it is very much harder to do this than to insert the correct number in the first place. In this sense, your attitudes and conduct now have much to do with your choice of husband or wife in the future.

That choice will require the keenest intelligence, the sharpest sensitivity, the most mature balance you possess. And all these invaluable traits can be enhanced by the insights of Judaism and of science. My highest hope in these chapters has been to supply you with at least the beginning of such skills.

No marriage is always perfect, because no human being is ever perfect. There are difficulties and tensions—anxieties and worries and quarrels—between every husband and wife. But two people who love each other maturely can solve any problem and move on together to unbelievable mountain peaks of happiness.

The reading of a book—or indeed, of many books—will not make a good marriage. The assimilation of wisdom which books may contain, however, can be of immeasurable help. We end where we began. Marriage can be the most exhilarating or the most devastating experience in life. May you think and act —now and in the future—in a manner that will make your marriage a creative joy.

Notes

1 • Marriage: heaven or hell?

1. E. M. Duvall, *Love and the Facts of Life,* pp. 78 and 81ff. Association Press, 1963.
2. J. McCary, *Human Sexuality—A Brief Edition,* p. 4. D. Van Nostrand Co., 1973.

2 • What is love?

1. F.A. Magoun, *Love and Marriage,* pp. 3, 4 and 7. Harper & Bros., 1956.
2. Eric Fromm, *The Revolution of Hope,* p. 40. Harper & Row Publishers, 1968.
3. Eric Fromm, *The Art of Loving,* p. 1. Harper & Bros., 1956.
4. *Ibid.,* p. 40.
5. *Midrash Aseret Hadibrot.*
6. *Sanhedrin* 72.
7. *Bereshit Rabbah* 54.
8. *Sanhedrin 105.*
9. *Pirkei Avot.* See Judah Goldin, *The Living Talmud,* p. 215. New American Library, 1957.
10. Eric Fromm, *The Art of Loving,* p. 26.
11. E. Borowitz, *Choosing a Sex Ethic,* p. 73. Schocken Books, 1969.

3 • Love and the family

1. *Zohar Chadash* IV:50b.
2. *Sanhedrin 22a.*
3. *Ruth Rabbah* I.
4. A.B. Shoulson (ed.), *Marriage and Family Life,* p. 62. Twayne Publishers, 1959.

5. A. Cohen, *Everyman's Talmud,* p. 160. E.P. Dutton & Co., 1949.
6. L. Newman, *Talmudic Anthology,* p. 124. Behrman House, 1945.
7. *Baba Metsiah* 59a.
8. *Ibid.,* 59a.
9. *Yevamot* 62.
10. A.B. Shoulson, *ibid.,* p. 63.
11. *Zohar* 233a.
12. *Or Yesharim,* p. 109.
13. Sidorsky, *Future of the Jewish Community in America,* pp. 78–80. Jewish Publication Society, 1973.
14. *Yevamot* 37.
15. *Sanhedrin* 22a.
16. *Song of Songs Rabbah* I.
17. M. Boyd, *Take Off the Masks,* p. 20. Doubleday & Co., 1978.
18. E.M. and S.M. Duvall, *Sex Ways in Fact and Faith,* p. 98. Association Press, 1961.
19. *Yad: Ishut,* 14:8.
20. S. Goldstein, *The Meaning of Marriage,* pp. 178ff. Bloch Publishing Co., 1942; A. Cohen, *Everyman's Talmud,* pp. 167–70.
21. *Yevamot* 37.

4 • A family is more than two

1. L. Newman, *Hasidic Anthology,* p. 45. Charles Scribner's Sons, 1935.
2. *Shemot Rabbah* I.
3. *Zohar Chadash* to *Lech Lecha.*
4. *Shabbat* 119b.
5. L. Newman, *ibid.,* p. 45.
6. *Ibid.*
7. *Shabbat* 10b.
8. *Zohar* I:50a.
9. *Bereshit Rabbah* 17:7.
10. L. Newman, *ibid.,* p. 304.
11. *Ibid.,* p. 118.
12. *Kiddushin* 31b, 32a.
13. *Kiddushin* 32a.
14. *Peah* 15c.
15. *Zohar* III:93a.
16. A. Cohen, *Everyman's Talmud,* pp. 180ff.
17. *Kiddushin* 31a.
18. *Yevamot* 6a.

5 • Old enough to love?

1. J.H.S. Bossard and E.S. Boll, *Why Marriages Go Wrong*, p. 101. The Ronald Press, 1958.
2. Bossard and Boll, *ibid.*, p. 110.
3. *The New York Times*, 21 June 1978.
4. Bossard and Boll, *ibid.*, p. 118.
5. *Zohar Chadash* I:4b.
6. *Redbook* magazine, March 1973.
7. *Ibid.*
8. E.M. Duvall, *Love and the Facts of Life*, pp. 38ff. Association Press, 1963.
9. S. Duvall, *Before You Marry*, pp. 10ff. Association Press, 1949.
10. E.M. Duvall, *ibid.*, pp. 249ff.

6 • How to make the right choice

1. *Yevamot* 63a.
2. L. Freehof, *Third Bible Legend Book*, pp. 80ff. Union of American Hebrew Congregations, 1956.
3. *Pesikta Buber* 11b, 12a.
4. *Pesachim* 49a.
5. S. Kaplan and H. Ribalow, *The Great Jewish Books*, p. 229. Horizon Press, 1952.
6. *Yevamot* 63a.
7. *Kiddushin* 70; *Pesachim* 50.
8. E.W. Burgess and L.S. Cottrell, *Predicting Success or Failure in Marriage*, p. 62. Prentice-Hall, 1939.
9. *Sanhedrin* 76.
10. *Yevamot* 101b.
11. J.L. Baron, *A Treasury of Jewish Quotations*, p. 296. Crown Publishers, 1956.
12. L. Newman, *Talmudic Anthology*, p. 256.
13. J.L. Baron, *ibid.*, p. 118.
14. A.B. Shoulson, *Marriage and Family Life*, p. 67.
15. F.A. Magoun, *Love and Marriage*, p. 229.
16. *Sotah* 2.
17. *Yalkut Shimoni*, 95.

7 • Recipe for success

1. United States Census Bureau; *The New York Times*, 2 May 1972.

2. *Statistical Abstract of the U.S., 1978.* U.S. Department of Commerce, Bureau of the Census.
3. James McCary, *Human Sexuality—A Brief Edition,* p. 6. D. Van Nostrand, 1973.
4. L. Newman, *Talmudic Anthology,* p. 269.
5. J.A. Peterson, *Toward a Successful Marriage,* p. 112. Charles Scribner's Sons, 1960.
6. *Kohelet Rabbah* 7.
7. J.A. Peterson, *ibid.,* p. 130.
8. *Yerushalmi Ketubot* 5, 6.
9. J.A. Peterson, *ibid.,* p. 98.
10. *The New York Times,* 2 October 1972.

8 • Sex is here to stay

1. *Bet Yosef, Tur Y.D.* 195.
2. *Tosafot, Shabbat* 13b.
3. Genesis 38:9ff.
4. Boyd Cooper, *Sex without Tears,* p. 26. Charles Publishing, 1972.
5. *The New York Times,* 28 June 1974.
6. *The New York Times,* 19 September 1973.
7. *The New York Times,* 21 September 1977.
8. Elizabeth Whelan, *Parents* magazine, February 1975.

9 • The same, yet different

1. W.B. Pomeroy, *Girls and Sex,* pp. 81ff. Delacorte Press, 1969.
2. E. Hamilton, *Sex before Marriage,* pp. 17–20. Meredith Press, 1969.
3. J. McCary, *Human Sexuality—A Brief Edition,* p. 205.
4. R. Hettlinger, *Living with Sex,* pp. 146ff. The Seabury Press, 1966.
5. E. Hamilton, *ibid.,* p. 28.
6. R. Hettlinger, *ibid.,* p. 148.
7. Deuteronomy 22:5.
8. Genesis 19:5.
9. Leviticus 20:13; also Leviticus 18:22.
10. J. McCary, *ibid.,* p. 243.

10 • Do all religions agree on sex?

1. I Corinthians 7:9.
2. I Corinthians 7:38.

3. D.S. Bailey, *Sexual Relations in Christian Thought,* p. 14. Harper & Bros., 1959.
4. *Ibid.,* pp. 23 and 99.
5. *Ibid.,* p. 63.
6. Matthew 5:27.
7. Regis Jolivet, *Introduction to Kierkegaard,* pp. 157. Translated by W.H. Barber, London, 1950.
8. *Guide for the Perplexed* 3:49.
9. S. Glasner, in *Encyclopedia of Sexual Behavior,* p. 576. Hawthorn Books, 1961.
10. E. Borowitz, *Choosing a Sex Ethic,* pp. 163ff.
11. *Even Ha'ezer* 76:1.
12. *Pesachim Rabbah* 17b.
13. *Responsa, Prague* #199.
14. A.B. Shoulson, *Marriage and Family Life,* p. 56.
15. *Ibid.,* p. 64.
16. *Ibid.,* p. 65.

11 • To wait . . . or not to wait

1. Exodus 22:15ff.
2. Deuteronomy 22:28ff.
3. *Shenei Luchot Haberit,* Otiyot, p. 89a.
4. *Yaarot Devash* I, 3, p. 22a.
5. L. Kirkendall and R. Whitehurst, *The New Sexual Revolution,* p. 97. Donald W. Brown, Inc., 1971.
6. *Ibid.,* p. 171.
7. *The New York Times,* 10 May 1972.
8. H. Katchadourian and D. Lunde, *Fundamentals of Human Sexuality,* p. 481. Holt, Rinehart & Winston, 1972.
9. *Los Angeles Times,* 30 November 1977.
10. *Reconstructionist,* February 1978.
11. J. McCary, *Human Sexuality—A Brief Edition,* pp. 105ff.
12. *Ibid.,* p. 102.
13. E. Borowitz, *Choosing a Sex Ethic.*
14. *Saturday Review,* 26 September 1953.
15. R.L. Tyler, in Delora & Delora, *Intimate Life Styles,* p. 397. Goodyear Publishing Co., 1972.
16. *Sexual Behavior,* March 1973.
17. *Parents* magazine, February 1975.
18. G.F. Gilder, *Sexual Suicide,* p. 5. Bantam Books, 1975.
19. *Parents* magazine, February 1975.
20. E. Fromm, *The Art of Loving,* pp. 54ff.
21. *Ibid.,* pp. 88ff.

22. E. Borowitz, *op. cit.*, p. 107.
23. *Ibid.*, p. 18.

12 • Not to wait

1. H. Christensen and C. Gregg, "Changing Sex Norms in America and Scandinavia," in A. Kline and M. Medley, *Dating and Marriage*, pp. 131–2. Holbrook Press, 1973.
2. J. Cuber and P. Harroff, *Sex and the Significant Americans*, pp. 43–65. Penguin Books, 1965.

13 • To wait

1. L. Linn and L.W. Schwarz, *Psychiatry and Religious Experience*, p. 143. Random House, 1958.
2. *Current Medical Digest*, January 1965, pp. 31ff.
3. I.L. Reiss, *Premarital Sexual Standards in America*, pp. 170ff. The Free Press, 1960.
4. H. Katchadourian and D. Lunde, *Fundamentals of Human Sexuality*, p. 7.
5. *Ibid.*, pp. 468ff.
6. L. Thomas, *The Lives of a Cell*, p. 137. The Viking Press, 1974.
7. R. Hettlinger, *Living with Sex*, p. 42.
8. R. May, *Love and Will*, p. 40. W.W. Norton & Co., 1969.
9. Anonymous, *Go Ask Alice*, p. 98. Prentice-Hall. 1971.
10. R. May, *op. cit.*, p. 84.
11. V.A. Demant, *Christian Sex Ethics*, pp. 100ff. Harper & Row, 1964.
12. P. and E. Kronhausen, *Sex Histories of American College Men*, pp. 227ff. Ballantine Books, 1960.
13. J. Huxley, *New Bottles for Old Wine*, pp. 218ff. Harper & Bros., 1957.
14. E. Borowitz, *Choosing a Sex Ethic*, p. 106.
15. H. Greenwald, *Decision Therapy*, pp. 235ff. David McKay Co., 1973.
16. E.W. Burgess and P. Wallin, *Engagement and Marriage*, pp. 371ff. J.B. Lippincott, 1953.
17. M.B. Loeb, "Social Role and Sexual Identity in Adolescent Males," in *Casework Papers*, National Association of Social Workers, 1959.
18. J. McCary, *Human Sexuality—A Brief Edition*, pp. 107ff.
19. I. Metzker (ed.), *A Bintel Brief*, pp. 201ff. Doubleday & Co., 1971.

20. Seymour Fisher, *Understanding the Female Orgasm,* pp. 187 and 195. Basic Books, 1973.
21. *Parents* magazine, February 1975.
22. *Ibid.*
23. *Sex, Science and Values,* Society for Information and Education in Sex (SIECUS), 1969.
24. *Sexual Behavior,* March 1972.
25. C. Leuba, *Ethics in Sex Conduct,* p. 82. Association Press, 1948.
26. *Talmud Kiddushin* 2b.
27. H. Katchadourian and D. Lunde, *op. cit.,* p. 259.
28. *Redbook* magazine, April 1962.
29. E. Borowitz, *op. cit.,* p. 69.
30. H. Katchadourian and D. Lunde, *op. cit.,* p. 256.

14 • New trends . . . and newer

1. *Talmud Nedarim* 20b.
2. *Talmud Kiddushin* 41a.
3. *Talmud Megillah* 14a.
4. *Talmud Sotah* 11b.
5. *Talmud Taanit* 23a, b.
6. *Talmud Betzah* 23b.
7. *Bereshit Rabbah* 17:7.
8. *Talmud Rosh Hashanah* 22a; *Talmud Sotah* 47b.
9. Numbers 27:8; *Talmud Baba Batrah* 110a, b.
10. H. Loewe, in C.G. Montefiore and H. Loewe, *A Rabbinic Anthology,* p. 656. Macmillan & Co., Ltd., 1938.
11. *Siddur Rashi,* #267.
12. H. Katchadourian and D. Lunde, *Fundamentals of Human Sexuality,* p. 484.
13. E.M. Duvall, *The Art of Dating,* pp. 67ff. Association Press, 1958.
14. *Talmud Shabbat* 62b.
15. G.D. Bartell, *Group Sex,* p. 26. Peter H. Wyden, Inc., 1971.
16. *Ibid.,* p. 43.
17. N. and G. O'Neil, *Open Marriage,* pp. 81–84. Avon Books, 1972.
18. *Ibid.,* p. 36 (adapted).
19. *Ibid.,* pp. 36ff. (adapted).

15 • The stakes are high

1. M. Fine & M. Himmelfarb (ed.), *American Jewish Yearbook* 1963, pp. 16–30, Jewish Publication Society.
2. E.M. & S.M. Duvall, *Sex Ways in Fact and Faith,* p. 61.
3. *Ibid,* p. 62.

4. C. Leuba, *Ethics in Sex Conduct,* pp. 127ff.
5. J.H.S. Bossard & E.S. Boll, *One Marriage, Two Faiths,* pp. 100ff., The Ronald Press, 1957.

16 • How important is religion?

1. J.A. Pike, *The Next Day,* p. 95, Doubleday & Co., 1957.
2. E.M. & S.M. Duvall, *Sex Ways in Fact and Faith,* pp. 88ff.
3. J.A. Peterson, *Toward a Successful Marriage,* p. 104.
4. *Ibid.*
5. J.A. Peterson, *ibid,* pp. 107ff.
6. *Genesis Rabbah* 8:9.
7. *Pirkei de R. Eliezer,* ch. 12.
8. F.A. Magoun, *Love and Marriage,* p. 420.
9. *The New York Times,* 31 January 1965.
10. I. Eisenstein, *What We Mean by Religion,* Behrman House, 1946.
11. L. Newman, *Hasidic Anthology,* p. 237.